THIS ~~I~~ HAS FLOWN

The Enduring Beauty of
Rubber Soul,
Fifty Years On

JOHN KRUTH

Backbeat Books

An Imprint of Hal Leonard Corporation

Published in 2015 by Backbeat Books
An Imprint of Hal Leonard Corporation
7777 West Bluemound Road
Milwaukee, WI 53213

Trade Book Division Editorial Offices
33 Plymouth St., Montclair, NJ 07042

Printed in the United States of America

Illustrations by Glenn Wolff
Book design by John J. Flannery

Library of Congress Cataloging-in-Publication Data

Kruth, John.
 This bird has flown : the enduring beauty of Rubber soul fifty years on / John Kruth.
     pages cm
Includes bibliographical references and index.
ISBN 978-1-61713-573-6
1. Beatles. Rubber soul. I. Title.
ML421.B4K8 2015
782.42166092′2--dc23
                                        2015030425

www.backbeatbooks.com

For Jayney Genius
and her pink and white Magnavox

"Unless you try to do something beyond
what you have already mastered, you will never grow."
—Ralph Waldo Emerson

Contents

Introduction
I Still Feel Fine

was nine years old and nothing else mattered, except for maybe . . . girls. Any interest I had in sports was instantly crushed on the night of Sunday, February 9,1964. One look at the Beatles on *The Ed Sullivan Show* and I immediately abandoned my (very brief) lifelong dream of playing third base for the New York Yankees—my future in pro ball was over before they finished singing "All My Loving."

Although I thought John Lennon was cool, bobbing up and down as if he were riding an invisible horse as he strummed his guitar, it was Ringo Starr, with his hair flying everywhere, laughing at the madness of the moment as he bashed the beat, that made my heart pound in double time. I had simply never seen anyone having that much fun before in my life.

"Trash," my pop grumbled as the mop-tops bowed in unison in their nicely tailored suits and pudding-bowl hairdos. "Nothing but a lotta noise." From my dad's response, it was clear my odds of getting a drum set for my next birthday were pretty slim.

That spring a bunch of us fourth graders got together and conspired to dress up like the Beatles to lip-synch "Twist and Shout" at the annual school talent show. I auditioned for the part of John, giving it my best shot, bobbing up and down on my own invisible horse while trying to strum a guitar. I had actually learned to play a couple folk songs, like "Kumbaya" and "Michael Row Your Boat Ashore," on a nylon-string guitar the previous summer at sleepaway camp, so I already knew how to form an A chord. I imagined the whole auditorium filled with screaming girls as I rocked as hard as a fourth grader could. But a minute later I got the thumbs down from my teacher, Mr. Grant. Crestfallen, I was heading dejectedly toward the exit when he caught my profile in the stage lights. "Ringo!" he shouted, inspired by my ample Semitic nose. (Richard Starkey, despite the many rumors at the time, was not Jewish.)

My friend Danny Schecter, whose parents had recently bought him a brand-new sparkling set of champagne-pink Rogers drums, had been slated to play Ringo, although he looked more like George. Schecter had even taken a couple of drum lessons and could actually stumble through the Surfaris' classic surf anthem "Wipe Out." But it was quickly decided, much to his dismay, that he would be George and that I should play Ringo, although I'd never sat behind a drum kit in my life.

The day of the show soon arrived. Backstage, dressed like four junior bankers in our nice, neat suits and ties, we waited for Mr. Grant to ceremoniously place the Beatle wigs over our crew cuts. That hair falling in our eyes seemed to give us an intoxicating new power—something TV and magazines called "sex appeal."

As the curtain rose, the girls immediately began to scream, even before Mr. Grant had the chance to drop the needle on a new 45 of "Twist and Shout." As the first chord of the song burst through the P.A., we broke into our well-rehearsed routine. Everything was going fine until, in the heat of the moment, I accidentally whacked the snare drum out of time, and everyone started to see through our little charade. I inadvertently slapped a cymbal and the crowd began to turn ugly. I noticed some of the older kids in the back pointing at us and laughing. Hoping to convince the scoffers, I began shaking my head like Ringo while waving the drumsticks in the air. Suddenly the wig went flying off my head and landed on the floor, where it laid like a dead cat. I sat there stunned, naked, my crew cut exposed. I tried to carry on, but my palms, slippery with sweat, could no longer hold the drumsticks. A moment later they fell out of my hands and came crashing down on the cymbals.

As the record ended "John," "Paul," and "George" all took their well-rehearsed bows as I bolted from the stage, down the hall, and out of the school door. From that day forth I was known as "Ringo," or, even worse . . . "the Spaz"!

After the Beatles appeared on *The Ed Sullivan Show*, the world was a different place. Girls across the country were suddenly taking a second look at their boyfriends and wondering what they were doing going out with such Neanderthals. Overnight crew cuts, Arrow shirts, and penny loafers had become relics of a square past. Bangs and pointy-toed ankle boots, previously a fashion essential of hoods and greasers, were now in vogue. You were gold if you could fake a British accent.

I never went anywhere without my ear glued to a transistor radio, listening to Bruce Morrow, aka Cousin Brucie, on the local Top 40 station WABC—or as he called it, W-A-"Beatle"-C—or Murray the K, who'd dubbed himself "the Fifth Beatle." I would do anything, even rake leaves, to get my mom to drive me to the department store, Two Guys from Harrison, to buy whatever new Beatles record had just come out.

Whenever a new song by the Beatles was released, Baldoni's pizza parlor was the first place in town to get it on their jukebox. So after school, I'd hop on my Schwinn and race over to check it out.

It was the Beatles—or rather, my total obsession with them—that made Mr. Baldoni blow his top one day and throw me out of his pizza parlor. I had just stopped by the bank, where I'd cashed in a dollar bill for ten dimes, which I then proceeded to pump, one after the next, into his jukebox, with the intent of playing the new Beatles' single, "I Feel Fine," ten times in a row. I'd actually made it to seven or eight, as I still had a couple of dimes left in my pocket when Mr. Baldoni began to scream in Italian as he threw open the door and tossed me out onto the sidewalk. Then he told me to stay out of his restaurant for good. "And don't-a come-a back-a no more!" he hollered.

I liked Mr. Baldoni, even though his pizza sucked. My mom's spaghetti beat his any day. But he liked music. His jukebox played lots of corny old Italian songs like Dean Martin singing "Amore" and the "Chairman of the Board," Frank Sinatra, who sang about "Chicago" and "Witchcraft." He had lots of old rock 'n' roll on there, too—Elvis Presley and Jerry Lee Lewis, Johnny Cash and sad, old Roy Orbison—music that greasers liked. He even had some black singers on his jukebox, like Ray Charles and James Brown. I think Baldoni's would've been the first integrated place in my hometown if there had actually been any black people living there.

I knew all the Beatles' songs by heart up to then, but there was something different about "I Feel Fine." From the very first note, it was mesmerizing. I had never heard anything like it before in my life. It leapt out of the speakers and stung me in the ears like a giant electric hornet. *Baahhrrraaaohhhwwwiiiiiinnnggggg!* It was something called "feedback," followed by a catchy, reverb-drenched guitar riff that sounded like the coolest surf band in the world. At the time, I was thumping away on my friend's sister's folk guitar, playing "Blowing in the Wind" and learning the Rolling Stones' "Satisfaction." But compared to that crude, repetitive three-note riff, "I Feel Fine," was *rocket science*.

You could learn a lot from listening to the Beatles' records, particularly about love and its ups and downs. From my naïve teenage perspective, the Beatles seemed to understand women pretty well. (Sometimes I wonder just how twisted and painful my love life might have become if I'd followed the Stones' misogynist idea of romance). Sure, there were a few heartbreakers in the bunch ("Not a Second Time," "Girl," and "No Reply," to name a few), but the birds described in their early songs usually possessed the warmth and understanding that a young bloke needed to make it in this tough world. And just the sight of Pattie Boyd in *A Hard Day's Night* showed you what to look for in a girlfriend. (Diane Keaton would adopt her cool, masculine fashion sense, more than ten years later in Woody Allen's *Annie Hall*.) If anyone was to blame for screwing up a relationship, it was usually Lennon, who seemed to have no qualms about admonishing himself for being jealous and cruel.

It took me a few years, but by the sixth grade I'd met a girl named Michelle. She even had a suede jacket. I soon found myself singing "I've Just Seen a Face" on the way home from school. I imagined her room being made of "Norwegian Wood." If I called her up and her line was "engaged," I'd try again until I got through. Possessive and arrogant as Paul McCartney in "You Won't See Me," I'd put her in her place, saying, "I've had enough, now act your age," and then hang up. . . . The whole script was right there in *Rubber Soul*, from the warm-hearted gush of "Michelle" to the perfect put-down lines of "Think for Yourself." Impressionable as I was, I always felt that John singing, "I'd rather see you dead" in "Run for Your Life" was definitely taking things too far (no matter how cool that guitar riff was). Our brief love affair suddenly came to an end a few months later in May of '66 with the release of the Beach Boys' *Pet Sounds*, when I went looking for a girl named Caroline.

1
Soul—Plastic and Otherwise

"What is soul?
It's like electricity. . . . It's a force that can light a room."
—Ray Charles, 1966

Essential yet elusive, soul is hard to define, and even more difficult to locate. You won't find it on any map or with an MRI. Some believe the soul is like a microchip embedded deep within our hearts, like a tiny piece of stardust that unites us all and reminds us of from whence we came.

Busking for spare change on the streets of Beaumont, Texas, in the 1930s, the holy-blues shouter Blind Willie Johnson begged of those strolling by:
"Won't somebody tell me,
Answer if you can,
Won't somebody tell me,
What is the soul of a man?"
Though Johnson died in 1945, his songs and searing slide guitar still haunt us today while his ghost patiently awaits the answer to his timeless question.

Another great bluesman, Chester Burnett, better known as Howlin' Wolf, was touring England in 1964 when he came across a clutch of long-haired louts from London who'd been popularizing (and cashing in on) the music he'd spent much of his hard life creating. After years of paying his dues in every ramshackle roadhouse from Clarksdale, Mississippi, to the South Side dives of Chicago, the Wolf could only shake his head in wonder while white chicks screamed their fool heads off as these skinny, sullen-faced London punks cranked out their earnest but lightweight versions of his music, born and bred in pain and desperation. "Plastic soul," he allegedly croaked in his trademark rasp. "Plastic soul."

The Wolf's adroit observation had undoubtedly lodged itself somewhere in the back of Paul McCartney's mind until

June 14, 1965, when the Beatles recorded "I'm Down." As the frenetic rocker fades out you can hear Paul exclaim "Plastic soul!," perhaps taking a shot at himself for his obvious imitation of Little Richard on the tune. The phrase would pop into McCartney's head once again while he searched for a clever title for his band's next album.

Brian Jones, the Rolling Stones' charismatic multi-instrumentalist, never cared much for formal education, but he was steeped in Howlin' Wolf's legend as deeply as that of King Arthur, Oliver Cromwell, or any other hero he might have learned about back in grammar school. And when the Stones performed on the popular weekly music TV show *Shindig*, in May 1965, they demanded their hero Howlin' Wolf get his share of the limelight as well.

Brian, whose golden locks glistened under the bright lights, introduced the bluesman while the Stones sat at their master's size twelves and gently clapped along to the rhythm of a band that included the likes of Billy Preston hammering the piano, Elvis Presley's guitar slinger James Burton, and Southern soul singer Delaney Bramlett on bass, looking slick, with his hair greased back in a pompadour. The Wolf did a mean take of Willie Dixon's "How Many More Years" (a song that Led Zeppelin would later pilfer—and eventually pay the price for plagiarizing— for their own very thinly disguised "How Many More Times").

Wolf's neck was thick, his head as heavy as a block of cement. His face resembled that of a vengeful Aztec god. When his eyes weren't bugging out of his head, they became inscrutable slits from which it seemed molten lava might suddenly burst forth. His teeth looked like they could raze a forest. People must have wondered if his necktie wasn't choking him near to death as sweat busted off his forehead while he delivered a regretful lament in a strangulated growl.

Although Jones revered him as "one of our greatest idols," Wolf was, as far as most people in television land were concerned, at best, a novelty act, some dirty old man doing a lascivious bump-and-grind as he wheezed asthmatically on his harmonica, while the Stones, on the other hand, were undoubtedly the genuine article. What was the white man gonna try and fool him with next? the Wolf must have wondered. How could these strange, lost boys ever understand what the blues meant anyway? Later the Shin-diggers (the show's troupe of caged, miniskirted go-go dancers, which included the comely actress Teri Garr) shook their moneymakers to the Stones' latest disaffected smash, "(I Can't Get No) Satisfaction."

It was a time when artists and critics alike wrestled over the conundrum of whether a white man could play the blues (as the old joke goes, white people can't *play* the blues; they *give* black folks the blues), but the point soon became moot thanks to a new generation of young (white) blues troubadours from Chicago to London.

While Muddy Waters and Howlin' Wolf were first amused by the novelty of a wiry, oily-haired harmonica wailer named Paul Butterfield and his pal, the Brillo-haired virtuosic guitarist Mike Bloomfield (the son of a multimillionaire), who mimicked their riffs, they soon watched, bewildered, as a new generation of white acolytes began to take their gigs. John Hammond Jr., the son of famed record producer John Hammond (responsible for signing the likes of Billie Holiday, Bob Dylan, and Bruce Springsteen to name but a few), surprisingly turned out to be one of the greatest interpreters of Robert Johnson's haunted Delta blues to ever come down the pike. Hammond's slashing slide work cut to the bone while his harmonica playing was second only to that of Jimmy Reed. If this wasn't enough to put the issue of race to rest, a pair of albinos from Beaumont, Texas, named Johnny and Edgar Winter played both blues and R&B with a ferocious virtuosity. Along with the Animals and the Celtic soul belter Van Morrison, whose band, Them, offered raw, somewhat sleazy renditions of Lead Belly, John Lee Hooker, and Ray Charles numbers, there was also a young guitar slinger from the UK named Eric Clapton, whose nickname, "God," was spray-painted on the tube station walls of London. As Muddy Waters pointed out, "It's not a matter of color. It's a matter of heart."

"Soul," Bhagavad Gita scholar and author Joshua M. Greene reminds us, "is the true self, the source of consciousness in the body. What we seek, through music, meditation, yoga and the study of wisdom texts, is to know ourselves beyond this one fleeting life. That self, which transcends any one lifetime, is called *atma* in the Sanskrit texts, or what we translate as *soul*."

Soul is hard to measure. There is no yardstick or thermometer capable of detecting who has the most. By the mid-sixties the competition had become rather stiff. Whether christened by a music critic in search of a catchy headline, or by a label's A&R department hoping to give its artists an aristocratic aura while moving more copies of their latest albums, legions of performers were suddenly awarded royal monikers designating them the reigning sovereigns of soul. While both Aretha Franklin and Nina Simone were dubbed the "Queen of Soul," Gladys Knight was baptized the "Empress of Soul," whereas Patti LaBelle respectfully became known as the "Godmother" of the genre. There have also been white Soul Queens as well, including Dusty Springfield and Carole King, the latter of whom, along with her ex-husband Gerry Goffin, wrote a plethora of classic soul and pop hits, including "Chains," which the Beatles recorded in 1963. In their early songwriting days, Lennon and McCartney had modeled their partnership after that of Goffin and King, although John and Paul wrote both lyrics and music, while Gerry focused on lyrics while Carole fashioned the melodies.

Sadly, Carole King is frequently overlooked as a true soul diva, perhaps due to her blue-jeaned earth-mother hippie image. But beyond her husky, honeyed voice and the righteous piano vamps of her 1971 album *Tapestry* (one of the most popular albums in the world, with sales estimated at over 25 million copies), King has written hits for everyone from Little Eva ("The Loco-Motion") to the Drifters ("Up on the Roof") to Aretha Franklin ("You Make Me Feel like a Natural Woman") to the Monkees ("Pleasant Valley Sunday"). The list goes on and on. She makes it seem so easy: as she sang in "The Loco-Motion," all you need is "a little bit of rhythm and a lotta soul."

James Brown, famously known as the "Hardest Working Man in Show Business," was hailed as both the "King" and the "Godfather of Soul," but it was his handle "Soul Brother Number One" that set the record straight, in case there was ever a shadow of a doubt after seeing the man in action.

Both Sam Cooke (another soul great deserving of the title "King") and Ray Charles (the "Genius of Soul") chose to avoid the hysteria and controversy surrounding rock 'n' roll in the early fifties and sixties by calling their music "soul," which brought both respect and an air of mystery to the music. No one demanded (or deserved) his "propers" more than the powerhouse vocalist Solomon Burke, who solemnly sat upon his throne wearing a velvet robe in the early '60s when he was ceremoniously crowned the "King of Rock and Soul" by Baltimore DJ Rockin' Robin.

One defining aspect of most soul singers is that they share roots in gospel, regardless of their own lifelong relationships to the church. No matter how convincingly Paul McCartney could howl like Little Richard (whose father, a Pentecostal preacher, threw his son out of the house, fearing he was possessed by the devil, for playing rock 'n' roll), the Beatles' brand of "northern soul" was somewhat anemic in comparison, as it lacked the true grit and feeling that could only come with the firsthand experience of having attended a black church, whether in Harlem or America's Deep South.

No matter where the music originated, whether in Detroit, Memphis, Philadelphia, or Muscle Shoals, Alabama; no matter who sang it or shouted it, from Jackie Wilson to Ben E. King to Solomon Burke, or whether it was smooth as silk or sweaty; no matter what label it was released on—Motown, Stax, or Atlantic, or any of the myriad of smaller labels that cranked out smoldering 45s at the time—soul was all about a sound, definitively black in origin, but so far-reaching and ultimately irresistible that it became a crucial tool in breaking down the walls of segregation.

Upon meeting Wilson Pickett, Ringo Starr earnestly begged the Alabama-born soul man, "What is soul? How do you know when you have it?" "Soul," the Wicked Pickett assured the world's most famous drummer, "ain't nothin' but a feelin'."

With the Supremes, the Temptations, and the Four Tops competing with the Beatles, Stones, and Beach Boys for the top of the charts, *soul* had become the buzzword of the day. Everybody from Catholic theologians to London's stylish mods (who were fond of Italian-made suits and custom scooters) and their rivals, the leather-clad bikers known as rockers, was in hot pursuit of *soul*. Soul bubbled with passion, imbued a sense of the divine. Soul is that immortal piece of your heart, a deep-down knowing in your bones. Soul was in the way your baby walked, how she danced. It's the genuine flavor you can only get from a home-cooked meal. *Soul*—it was a weekly TV show (which aired from September '68 through February 1973 and featured King Curtis as its musical director). It was even a finger—although nobody was sure exactly which one—thanks to the Bar-Kays' Top 20 smash hit "Soul Finger," which featured their trademark horns (famous for backing up Otis Redding) and a gang of neighborhood kids who jubilantly chanted its title in exchange for a couple cold bottles of Coke.

Soul—plastic, rubber, or otherwise—had long been part of the Beatles' repertoire, since the group's early days at the Cavern Club. Their set list regularly included a handful of Motown numbers, with John belting out righteous renditions of "Money" and "Mr. Postman" (Smokey Robinson was a favorite of both Lennon and McCartney's).

The quirky title of their sixth album, *Rubber Soul* (which many considered nothing more than a dumb pun), was not just a tip of the hat to the music they dearly loved and their earnest attempt as a clutch of pale-faced Brits to play it with respect and passion, but a clever nod to their famous Beatle boot, which they'd been wearing since 1961, after John and Paul commissioned shoemakers Anello & Davide to craft four pairs, complete with custom Cuban heels, after discovering them in a London shopwindow.

Then there was the far-flung theory amongst a few of their hormone-addled teenage fans that "Rubber Soul" was poetic code for falsies, or a padded bra. When you finally got to "second base" with a girl you desperately desired and wound up with nothing but a handful of foam, you were sure to instantly understand its mysterious meaning. After all, weren't the boys all gleefully singing "tit, tit, tit" on the backup vocals to John's "Girl?"

"There's no great mysterious meaning behind all of this," Lennon said years later. "It was just four boys, y'know, working out what to call a new album."

"The title," Paul McCartney said in an interview on November 1, 1965, could easily have been "'*It's the Bloody Beatles Again!*'" or '*Eight Feet Away.*'" Years later, when talking with Barry Miles for his biography *Many Years from Now*, Paul pointed out that *Rubber Soul* "was a reference to rubber-soled shoes as well as soul music."

Originally pressed in an edition of 750,000 copies, *Rubber Soul* was released on December 3, 1965, in the UK by Parlophone Records (in both mono and stereo versions). Three days later the record reached America's shores. Although it featured the same title and album cover as the UK version, it was hardly the same record. While both editions shared ten titles—"Norwegian Wood," "You Won't See Me," "Think for Yourself," "The Word," "Michelle," "Girl," "I'm Looking Through You," "In My Life," "Wait," and "Run for Your Life"—the American version of *Rubber Soul*, it turned out, represented the first and only time Capitol's habit of meddling with the playlist made any artistic sense. Whether a case of buffoonery or kismet, the label inadvertently created a folk-rock masterpiece by deleting what they deemed the "electric songs" ("Drive My Car," "Nowhere Man," "What Goes On," and "If I Needed Someone") and replacing them with a pair of tunes from the British pressing of *Help!*—Paul's breezy "I've Just Seen a Face" and John's mawkish ballad "It's Only Love," along with another McCartney number, "Wait," an outtake, also from *Help!*, that suddenly came in handy when the band came up one song short of finishing *Rubber Soul*.

Capitol, the Beatles' label in the States, had routinely interfered with the order and content of the band's every release, beginning with 1963's *With the Beatles* (which was actually their second LP in England but their first in America, better known as *Meet the Beatles*) and continuing up to *Sgt. Pepper's Lonely Hearts Club Band* in June 1967. With the remaining tracks they edited from the original British versions, Capitol would later release poorly conceived compilation albums that devoted fans bought regardless of how slapdash the production and second-rate the graphics were (some of which, like *The Beatles' Second Album, Something New*, and *Beatles VI*, had all the aesthetic charm of a cereal box).

Their worst offense came with the American release of *Help!* While the British pressing included a gentle ballad called "Yesterday" amongst its fourteen titles (Paul's ballad remained unavailable in the U.S. until it was issued a month later by popular demand as a single on September 13, 1965), Beatle fans in the States were unfortunately stuck with the official movie soundtrack album, which included a mere seven new songs from *Help!*, plus five forgettable James Bond theme–like instrumentals, incidental music from composer Ken Thorne.

"*Rubber Soul* was my favorite album," George Harrison proclaimed. "I think that it was the best one we made; we certainly knew we were making a good album. We did spend a bit more time on it and tried new things. But the most important thing about it was that we were suddenly hearing sounds that we weren't able to hear before. Also, we were being more influenced by other people's music and everything was blossoming at that time, including us, because we were still growing."

"This was the departure record," Ringo concurred. "A lot of other influences were coming down and going on the record . . . . We were expanding in all areas of our lives, opening up to a lot of different attitudes. . . . I felt we were progressing in leaps and bounds, musically. Some of the material on *Rubber Soul* was just brilliant. What was happening elsewhere [at the time] was nothing like it." Written and recorded at breakneck speed, between October 12 and November 11, 1965, *Rubber Soul* was a game changer, not just for the Beatles themselves, but as a work whose sound and ideas went on to last for decades, impacting nearly everything that transpired in popular music in its wake.

Capitol believed so strongly in *Rubber Soul*'s impending success that they didn't bother to release a single from the album. While this was typical of record companies in England, it was unusual, to say the least, in America. DJs from coast to coast soon made the decision for themselves, choosing "Michelle" as the lead-off song. To help facilitate sales, Capitol quickly slapped a bright yellow sticker on its cover announcing HEAR PAUL SING "MICHELLE."

Newsweek hailed the Beatles as "the Bards of Pop," while critic Greil Marcus claimed *Rubber Soul* was "the best album they would ever make." For Traffic's Steve Winwood, the Beatles' sixth studio record "broke everything open. It crossed music into a whole new dimension and was responsible for kicking off the sixties rock era." Somehow, they seemed to intuitively understand, as Jimi Hendrix would sing years later, that "with the power of soul anything is possible."

But not everyone was quite so ecstatic over the Beatles' latest. *Melody Maker* initially panned *Rubber Soul*, calling the album "monotonous." Some fans loathed the warped cover photograph and wrote to their fanzine, *Beatles Monthly*, complaining that their favorite group "looked dead."

Petty grievances and gallows complexions aside, the latter of which may have had something to do with the grueling hours spent in the studio ("The Beatles have come to accept that recording is their way of life," producer George Martin surmised, likening the long hours and intense work schedule to "voluntary imprisonment.") and the "very impossible" task of creating a fresh body of work under a looming deadline—seven of the album's songs were composed in just one week!—the Beatles had created their first masterpiece.

2
The Times They Were A-Changin'

"Be groovy or get out!"
—*Bob Dylan to the assorted hangers-on in his London hotel room,*
Don't Look Back, *1967*

Nineteen sixty-five was a tumultuous year, the tipping point in a decade of constant change. New levels of activism and consciousness followed the assassination of Malcolm X, the escalation of the Vietnam War, and the Watts riots in L.A. Despite the raging chaos, a sense of purpose and optimism prevailed amongst those who chose the path of nonviolent protest as epitomized by Dr. Martin Luther King. The popular slogan of the civil rights movement, "Keep your eyes on the prize" (originally heard in "The Gospel Plow," an African-American folk song discovered by ethnomusicologist Alan Lomax, dating back to the first decade of the twentieth century), seemed to sum up the attitude of those taking a stand against the establishment, whether confronting issues of segregation or refusing to participate in an amoral war.

In pop music the year had begun with an innocuous promise: Petula Clark's "Downtown," a perky ode to an earthly paradise, which, for at least three minutes and five seconds, provided an oasis where you could "forget all your troubles, forget all your cares." Originally released in November 1964, "Downtown" eventually climbed to the number one slot on January 23, 1965, making Clark the first British female pop star to top the American charts. The song echoed out of every dashboard speaker and transistor radio from coast to coast for another week before being bumped off by Phil Spector's grandiose production of the Righteous Brothers' "You've Lost That Lovin' Feelin'."

Throughout the 1940s and fifties, white singers had found great success in popularizing songs by black artists, and although their "cover" versions, as they were called, rarely matched the feeling of the original, they routinely received more airplay and publicity while generating considerably more money. Most kids who heard Pat Boone's insipid renditions of "Tutti Frutti" and "Ain't That a Shame" actually believed the clean-cut great-grandson of the famous coonskin-capped explorer, Daniel, had invented rock 'n' roll. Boone, who was more comfortable with hymns and "safe as milk" ballads, claimed he only sang that rowdy rock 'n' roll with its "nonsense lyrics" at the incessant prodding of his producer. Pat had even suggested changing the title to Fats Domino's hit song "Ain't That a Shame" to the more grammatically correct "Isn't That a Shame," in hopes of not offending his admirers with any backwoods colloquial-isms. Despite the rampant whitewashing within the music business, Boone's fans seemed to know little of (nor care about) the injustice and indignity the music's true innovators, such as Little Richard, Fats Domino, and Chuck Berry, suffered at that time. Ironically, Fats claimed to like Boone's rendition of his song. He even invited the great white buck-shoed wonder to sing with him onstage while showing off a gold ring he'd recently bought with the royalties from the sales of his song.

After the hell-bent country star Ira Louvin branded Elvis Presley "a white nigger," the time had clearly come for a more user-friendly term to ease the stigma suffered by white musi-cians who played R&B. A Philadelphia DJ named Georgie Woods came up with the catchy handle "blue-eyed soul." The Righteous Brothers liked the ring of Georgie's poetry so much they immediately titled their 1964 LP *Some Blue-Eyed Soul.*

While Stax and Motown hits had been part of the Beatles', the Stones', the Who's, and the Kinks' early repertoires, Van Morrison, the Animals' Eric Burdon, and a teenage prodigy named Stevie Winwood of the Spencer Davis Group (who was just eighteen when he recorded the classic frat-house rocker "Gimme Some Lovin'") would also bring an added credibility to the newly dubbed genre.

In the States, the premier blue-eyed-soul band of the day was the Young Rascals, a trio of Italians from Long Island, rounded out by a Canadian guitarist. "Nobody in the band even had blue eyes!" singer/organist Felix Cavaliere pointed out. Following the success of their rowdy garage rocker "Good Lovin'" in 1966, the Rascals would drop the "Young" from their name, along with their cute uniform of schoolboy knickers and caps, and quickly begin to stir up controversy by demanding their favorite black bands share the bill with them. Whatever their motive, whether musical or political, the band inadvertently would become relentless advocates for equal rights.

"The Rascals had crossed the line," Felix said. "They played us on the black stations. The classic story is when Otis Redding came into the studio [at Atlantic Records in New York] and said, 'My God, guys are white! Until we saw you, how could we be sure? We had no clue.'

"We did a gig with the Friends of Distinction, who had a hit with 'Grazin' in the Grass,'" Cavaliere recalled. "They came up to us backstage and said, 'Thank you for puttin' us on the show because we don't get a chance to play too much for white people. We're always in the black thing and our music is cross-over music like yours, only we're goin' the other way.' I said, 'Bingo! We gotta bring the people together through the music.' I had no idea at the time of the implication of what I was saying."

In 1968 Felix and the Rascals' singer/songwriter Eddie Brigati responded to the combined tragedies of the Martin Luther King and Bobby Kennedy assassinations by writing and recording "People Got to Be Free," a steamin' hunk of funky message music that shot straight to number one and topped the *Billboard* charts for five weeks. Ironically, Atlantic Records had balked at the first hearing of the song, thinking the public would scoff at such idealistic lyrics, coming from a group of white boys famous for three-chord odes to adolescent love. But "People Got to Be Free" soon became the Rascals' hottest disc to date. It was also the last time they'd reach number one.

The sophisticated lyrical themes of *Rubber Soul* would inspire the Rascals to grow and write more introspective numbers like "Groovin'" and "It's a Beautiful Morning." "Without the Beatles none of this would have happened," Felix concurred. "It's not like they were the end-all and be-all of music, but their contribution was beyond words. The radio *had* to play the Beatles. So when they stretched out, everybody else could stretch out. And the doors they opened? There's no words that can say. They were brilliant and beautiful. If a duck sang it, it would still be great!"

Long before John was indoctrinated into leftist politics by
Abbie Hoffman and Jerry Rubin in the early 1970s, spewing
radical slogan songs like "Attica State" and "Power to the
People," Lennon and his fellow Fabs took a not-particularly-
well-publicized stand against racial discrimination when they
refused to perform at the Gator Bowl in Jacksonville, Florida, on
September 11, 1964, after having learned that stadium seating
was to be prioritized on the basis of their fans' skin color. The
Beatles soon discovered their hotel reservations had been
mysteriously canceled. When asked by a reporter about the all
hubbub, George Harrison replied frankly, yet cautiously: "We
don't know about our accommodations at all. We don't arrange
that. But, you know, we don't appear anywhere where there is . . .
[discrimination]."

"We don't like it if there's any segregation or anything
because we're not used to it," Paul told Philadelphia journalist
Larry Kane. "I just seems daft to me. . . . You can't treat other
people like animals," he said, adding, "Some of our best friends
are colored people."

This was just the beginning of the Beatles' tenuous relationship
with the American South. British journalist Maureen Cleave had
written a weekly series called "How Does a Beatle Live?" for the
London Evening Standard based on interviews with "the darlings of
Merseyside," as she'd dubbed the boys. But things suddenly took
an unexpected spin out of control when Lennon, who was in the
midst of reading Hugh J. Schonfield's *The Passover Plot*, espoused:
"Christianity will go. It will vanish and shrink. I needn't argue
about that; I'm right and I'll be proved right. We're more popular
than Jesus now; I don't know which will go first—rock 'n' roll or
Christianity. Jesus was all right but his disciples were thick and
ordinary. It's them twisting it that ruins it for me."

While nobody in England gave neither feather nor fig about
Lennon's pompous pontifications, folks in the American South
were not about to take such careless mouthing off about their
messiah lying down. Five months later all hell broke loose when
the August 1966 issue of *Datebook*, an American teen magazine,
hit the stands with John's blasphemy blazing across its otherwise perky cover. In no time the Beatles were banned from radio
stations from Alabama to Texas (outraged citizens of Spain and

South Africa quickly followed suit). Hastily constructed bonfires blazed so angry mobs could dispose of their Beatle "trash" quickly and conveniently. Sequestered away in their hotel rooms, the Fab Four watched nervously as the nightly news reported mass "Beatle Burnings" across an enraged Dixie. Although protests were staged over their Memphis Mid-South Coliseum show, the concert went off without a hitch, despite the presence of the KKK and the occasional burst of firecrackers (which caused them to flinch, as they understandably thought they might be gunshots).

For most musicians around Memphis, the struggle for civil rights had finally begun to bring about a much-needed change for the better. An atmosphere of new possibility flourished in an old movie theater at 926 East McLemore Avenue, whose marquee proudly boasted the words SOULSVILLE U.S.A. in big red plastic letters. In 1965, Stax Records was a tiny oasis of musical and racial harmony in a segregated city in the Deep South. Run by the brother-and-sister team of Jim Stewart and Estelle Axton (whose names together created the anagram Stax), the label became home to the likes of Rufus Thomas, Albert King, and Otis Redding, to name a few. Steve Cropper, guitarist with Booker T. and the MGs, believed the Stax signature sound (a tasty gumbo of Southern music, blending gospel and blues with the occasional touch of country twang) was just "one of those accidents" that happened thanks to "a melting pot of musicians from all different walks of life and different styles." Stax, while hardly a perfect model of integration, showed the world that a New South was, at last, on the rise—at least until the assassination of Dr. Martin Luther King, which occurred across the street from Stax Records at the Lorraine Motel on April 4, 1968.

While Marvin Gaye, Stevie Wonder, and even the Supremes began singing politically conscious "message" songs (despite the initial protests of Motown's producer, Berry Gordy), no Stax artist ever openly addressed the everyday troubles that African-Americans faced. But according to Fontella Bass, there was a lot more going on below the surface of most songs played on pop radio at the time. Her smash hit "Rescue Me" was "not just a love song," she pointed out. Apparently her number one smash was rife with "political overtones. . . . A lot of things were goin' on in '65, [including] Vietnam, the Watts riots, everybody was in turmoil. That was the thought behind the record," she explained. "C'mon baby let's get it together!"

While the British Invasion had taken America by storm, initially boasting a string of would-be pedigreed bands like the Beatles, the Stones, the Animals, and the Kinks, within a year the gene pool had plummeted to such dismal depths as to include the Manchester group Freddie & the Dreamers (purveyors of a popular spastic dance craze known as "The Freddie"), who soared to number one that April with their rinky-dink anthem of twisted dependency, "I'm Telling You Now."

The dreadfully chipper Herman's Hermits would also have two number one hits in the States, with the terribly trite "Mrs. Brown, You've Got a Lovely Daughter" and "I'm Henery The Eighth, I Am." The latter was a British music hall ditty by Harry Champion from 1910, which the granddad of lead singer Peter (aka Herman) Noone used to sing to him when Peter was a boy. The insidiously infectious "Henery" would become the fastest-selling song in history of popular music at the time.

On the other end of the spectrum was the sinister hook of "(I Can't Get No) Satisfaction," which, according to Mick Jagger, "really made the Rolling Stones . . . changed [them] from just another band into a huge, monster." Beyond its "great guitar sound," Mick believed "Satisfaction" (released in May of '65) captured "a spirit of the times . . . which was alienation." Keith Richards's secret weapon, which seared that three-note rocker into our brains, was the new Gibson Maestro fuzz box.

But the real game changer of the day was Bob Dylan's latest song, "Like a Rolling Stone," which not only revolution-ized everyone's concept of what song lyrics could do but also single-handedly challenged the accepted format of pop music as well. Coming in at over six minutes long, Bob's latest opus confronted the strict limitations of both AM radio and jukebox play, which dictated the length of a pop tune be no longer than three minutes. Columbia, Dylan's label, refused to press the song on one side of a single. Perhaps their concern was over the record's lack of fidelity. This was a matter of simple physics: the longer a record is, the more volume is required to compensate for its softer sound, so it would be necessary to turn it up. On the other hand, they feared their willingness to accommodate Dylan would encourage every band or singer of the time who suddenly considered themselves "recording artists" to follow their whims and cut a five-minute record. And so "Like a Rolling Stone" was initially released as a two-part single (inadvertently turning it into a highly desirable collector's item) that forced disc jockeys to stop and flip the record over in order to play the second half of the song. But Dylan had only begun to push the boundaries of his artistic vision. With his hypnotic surrealist prayer "Sad Eyed Lady of the Lowlands," Bob would unleash a twelve-minute rambling poem long enough to fill the fourth side of his 1966 double album *Blonde on Blonde*, once more bending everyone's notion of the modern song far beyond all recognition.

Dylan was growing in leaps and bounds. Having shed his Woody Guthrie, weary-dust-bowl-balladeer image, he suddenly appeared as an immaculately hip aristocrat, dressed in tailored shirts, sports jackets, and Ray-Bans. Gone too were his bumpkin Okie accent and acerbic protest songs. While his raspy harmonica and acoustic guitar remained essentially the same, Bob's lyrics were now infused with stream-of-consciousness images that gushed from the same well of inspiration that illuminated the timeless work of French symbolist Arthur Rimbaud and Beat poet Allen Ginsberg, who had recently appeared in a short promotional film with Bob and on the back of his new album's sleeve, as well.

Released on March 27, 1965, Dylan's *Bringing It All Back Home* was divided into two sets, while a handful of acoustic songs graced side two. The album opened with a rollicking electric band performing the mad, rambling "Subterranean Homesick Blues," Bob's first single to make the *Billboard* charts, clawing its way up to number thirty-nine. The album's mesmerizing cover portrait by Daniel Kramer revealed Bob temporarily taking shelter from the storm as he clutched a smoke-gray kitten inside his inner sanctum. Beside him lounged a beguiling lady in red with a Mona Lisa smile, Sally Grossman, the wife of his infamous manager, Albert. You can almost smell the perfume lingering in the air. The startling sight of Dylan's French cuffs and perfectly coiffed hair made you wonder for a moment which one of them was wearing it.

In 1965 Bob Dylan was at the center of a media circus. His press conferences from this time are particularly brilliant. Asked everything from his political views to whose shirts he preferred, Dylan confused and skewered interviewers with one-liners that seemed to perfectly reflect the absurdity of fame. Grilled by a horde of reporters at a San Francisco press conference in December of that year, Bob was asked, "Do you think of yourself primarily as a singer or a poet?" Without skipping a beat, Dylan quipped, "I think of myself as a song-and-dance man." Grinning as he chain-smoked, Bob seemed resigned to life in the eye of the hurricane, at least for the time being. Everything, as portrayed on the cover of *Bringing It All Back Home*, seemed to swirl around him in a strange druggy haze. Images abound. Albums are strewn everywhere, from Robert Johnson's *King of the Delta Blues Singers* to *The Folk Blues of Eric von Schmidt* and records by Lotte Lenya and the Impressions. Atop the mantelpiece rests a record by the brilliant stand-up philosopher Lord Buckley.

Dylan was showing everybody his hand, openly sharing his influences with his fans, as the Beatles would two years later with the cast of characters they assembled and posed with for the cover to *Sgt. Pepper's Lonely Hearts Club Band*. Bob's previous album, *Another Side of Bob Dylan*, was also amongst the pile, as if, perhaps, to point out that he was just another link in the chain of the writers, poets, and singers who inspired him. Tossed into the mix was a black and yellow fallout shelter sign, along with a recent issue of *Time* with then president Lyndon Baines Johnson on the cover, reminding his fans that the harsh realities of the day were never very far off.

Composing at odd hours, after gigs, on the road, and during early-morning sessions, and fueled by endless cigarettes and plenty of pot and cheap Burgundy, Dylan sat hunched over his typewriter, pecking out startling surrealist verse that included "Gates of Eden" and "Mr. Tambourine Man," the latter a rambling poem inspired by session guitarist Bruce Langhorne's

Turkish tambourine, which Bob years later described as being "big as a wagon wheel."

Bob's freewheeling, free-spirited writing style spilled over to the recording studio, where he took a loose, organic approach to the record-making process. As photographer Daniel Kramer recalled: "Dylan bounced around from one man to another, explaining what he wanted, often showing them on the piano what was needed until, like a giant puzzle, the pieces would fit and the picture emerged whole."

By this point Dylan was so influential that it took just a single word from his mouth to forge a multimillion-selling chart-topping smash. And that word was *babe*. *Babe*, the only bit of warmth and assurance that Bob could offer his jilted lover in his bitter 1964 breakup ballad "It Ain't Me Babe." Although recorded by both the Turtles and the Byrds, it was the Man in Black's version that exuded genuine soul. The word *babe* came tumbling off Johnny Cash's nicotine-stained lips. Sonny & Cher immediately picked up on Dylan's *babe* and turned it into the buzzword of the moment with a tune cowritten by Sonny and Phil Spector, "I Got You Babe." "Babe" they intoned, gazing lovingly into each other's eyes (for at least a couple of seasons). The counterculture couple's signature song quickly soared to the top of the *Billboard* charts in August 1965, where it spent three weeks, selling more than a million copies.

Then, on July 25, 1965, came the Newport Folk Festival, featuring Bob Dylan as the much anticipated headliner, backed by organist Al Kooper, Barry Goldberg, on piano and America's greatest guitar slinger of the day, Mike Bloomfield of the Paul Butterfield Blues Band.

Seldom does a musician's quest for a new mode of expression culminate in such a fervent display of spontaneous mayhem from his or her audience. The most notorious instance in the twentieth century came with the riotous premiere of Igor Stravinsky's *Le Sacre du printemps* (*The Rites of Spring*) in Paris on May 29, 1913. Inspired by pagan rites, "the Prince of the Avant-Garde," as Stravinsky had become known, jolted his audience with strange dissonant chords and asymmetrical rhythms, inspiring Henri Quittard, a leading critic of the day, to write a scathing review in the conservative French daily newspaper

Le Figaro declaring, "We are sorry to see an artist such as M. Stravinsky involve himself in this disconcerting adventure."

The trouble erupted when the audience split into two groups and began arguing with each other over an atonal bassoon passage, as well as the unconventional dance steps that accompanied it. But the rowdy crowd soon united to aim their pent-up aggression at the orchestra, throwing whatever wasn't nailed down at the musicians. The police eventually arrived to break up the brawl while Stravinsky fled in dismay. Although met with a barrage of nasty hoots and catcalls, the performers and the band gallantly played on.

A little over fifty years later, Bob Dylan would understand what it felt like to walk a mile or two in Stravinsky's shoes, when he donned a black leather jacket, plugged in his Stratocaster, and shocked his audience at the Newport Folk Festival. Things began to go awry from the moment that Peter Yarrow of the famed folk trio Peter, Paul and Mary boldly announced in the film *Festival!*, "We are now approaching the genius!" A portion of the crowd (roughly over half the audience, depending upon who you ask) began to erupt in outrage and anger. In the most commonly told version of this modern-day myth, the banjo-strumming King of the Sing-Along, Pete Seeger, stormed off in search of an ax with the intent of whittling the soundboard into kindling. The message *this machine surrounds hate and forces it to surrender* had been written in bold letters on the face of the instrument that Seeger's name was synonymous with. But Pete, a tireless champion for change and freedom of speech, was now looking for the quickest way to muzzle Dylan. Thankfully Seeger was subdued by the Israeli folk singer Theodore Bikel. Though a member of "the old guard," Bikel knew a game changer when he saw it, and admonished his friend, "You can't do that, Pete! You can't stop the future!"

For most of Dylan's peers, his abrupt change of style was not so earth-shattering. "The popular misconception is that most folkies didn't listen to rock 'n' roll," the Lovin' Spoonful's John Sebastian chuckled. "Both Zali [the Spoonful's singer/guitarist Zal Yanovsky] and I had been playing electric guitar with sax bands before we ever strummed acoustics. We loved Duane Eddy and Link Wray! So it wasn't like we came from out of a folk tradition and then just plugged in."

But at least half of the crowd on that hot summer night felt deeply betrayed by their boy wonder. Before them stood Bob Dylan, like Judas in Beatle boots, defiantly flailing away on his Fender while crowing, "I ain't gonna work on Maggie's farm no more!" His message came across loud and clear. Bob had apparently turned his back on "the cause." Dylan might have sold out to rock 'n' roll, as many claimed, but he also happened to be playing some of the greatest music of his life. Bob had apparently moved on. His art was no longer about fighting isms. Over the next year, his lyrics would become more poetic and mystical.

"I knew Bob as long as I knew Michael [Bloomfield]," blues guitarist/singer John Hammond said. "They weren't really playing the blues, and it wasn't the Dylan I'd known before. Honestly, I wasn't impressed."

"I'd been at the afternoon sound check and Mike had this real intensity. He was leaning over his guitar, looming around like he was about to fall off the stage. I was wondering what was going to happen," recalled Betsy Siggins Schmidt, founder of the New England Folk Music Archive. "Then, later on Pete Seeger *did* try and stop the performance. Dylan got booed. He was upset. I was there! Afterward Bob came backstage and sat and on my lap."

"My take on it was it was mixed. There was some positive reaction," said Dylan's pianist Barry Goldberg. "I thought 'Like a Rolling Stone' was really great, mostly because of Bob's voice. Michael [Bloomfield] was just blazing away. But we were playing a folk festival and they didn't know how to mic a rock band. It all came as a surprise and when you break rank and do something really great like that, people are going to react in all sorts of ways. Bob was in the hot seat. I think the crowd's reaction was more political than about the music but folk rock and Bob's new career were born at Newport!"

Al Kooper believed the fracas ensued due to lousy sound and that Dylan left the stage after only fifteen minutes. Kooper refutes the claim that the riotous atmosphere at Newport had anything to do with "Dylan going electric," as the moment will forever be known in history, but maintains "the crowd was going bonkers for an encore. . . . I was standing right there," Al explained in his myth-busting memoir *Backstage Passes & Backstabbing Bastards*.

"Damn right they booed. But not at Bob," Kooper pointed out; "rather, at whoever was seemingly responsible for yanking him offstage after fifteen minutes. We had just run out of rehearsed material and that's why we stopped." No matter whose version you care to believe, Bob Dylan's brief set at Newport, on the evening of July 25, 1965, had suddenly pulled the rug out from under the folk revival.

That summer the Beatles would change a few rules of the game themselves when they performed at Shea Stadium on Sunday, August 15, kicking off their second American tour by whipping 55,600 fans into a frenzy. As in a lost scene from *A Hard Day's Night*, the band left the Warwick Hotel, piling into a limo before sailing above the Manhattan skyline in a red, white, and blue helicopter (George Harrison, who loathed flying, said he'd rather take his chances fighting the heavy traffic next time). Landing at the World's Fair grounds in Queens, they were immediately ushered into an armored car, where, on their way to the stadium, the band were deputized with Wells Fargo badges, something of a warm-up for the MBE medal they were soon to receive from Her Majesty Queen Elizabeth that October.

DJ Cousin Bruce Morrow introduced promoter Sid Bernstein, who first brought the Beatles to Carnegie Hall on February 12, 1964. Bernstein then introduced Ed Sullivan, who finally announced the Beatles, who followed a series of brief sets by Brenda Holloway (who'd had a minor hit with "You Made Me So Very Happy," before Blood Sweat & Tears made it famous), Cannibal and the Headhunters, Sounds Incorporated, and Bernstein's latest pop sensation, the Young Rascals. (Sid, anxious to hype his new group, angered the Beatles' manager Brian Epstein, who demanded the banners announcing the Rascals' imminent arrival be taken down immediately, as not to draw one iota of the fans' obsession away from his boys.)

CANNIBAL & THE HEADHUNTERS

IT WAS PAUL MCCARTNEY who urged Brian Epstein to secure Cannibal & the Headhunters (or, as he called them, the "Nah Nah Boys," referring to their recent hit, a cover of Chris Kenner and Fats Domino's "Land of a Thousand Dances") to open up for the Beatles on the band's 1965 tour. The song's insidious hook, the extended "nah nah nah nah nahs," was actually a mistake that stuck after Frankie "Cannibal" Garcia (nicknamed "Cannibal" after he allegedly bit somebody in a street fight) forgot the lyrics when recording the tune.

While racial tensions in Los Angeles had reached a fever pitch, culminating in six days of violence and looting in the predominantly African-American neighborhood of Watts, a Chicano combo from the projects of East L.A. took the stage at Shea Stadium as if in a dream. Not only were they opening for the most famous band in the world, they were accompanied by the great soul/jazz saxophonist King Curtis and his band.

Cannibal and the boys then traveled with the Beatles, flying to seventeen states. "George was pretty quiet," Cannibal Richard "Scar" Lopez recalled in an interview. "Ringo was a crack-up, [he'd] tell a lot of jokes. Of course John Lennon was a joke teller. The one that I got along with really good was Paul McCartney. . . . I used to sit with him quite a bit on the plane and talk to him. . . . We used to talk a lot about my neighborhood and his neighborhood [in Liverpool]. As a matter of fact, I even invited him to the neighborhood one time, but of course he didn't come. . . . I don't remember which person it would be on the plane, but somebody would be on the plane and all of a sudden go 'Nah, nah, nah, nah, nah' and everybody would join in. But I can't say exactly who would kick it off." Two weeks after Shea Stadium, the "Nah Nah Boys," as Paul called them, were welcomed home and regaled as local heroes when they opened for the Fabs on August 30 at the Hollywood Bowl.

Over the years there's been a lot of speculation as to whether Paul's inspiration for the famous coda to "Hey Jude" was lifted from the catchy refrain of the Headhunters' chart-topping tune (and as to whether the Beatles owed a sizable debt to Frankie "Cannibal" Garcia and his rocking crew).

Bernstein ceremoniously honored Ed Sullivan as "one of our finest newspapermen," calling him "the number one showman of the world" before adding, "and most important of all, a truly great American." In doing so, perhaps Bernstein hoped to clarify once and for all that there was nothing "un-American" about rock 'n' roll to those naysayers who since the 1950s had despised and demonized the music. Despite all the wild accusations from teachers, preachers, and other upstanding citizens, rock 'n' roll, it turned out, was neither a Communist nor an African American plot.

Meanwhile the Beatles, as they huddled in the dugout before storming the stage, reportedly began to shiver. As it was

a hot, muggy August night, their nervous response was triggered by neither stage fright—they were way beyond that—nor
the weather, but by the amount of sheer electricity in the air.
Bedlam ensued as the Fab Four sprinted, guitars in hand, across
the field to the stage at second base.

According to one fan interviewed years later, the entire
stadium "actually started shaking."

"The whole upper deck of the stadium was bouncing," Frank
Branchini, another fan, concurred.

While some recalled the music as "wonderful," very few
could actually hear the Beatles above the ensuing hysteria.
Arthur Aaron, who was in the stands that night, compared the
relentless din to "Niagara Falls." The sound, he explained was "a
constant roar [that] never stopped. It never subsided the entire
three hours that I was there."

"The Beatles at Shea Stadium was the most remarkable
moment in my career," Cousin Bruce Morrow said. "All these
years later I can still feel the vibrations and electricity racing
through my body. That's how powerful it was. There will never
be another concert or moment like that again!"

Even their new custom 100-watt Vox amplifiers were no
match for the caterwauls emitting from their delirious crowd.
Everyone, it seemed, had come to *see* the Beatles—as hearing
them was simply out of the question. Their short set list of
twelve songs was comprised of recent hits, from "I Feel Fine,"
"Ticket to Ride," "Can't Buy Me Love," "She's A Woman" and
"Help!" to a batch of the band's favorite covers, which included
everything from soul tunes to rockabilly and C&W numbers.
Thanks to the Beatles, a younger generation of Americans inadvertently discovered some of their country's greatest music,
which otherwise would have slipped through the cracks into
obscurity. Having topped the charts with their version of the
Isley Brothers' "Twist and Shout," the Beatles covered no fewer
than three songs by New Orleans R&B pianist Larry Williams,
including "Bad Boy," "Slow Down," and, most recently, "Dizzy
Miss Lizzy," which John belted at the top of his lungs at Shea.
George (whose vocal cords never packed the wallop of either
Lennon's or McCartney's) gave his best on Carl Perkins's "Everybody's Trying to Be My Baby" (from *Beatles '65*), while Ringo sat

upon his drum throne like "the biggest fool who ever made the big time" warbling the Buck Owens cover "Act Naturally."

By the set's last number the band had become giddy as John, imitating Jerry Lee Lewis, played the organ with his elbows, smearing glissandos of notes as McCartney wailed "I'm Down." The next thing everyone knew, they were gone. Girls wailed like grief-stricken banshees as two thousand security guards attempted to control the frantic mob, while a Wells Fargo truck carted its precious human cargo off into the night.

The Beatles had taken the stage at approximately 9:15 p.m. Fifty minutes later, the band and their manager were $160,000 richer. The first arena rock show was an enormous success (even though not a single tour T-shirt was sold—they hadn't been invented yet), and rock 'n' roll was now securely in the hands of big business.

Ringo, who'd always been criticized as the band's weak link for his wobbly voice and his loosey-goosey drumming style, which, although slightly erratic, brimmed with soul and character, held the music together that night, as it was impossible for Lennon, McCartney, and Harrison to hear themselves, let alone each other. Having played "eight days a week" back in Hamburg's Reeperbahn, the Beatles proved they could rock a tight set under any circumstances, whether in their sleep or, in this case, a swirling nightmare. How were they supposed to connect with their audience, who seemed like they were sitting a mile away and were clearly out of their minds?

"The commotion," Paul explained, "doesn't bother us anymore. It's like working in a bell factory. You don't hear the bells anymore."

A documentary of the concert, titled *The Beatles at Shea Stadium*, was filmed by Ed Sullivan's production team, in cooperation with Brian Epstein's NEMS Enterprises and first premiered on BBC One in England on Tuesday, March 1, 1966. American fans would have to wait until January 10, 1967, to see it. By then, the Beatles had changed drastically from their former selves. Physically they were nearly unrecognizable, having sprouted mustaches and beards, while donning a mix-and-match psychedelic wardrobe of garish polka-dot and paisley designs. Musically they had transformed as well—John's "hazy, impressionistic" psychedelic masterpiece "Strawberry Fields Forever" was recorded a month before the Shea Stadium special hit the air.

On January 5, 1966, the Beatles arrived at London's CTS (Cine-Tele Sound) Studios to clean up the live tape for the Sullivan documentary. McCartney overdubbed new bass lines on "Can't Buy Me Love," "Baby's in Black," "Dizzy Miss Lizzy," and "I'm Down," to which John also replayed his organ part, replacing his frenetic, near slapstick live performance with something a bit more musical.

At George Martin's insistence the band cut entirely new versions of "I Feel Fine" and "Help!" with a bit more spontaneous, live feel than heard on the previous studio recordings. Watching the footage, the Fabs did their best to synch their vocals, delivering their trademark harmonies while trying to re-create the excitement of a live performance.

While George's "Everybody's Trying to Be My Baby" and Paul's "She's a Woman" ultimately wound up on the cutting-room floor ("because," as Michael Adams, the son of the documentary's director, explained, "they had to change the film during the song"), Ringo's moment in the spotlight, "Act Naturally," was linked up with the Beatles' earlier studio recording of the song. It worked surprisingly well for most of the performance, until Starr is seen momentarily singing with his mouth closed.

Although John wanted to recut "Ticket to Ride" for the film, he was outvoted. There is some speculation over whether the song, as it appeared in the movie, was played as such or whether the Beatles overdubbed new guitar parts to give it a crisper, cleaner sound.

As far as the opening number, "Twist and Shout," was concerned, George Martin opted to use the recording of their concert at the Hollywood Bowl, which took place two weeks later, as it had a far superior sound quality. But the whole affair was kept very hush-hush—Brian Epstein wanted everyone to believe his boys' performance was flawless despite their having to play under near battlefield conditions.

On October 26, 1965, the Beatles were chauffeured in a Rolls-Royce (the ultimate symbol of English establishment) over to Buckingham Palace, where they were ceremoniously awarded the MBE (Member of the Order of the British Empire) by Queen Elizabeth herself.

While "the spokesman of his generation" as Dylan was dubiously dubbed, embodied nonconformity and rebellion, the carefully coiffed Beatles were now lauded by the very establishment that stood steadfastly against everything that they and rock 'n' roll had represented. Some members were so infuriated that a bunch of longhairs had been invited into their elite club that they immediately returned their medals along with an assortment of terse sentiments. Hector Dupuis, from the Canadian Parliament, felt the Beatles' appointment was an outright insult to all men who bravely served their country. Dupuis (a Liberal!) was dismayed that gallant war heroes should be considered "on the same level as vulgar nincompoops," while a retired British colonel abruptly canceled any hope of a postmortem donation to England's Labour Party. Meanwhile, outside the palace, hysteria and mayhem ensued as usual, as throngs of screaming, fainting girls had to be subdued by an army of bobbies. While the award seemed to mean the world to Brian Epstein—as well as Paul (later *Sir* Paul), who would later write "Her Majesty" in honor of the Queen—George Harrison felt the bestowal of "that bloody old [medal]" was, at best, a transparent gesture to the band, in return for "selling all that corduroy and making [London] swing." (As for John, he would have his chauffeur Les Anthony return the dubious badge to Buckingham Palace on November 25, 1969, "in protest against Britain's involvement in the Nigeria-Biafra thing, against our support of America in Vietnam and [his latest single] 'Cold Turkey' slipping down the charts."

Despite the day-to-day chaos of the world, there seemed to be a brief moment in 1965 when popular music (thanks to the Beatles' irrepressible spirit and sense of inventiveness) was rife with possibility, before the Fabs dove off the deep end into some seriously weird territory, singing the praises of pot and LSD, before Lennon and his Japanese conceptual artist girlfriend, Yoko Ono, began occupying large bags and hotel rooms, in the name of peace . . . before Paul McCartney started that other band, before George Harrison traded in his guitar for a garden hoe, and before Ringo became famous to a new generation as "Mr. Conductor," the bearded jovial railroad engineer from *Shining Time Station*.

3
Beatles '65

"The Beatles saved the world from boredom."
—George Harrison

Released just ten days before Christmas, 1964, the Fabs' new album *Beatles for Sale*—or *Beatles '65*, as it was known in the States—was a mixed bag of the band's latest originals, rounded out by a batch of old rock 'n' roll numbers, some of which the band had been playing since their early days in Liverpool as the Quarrymen. While the records shared eight titles between them, the American pressing lacked their recent hits "Eight Days a Week" and "I Don't Want to Spoil the Party," along with a pair of forgettable B-sides, "Every Little Thing" and "What You're Doing." There were also a batch of great cover tunes, including a sweat-busting medley of Leiber and Stoller's classic "Kansas City" mashed up with Little Richard's "Hey Hey Hey," which featured McCartney's searing falsetto, as well as a tender cover of Buddy Holly's "Words of Love," sung in a low, breathy, sensual whisper that was nothing short of mesmerizing. But Americans would have to wait to hear those tracks until June 14, 1965, when Capitol released the rather shoddy collection *Beatles VI*.

Beatles '65 kicked off with a bitter bossa-nova breakup number called "No Reply." Over a gently strummed acoustic guitar John Lennon's voice reveals the influence of Dylan's weary rasp as he recounts the pain he's suffered at the hands of a heartless girl.

Themes of separation and uncontrollable jealousy appeared in Lennon's songs throughout his life, from "I'll Cry Instead" and "I'll Get You," (two of *A Hard Day's Night*'s creepier moments) to his last album, *Double Fantasy*, released in 1980, the year of his murder, which included the dark, claustrophobic "I'm Losing You." Unable to let go of a girl who has apparently already moved on without him, the singer repeatedly calls her on the telephone while spying on her house, in order to keep track of who is coming and going. Perhaps the object of his obsession made the right choice after all, refusing to have anything to do with him, as, in his self-absorbed misery, he's become nothing more than a creepy stalker.

For the Byrds' bassist/mandolinist Chris Hillman, "No Reply" represented the Beatles "at the top of their game. . . . There is no rock blueprint for this," he told *Mojo* magazine. "That rhythm Lennon and Harrison are playing on their guitars is funky, out of left field. This is the stuff which got us all over here to put down the mandolins and banjos and plug in and pay attention to rock again."

Like the Byrds, who topped the charts with their "Beatl- ized" Dylan anthems, everyone borrowed and exploited the Fabs' sound and style, including the Tex-Mex rockers known as the Sir Douglas Quintet, who donned collarless jackets (with cowboy boots) and gave their group an aristocratic name to help encourage airplay at a time when America was obsessed with and overrun by British culture. Fronted by Doug Sahm, the band had a funky 1965 hit single, "She's About a Mover," which bore a strong resemblance to McCartney's "She's a Woman," while the Beau Brummels from San Francisco, with their cleverly anglicized name and sound, peaked at number fifteen on the *Billboard* charts with "Laugh, Laugh" (produced by Sylvester Stewart, soon to be the world-famous Sly Stone). Other Brit wannabes of the day included the Buckinghams, a Chicago combo whose "Kind of a Drag" went gold in February '67, while the most eclectic and noncommercial band to cash in on the trend was a Boston-based bluegrass group known as the Charles River Valley Boys, who cut an album for Elektra Records called *Beatle Country*, of tightly arranged Lennon/McCartney hits played on acoustic guitar, banjo, and mandolin and sung in a plaintive high lonesome style.

John Lennon's "I'm a Loser" was a rather brutal self-portrait, at the low point of what he dubbed his "fat Elvis" period. The catchy country shuffle features John stretching out vocally, begin- ning the tune with a hoarse a cappella before scraping the bottom of his range in his best imitation of Johnny Cash, as McCartney's walking bass buoyantly bounces the song along. Lennon growls on his harmonica à la Dylan while George Harrison offers some fine Merle Travis–style picking. "I'm a Loser" unceremoniously lifted the carefree mask worn by the leader of the world's most popular band, to reveal a rather unhappy bloke. There's nothing very new or original about a clown "wearing a frown." As writing goes, it's rather trite. We'd certainly heard it plenty of times before, ten years earlier from the Platters with "The Great Pretender," and from Smokey Robinson, who offered "My Smile Is Just a Frown (Turned Upside Down)"; in 1967, he would deliver the similarly themed "The Tears of a Clown." But it's Lennon's willingness to reveal his vulnerability that's most surprising. He actually seems to be singing about himself for a change, rather than a fictional character or fabricated scenario. And it's powerful stuff. Perhaps John was inspired by Roy Orbison, a man who was fearless when it came to wearing his heart on his sleeve in an era when male role models were forged by Humphrey Bogart–style tough guys who silently sucked up their pain and nursed their wounds by chain-smoking and knocking back one shot of booze after the next until there was little or nothing left to feel.

"I'm a Loser" matters because it was the forerunner to John's early milestone songs like "Help," "Nowhere Man," "In My Life," and "Strawberry Fields Forever," in which the singer stands naked, shedding all artifice of fiction as the song—swirling with mellotrons, brass, cellos and exotic Indian instruments—creates a dreamscape where "nothing is real."

"Part of me suspects that I'm a loser," Lennon later told *Playboy*. "And the other part of me thinks I'm God Almighty."

Arguably the most morbid song in the Beatles' catalog (other than 1967's "A Day in the Life," in which Lennon laughs after reading the news that his friend Tara Browne, the heir to the Guinness fortune, was killed in a car crash), "Baby's in Black" paints the portrait of a grief-stricken widow (perhaps Astrid Kirchherr bereft over her poor doomed Stuart Sutcliffe) and a helpless friend, who awkwardly searches for the proper words to comfort her. The song came as something of a surprise, blending a twangy country waltz with a chorus worthy of an Irish pub sing-along. "Baby's in Black" contained some of the Beatles' best close-harmony style singing to date, undoubtedly influenced by the Everly Brothers, who grew up admiring the Louvin Brothers, a white country gospel duo from Sand Mountain, Alabama, who not only influenced Don and Phil Everly, but were a huge favorite of Elvis Presley's as well.

Ira and Charlie Louvin's songs were often morbid to the point of absurdity. Their fundamentalist Christian morals were so extreme that the songs often seemed to border on parody. When the Gram Parsons–led Byrds recorded their song "The Christian Life" in 1968 for their country-rock masterpiece *Sweetheart of the Rodeo*, Byrdmaniacs (as fans of the band were known) had to stop and scratch their heads and wonder if they were joking or not. Perhaps . . . but within a decade Roger McGuinn would become a born-again Christian and, along with T-Bone Burnett, would lead Bob Dylan to see the light in 1978, when the "voice of a generation" would suddenly become a disciple of Christ following a soul-crushing divorce from his wife Sara.

Recorded on August 11, 1964, just as *A Hard Day's Night* was topping the charts, "Baby's in Black" was the first tune cut for the *Beatles for Sale* sessions. The song took fourteen takes as John and Paul insisted on singing their parts together, live, into the same microphone, in hopes of capturing an authentic country-western sound. Their voices were so deeply entwined it's difficult to tell who sang lead and who carried the harmony. Oddly enough, "Baby's in Black" became a staple of the Beatles' live shows from late 1964 through their final show in August 1966. Never sure what their audience might think about this peculiar tune, McCartney, ever the band's charming emcee, routinely introduced it as "something different."

"Baby's in Black" had a remarkably long life, which stretched beyond the band's breakup in the spring of 1970; it was resurrected once again in 1996 with a live recording of the song released as the B-side to the Beatles' final single, "Real Love," a posthumous project on which the group's three surviving members overdubbed their instruments and voices on an unreleased John Lennon track.

The next cut on *Beatles '65* featured Lennon shredding his larynx on a kick-ass cover of Chuck Berry's classic "Rock 'n' Roll Music."

JOHN LENNON'S ROCK 'N' ROLL ROOTS

IN SEPTEMBER OF '69, barely a month after completing the *Abbey Road* sessions, John Lennon received a call from a festival promoter in Toronto asking him to be the emcee for a large rock 'n' roll revival stadium show the very next day. Lennon remarked that he'd rather play.

On a whim, Lennon threw together the Plastic Ono Band, which featured Eric Clapton on guitar (George Harrison had allegedly refused to drop everything and fly to Canada at a moment's notice); Lennon's wife, Yoko Ono; famed illustrator/old friend from Hamburg/bassist with Manfred Mann, Klaus Voormann; and drummer Alan White. With two rehearsals, (one of which took place on the plane), the band was ill-prepared to perform on a bill that showcased nearly every living legend of 1950s rock 'n' roll, including Little Richard, Jerry Lee Lewis, Chuck Berry, Fats Domino, Bo Diddley, and Gene Vincent, along with the Doors and Alice Cooper. Lennon, who was allegedly a nervous wreck, as he hadn't played a concert in nearly five years, threw up before taking the stage at Varsity Stadium to sing for twenty-five thousand people. "We're just going to do numbers we know, you know, because we've never played together before," Lennon stammered. A moment later the band lurched into a raucous rendition of "Blue Suede Shoes," which allegedly made Carl Perkins tell Lennon it was "so beautiful you made me cry." John and the Plastic Ono Band also rocked Barrett Strong's "Money" and Larry Williams's "Dizzy Miss Lizzy," both of which he performed in the early Beatles repertoire. The rest of the set would include "Yer Blues" (which he had performed with Clapton for a small crowd the previous December at the ill-fated Rolling Stones Rock and Roll Circus) plus a pair of his first solo songs, including "Cold Turkey" and "Give Peace a Chance" before John handed the mic over to Yoko, whose avant-garde caterwauling, framed with shrieking feedback from Lennon and Clapton's guitars, only alienated the enthralled crowd. The ensuing document of the concert, *Live Peace in Toronto 1969*, reached number ten on the *Billboard* charts.

Having released a handful of experimental albums with Yoko, and unsatisfied with the response to his solo efforts, John recorded the back-to-basics *Rock 'n' Roll* in 1975, produced by Phil Spector. Amongst this set of favorite oldies was Fats Domino's "Ain't That a Shame," the first tune Lennon had learned to play.

"I always liked simple rock and nothing else. . . . Really I like rock 'n' roll and I express myself best in rock," Lennon told *Rolling Stone* in December 1970.

Years later John would return to straight-ahead rock 'n' roll once more, singing his last single, "(Just Like) Starting Over," in a reverb-drenched, herky-jerky style he jokingly dubbed "Elvis Orbison."

John adored Chuck . . . perhaps a little too much. With "Come Together," the lead-off song from 1969's *Abbey Road*, Lennon nicked the line "Here comes old flat-top" from Berry's 1956 rocker "You Can't Catch Me" and wound up with a plagiarism suit on his hands. As a settlement with Berry's publisher, the notoriously devious Morris Levy, John agreed to record three of Chuck's songs for his following album. (While Lennon recorded three, only two were released during his lifetime.) But everybody would kiss and make up after John and Yoko moved to New York; in early 1972 they cohosted *The Mike Douglas Show* and invited Chuck Berry to perform with them, along with their motley street band, Elephant's Memory. Despite Lennon's newfound, all-inclusive proletariat philosophy, which encouraged amateurs to share the same stage with genuine legends, this ragtag amalgamation, which also featured Yippie instigator Jerry Rubin, gleefully pounding away on a tom-tom, managed to deliver rousing renditions of two Berry classics, including "Memphis" and "Johnny B. Goode," although Chuck appeared truly perplexed by Yoko's random primal shrieking into the microphone.

The Beatles would rework a handful of fifties classics on *Beatles '65* including two Carl Perkins numbers, "Everybody's Trying to Be My Baby," sung in a Sun Records–style reverb-drenched voice by his disciple, George Harrison, along with the good-time shuffle "Honey Don't," which featured Ringo's ebullient vocal and the classic ad lib "Ah rock on George for Ringo one time!"

Most of the album's songs by this point were over ten years old, relics from a bygone decade that the Beatles, along with Bob Dylan, had done more than anybody else to raze. Yet they played and sang old-school rock 'n' roll with true passion and abandon. Even their famously genteel producer George Martin let his perpetually well-groomed hair down for a hot minute, hammering the eighty-eights on "Rock 'n' Roll Music," like Professor Longhair after one too many cups of Earl Grey. These tracks still stand as evidence today as the sort of chain lightning the Beatles regularly unleashed in their live act.

McCartney's sentimental farewell, "I'll Follow the Sun," was sung from the point of view of an easygoing beachcomber with a live-for-today philosophy, despite losing "a friend in the end."

Paul had written the tune years before on the piano when the Beatles were paying their dues in Hamburg. Recorded four years later, on October 18, 1964, the combination of acoustic guitar with a pair of lightly clicking claves lays down a sweet Buddy-Holly-with-sand-between-his-toes groove, as George's nicely phrased lead quotes the melody.

One of the corniest tunes in the Beatles' repertoire (complete with a cheeseball skating-arena organ solo played by Paul), Georgia R&B singer Roy Lee Johnson's "Mr. Moonlight" still manages to pack a punch to this day thanks to Lennon's killer vocal delivery. John's nearly feral plea to the frozen lonely orb hovering above the star-crossed lover proves what a great torch singer he was.

A leftover from *A Hard Day's Night*, "I'll Be Back," could easily have been titled "No Reply Part Two." This time Lennon warns his lover that if she cuts him loose he'll "be back again." The lyric hints at revenge as he promises that "he's got a big surprise" planned. Built on pair of strummed acoustic guitars and a buttery two-part harmony, the song evokes the Everly Brothers in a dark mood.

"Fucking hell, it's a ghost!" McCartney cried as wild distortion suddenly shook the studio walls after Lennon absentmindedly left his guitar leaning against his amp. Never a band to let a happy accident go by, John fashioned the unwieldy sound into the opening riff of "I Feel Fine."

Backed with McCartney's funky rocker "She's a Woman," "I Feel Fine" was released as the Beatles' new single on November 23, 1964. Inspired by Bobby Parker's "Watch Your Step," a song that Lennon considered "the next move after [Ray Charles's] 'What I'd Say,'" John confessed that the Beatles had used Parker's infectious riff "in various forms."

"People liked that lick. I've heard fifty-seven different arrangements of it, from Santana to Jimmy Page," Bobby Parker sighed in the 2004 documentary *John Lennon's Jukebox*.

JOHN LENNON'S JUKEBOX

CHRISTOPHER WALKER's fascinating documentary *John Lennon's Jukebox* delves into the history of a Swiss-made KB Discomatic portable jukebox that

John Lennon bought in 1965 and took on tour with him to keep the music he loved within earshot. John stocked his state-of-the-art machine with forty of his favorite singles (the compact cassette tape player wouldn't hit the market for another year), mostly comprised of soul records by Smokey Robinson and the Miracles, Otis Redding, Wilson Pickett, the Isley Brothers, and Gary U.S. Bonds, as well as some old-school rock 'n' roll hits from Little Richard, Buddy Holly, Chuck Berry, and Gene Vincent. Curiously, the collection included nothing by Elvis. Of his fellow Brits, Lennon chose Donovan and the Animals (nothing by the Stones, Yardbirds, or Kinks), along with a few of his favorite American peers, Bob Dylan, the Lovin' Spoonful, and even Paul Revere and the Raiders. Interestingly, "Rescue Me" by Fontella Bass was the only song on Lennon's jukebox sung by a woman.

"That was the beginning of 'I Feel Fine.' That particular introduction did a lot for their song," Parker pointed out. Although Bobby claimed he was "flattered" that the Beatles borrowed the trademark riff he'd been known for around Washington, DC, club circuit since 1961, he felt, "in the back of his mind," that he "should have gotten a little more recognition."

The most popular album of the year, *Beatles '65* spent nine weeks at number one on the *Billboard* charts, beginning on January 9. The album unexpectedly created a trend, inspiring everyone from Sinatra to Duke Ellington to Sergio Mendes to tack the year '65 onto their name as the snazzy title for their latest albums.

4
The Cover Story

*"We all think it's just about our best LP.
The picture on the front is pretty good."*
—George Harrison

The Robert Freeman photograph that graced the sleeve of *Rubber Soul* perfectly captured the time in which it was made. Freeman, who had been photographing the Beatles since their first American release, *Meet the Beatles*, claimed that with this cover he was searching for "another angle" and a "different tonality."

While his photo for the band's previous album, *Beatles for Sale*, portrayed the band looking windblown and weary (undoubtedly exhausted from the mad pace of touring, recording, and, more recently, acting in their first feature film), the photo, taken as the light was fading on a winter day, was deemed too unforgiving for the American market and was replaced in the States with a series of images of the group posing coyly beneath umbrellas, safe, for the time being, from whatever storm might have been brewing outside the studio.

With *Rubber Soul*, gone were the Fabs' cute matching jackets and ties. The band stood shoulder to shoulder, huddled together in the cool autumn air, like a clump of wild mushrooms. George, "the soul horse," as beat poet Allen Ginsberg called him in his poem "Portland Coliseum," hollow-cheeked, eyes distant, sporting that solemn "Don't Bother Me" look that he'd perfected to combat the lunacy of Beatlemania, appears aloof, as though he had some place he'd rather have been than messing around with all this stupid pop-star nonsense. Beside him, John, the only Beatle to make eye contact with the camera, gazes down his long, thin nose through Freeman's lens, into the window of your soul, as if he knew the answer to everything but (for a change) wasn't talking. Slightly behind Lennon stands Ringo, also in suede, content to go along for the ride. To his left, Paul, sincere as always, doe-eyed cute from any angle.

There's something ghostly about the image, not just in their drawn, stretched-out faces, but in the way the boys lean together, pale, washed out, like old tombstones. You can almost feel the chill in the air. A closer look at the full-frame image, released several years later, reveals John with his hands shoved down into the pockets of his blue jeans, while Paul's jacket is pulled down over his hands to protect them from the cold. Their hair, hanging in their eyes, falling over their collars, creeps toward their shoulders like wild vines.

Incidentally, a quick glance at the cover of *The Freewheelin' Bob Dylan* shows the song-poet trudging up Jones Street on a winter's day in Greenwich Village, with his long-haired bohemian girlfriend, Suze Rotolo, at his side. Bob is also wearing a suede jacket with his hands thrust deep into the pockets of his jeans against the freezing wind.

According to journalist Maureen Cleave, John Lennon's iconic suede jacket was later sold to National Museums Liverpool for £28,000. "There's a worn patch in the lining where his arm moved, strumming the guitar," she said. "At the auction it was held up by a young curator in white gloves, as though it were a holy relic."

Bob Freeman's career as a professional photographer began back in 1961, when he shot American jazz legends John Coltrane and Julian "Cannonball" Adderley while they performed in British clubs. Two years later he met the Beatles during their first tour of England. Freeman's stark portrait of the mop-tops on *With the Beatles* (known as *Meet the Beatles* in the States) was the image that literally introduced millions of people to the band. Freeman was then hired to film and edit the fast-paced opening credit scene of *A Hard Day's Night*. At the time, Bob was married to a German model named Sonny Spielhagen, whose provocative poses graced the popular Pirelli Tire calendar back in the early sixties. More than forty years later, in an interview with Philip Norman for his recent biography *Lennon*, Sonny claimed to be John's inspiration for "Norwegian Wood."

Although a fine portrait of the band, a happy accident that no one could have foreseen would transform Freeman's photo into the iconic image it soon became. As Paul recalled: "Whilst projecting the slides on to an album-sized piece of white cardboard, Bob inadvertently tilted the card backward. The effect was to stretch the perspective and elongate the faces. We excitedly asked him if it was possible to print the photo in this way."

In an interview with *Mojo* in 2006, McCartney picked up the story again, this time a bit more colorfully: "The card fell backward about 25 degrees and just stayed there, and we all went, 'Fucking hell!' 'Cos our heads had all stretched, because of the angle. We all went, 'Shit! That's fantastic!' Now I maintain that other people would have gone, 'Oh bloody hell, the card's fallen down,' and I maintain that that's the genius of the Beatles encapsulated in that."

Freeman believed "the distorted effect was a reflection of the changing shape of their lives." While ultimately "disappointed with the image quality," Bob felt that *Rubber Soul* was the band's "most successful cover" to date, thanks in part to Charles Front's innovative typography. An unknown art director (soon to become a children's book illustrator, whose work includes Barbara Sleigh's popular *Carbonel & Calidor*), Front was contacted by Bob Freeman to create the trippy-drippy lettering for the Beatles' new record jacket. Although most folks assumed his iconic calligraphy was either inspired by the effects of LSD or the often-imitated Art Nouveau posters of the Moravian painter Alphonse Mucha, Charlie (as he was known to friends and students) claimed the album's strange title led him to do some research on rubber manufacturing. "If you tap into a rubber tree then you get a sort of globule," Front told journalist Lisa Bachelor of the *Observer* in 2007. "So I started thinking of creating a shape that represented that."

Regardless of the album cover's striking originality, it was the last time that Freeman would work with the Beatles. Perhaps Sonny Spielhagen had actually made Lennon "sleep in the bath," as John suggested in the lyrics to "Norwegian Wood."

Though the Rolling Stones had a rough-edged style all their own, John Lennon often accused the band of taking artistic cues from the Beatles (check out the lyrics to "I Dig a Pony," John's caustic put-down of Jagger/Richards and company, in which he calls them out for imitating "everyone you know"). Released barely over a year after *Rubber Soul*, in January 1967, *Between the Buttons* featured a remarkably similar cover shot of the Stones taken by Gered Mankowitz on London's Primrose Hill. Smearing the edges of his lens with Vaseline, to create the feeling of a blurry, lost autumn afternoon, Mankowitz captured "the ethereal, druggy feel of the time." But the wild wind that tousled the Stones' scraggly hair wasn't the only reason they appeared so utterly disheveled. This was the first glimpse the public had of just how badly the band's dandy, Brian Jones (whose predilection for mixing booze and pills would lead him to an early grave), had deteriorated. Standing on the edge of the photograph as if upon a treacherous precipice, Keith Richards grins maniacally behind a pair of shades as Charlie Watts, looking like a hit man, eyes distant, leans into the wind in his black overcoat, while hollow-cheeked, heavy-lidded, Bill Wyman stands like a zombie, aloof in the rear. Haggard and agitated, Mick Jagger exhibits a barracuda grimace that looks as if he might eviscerate you at any moment.

Rubber Soul was just one of many Beatles album covers the Stones imitated over the years. Hounded by the police in 1967 and enduring a series of sensationalized drug busts that saw Jagger, Richards, and Jones hauled in and out of prison and brought before pompous magistrates determined to make an example out of them, the band needed something catchy to wrap their psychedelic misadventure *Their Satanic Majesties Request* in. Stunned by the fantastic imagery and detail of *Sgt. Pepper*, the Stones immediately hired Michael Cooper, the same photographer responsible for shooting the Beatles' intricate cover. But unlike the Beatles (who chose the images that comprised the colorful set and then posed for the famous photograph), the Stones actually built their own fantasy land over a three day period, constructing a flimsy magic castle, shimmering mountain peaks, and a dangling Styrofoam Saturn from, as Keith recalled, "God knows what . . . millions of bits of sequins, rhinestones and beads." Photographed by Cooper with a 3-D camera, the holographic image, when tilted, caused the band's faces to turn and look at one another, with the exception of Jagger, who sat center stage, shrouded in a purple cape, wearing a peaked wizard's cap. Originally dubbed *The Cosmic Christmas* (at the end of side one, strains of "We Wish You a Merry Christmas" can heard, played on a woozy synthesizer by Brian Jones), *Satanic Majesties* was released in December 1967. Deemed "a strange electric holocaust" by the *New Musical Express* (popularly known as *NME*), the album was unanimously panned by the press as well as by John Lennon (who, along with Paul McCartney, loaned his vocals to the record). Images of all four Beatles can be found on the cover, hidden within the mounds of flowers that engulfed the band.

No one was more brutal in their assessment of the Stones' brief dalliance with psychedelia than Keith Richards, who dismissed *Satanic Majesties* as "a load of crap." Richards tried his best to distance himself from the Stones' flawed concept album, claiming, "I can remember virtually nothing of those sessions. It's a total blank." Even Charlie Watts's mother, Lilian, took a shot at the album, when she quipped, "It was at least two weeks ahead of its time."

THE PREFAB FOUR

RELEASED IN JANUARY 1967, the cover of the Monkees' sophomore effort, *More of the Monkees*, suspiciously mimicked Robert Freeman's portrait for *Rubber Soul* with its groovy design and wide-angle outdoor portrait of the band, even as it was originally shot for a JCPenney fashion spread.

It was no secret that everything the Monkees (deridingly known as the "Prefab Four") did was a knockoff of the Beatles. Their weekly TV show, *The Monkees*, which ran from September 1966 to March 1968, was nothing more than a pale but charming imitation of *A Hard Day's Night*. No matter how they complained, the show made enormous stars out of Davy Jones, Mike Nesmith, Mickey Dolenz, and Peter Tork, who edged out his friend Stephen Stills for the role as the band's jovial bassist—allegedly, he was picked because he had more telegenic teeth.

The Monkees weren't a real band; they were actors from diverse backgrounds who were thrown together to play a band on a TV show. Oddly enough, the diminutive British front man, (former jockey) Davy Jones, was the best drummer of the lot, but the show's producers, Bob Rafelson and Bert Schneider, were concerned that he'd be lost behind the drum kit. So the group's best vocalist, Mickey Dolenz (who, as a child starred in the 1950s TV show *Circus Boy*), was handed the sticks and given some drum lessons. Peter Tork, who performed at various Greenwich Village coffeehouses before moving to L.A., was actually a better guitarist than Mike Nesmith, while Nesmith had actually played bass professionally before the Prefab Four were concocted. The group soon mutinied, having decided they wanted to be a real band and actually sing and play their own instruments rather than just lip-synch their hits and rely on session men. They were met with serious resistance from their creator, Don Kirshner.

When the Monkees flew to Hawaii to first test the waters as a live act, Kirshner—the mad doctor responsible for this monster—released their second album, *More of the Monkees*, without a word to the band. Although it included a couple Michael Nesmith originals (along with Neil Diamond's "I'm a Believer," which would be a massive hit for them), the Monkees felt betrayed.

When Kirshner had finally had enough of dealing with real people whom he couldn't control, his solution was to create an animated band called the Archies, based on the popular comic strip *Archie*, first published in 1941. Kirshner gave this lovable gang of high school kids a makeover, updating their image with sixties-style clothes, guitars, and a set of drums. By 1969, their bubblegum smash "Sugar Sugar" topped the charts in nine countries world-wide; the song ultimately sold six million copies. Not surprisingly, Kirshner's latest commercial brainstorm also owed a debt to the Beatles.

The following year, the Stones' cover concept—a filthy toilet with graffiti scrawled on a stained wall announcing the band's name with the album title—was not surprisingly scrapped by their label, Decca Records. Despite infuriating the Stones and delaying the record's release, their conservative company preferred a more dignified cover—a formal invitation that read in elegant italic script: *Rolling Stones, Beggars Banquet, R.SV.P.* Released on December 6, exactly two weeks after *The Beatles*, a double album with a minimalist white jacket, the Stones' new record (great as it was) quickly became known as "The Other White Album."

It's no wonder that John Lennon groused, "Everything we do, the Stones do four months later."

5

"Yesterday"

*"For something that just appeared in a dream, even I have to
acknowledge that it was a phenomenal stroke of luck."*
—*Paul McCartney*

It is said that the song had mystical beginnings in the attic of
the Asher family house on Wimpole Street, where Paul lived in
May 1965. McCartney claimed to have awakened one morning
with the melody ringing in his head, complete. All he had to do
was climb out of bed, sit down at the piano, which was only a
few feet away, and figure out the chords. Lyrics were never Paul's
strong suit. He certainly has had plenty of brilliant ideas over
the years, and his sense of melody and arrangement was second
to none (other than perhaps Brian Wilson), but his words were
often light, as much of Paul's solo career would later attest.

Although the music flowed freely, McCartney often drew a
blank when it came to finding something to say. But inspiration soon struck as Paul played his latest opus for Alma Cogan
(whose giggly voice made her the most popular British female
singer of the 1950s but who was suddenly deemed out of style
with the arrival of the new mod decade). Paul quickly improvised a few lines at Cogan's home while her mother whipped
up a batch of scrambled eggs for her daughter and their famous
guest.

"Scrambled eggs . . ." he began to sing. "Oh baby how I love
your legs . . ."

Paul's girlfriend at the time, the actor Jane Asher, would claim
the song had nothing to do with her, as her legs were hardly
worthy of such praise. As the tune first came to McCartney fully
realized in a dream, he was rather nervous about its origins, afraid
there might have been a bit of plagiarism taking place, whether
of the subconscious or unconscious variety—a phenomenon
known as cryptomnesia. Determined to steer clear of potential
lawsuits (both John and George would later be charged with

nicking a bit too much inspiration from fifties hit makers Chuck Berry and Johnny Otis, respectively), Paul played the song for everybody he could, from his bandmates to friends, asking if they'd ever heard it anywhere before. "I couldn't believe it," McCartney remarked. "It came too easy."

Not surprisingly, there were multiple versions of the song's miraculous "virgin birth." While George Martin believed Paul wrote "Yesterday" at a hotel in Paris in January 1964, Muriel Young from the British TV show *The Five O'Clock Club* recalled McCartney working out the words, playing a guitar upside down, as there was no left-handed model available in Albufeira, a small fishing village in Portugal.

As Paul later told journalist Brian Matthew in March 1967, he originally forged the melody on a "medieval guitar" while on a holiday in Corsica. Once more he facetiously sang "Scrambled eggs" but recalls having some crucial input from his partner. "I never could finish it, and eventually I took it back in. With the ancient wisdom of the east, John came out with [sings] 'Yesterday.'"

No matter how enormous "Yesterday" became, Lennon claimed he wanted no part of it. "That is Paul's song, of course, and Paul's baby. Well done," John said in an interview many years later. "Beautiful," adding coldly, "and I never wished I had written it."

In 1965 Paul McCartney was a man with a truly deep connection to his art. On one day, June 14, he recorded three top-notch songs, each one quite different from the next: "I've Just Seen a Face," "Yesterday," and (just in case you thought he'd lost his rock 'n' roll edge) the frenetic "I'm Down."

June 14 also saw the American release of *Beatles VI*, another hodgepodge of hits and B-sides compiled by Capitol (including "Eight Days a Week" and "I Don't Want to Spoil the Party") along with a batch of cover songs (including a rocking rendition of Larry Williams's "Bad Boy") that had been left off *Beatles for Sale*.

With the release of *Beatles '65* in December 1964, Capitol had begun flooding the market with Beatles albums every couple of months: *The Early Beatles* arrived in March, followed by *Beatles VI* in June, *Help!* in August, and finally, *Rubber Soul*, just in time for Christmas of 1965. As the comedic folksinger

Allan Sherman (best known for "Hello Mudduh, Hello Fadduh," which charted at number fifty-nine in 1964) complained in his parody "Pop Hates the Beatles" (sung to the tune of "Pop Goes the Weasel"): "There's Beatle books and T-shirts and rings and one thing and another. To buy my daughter all of these things, I had to sell her brother."

While some might pinpoint "Yesterday" as the precise moment when the Beatles began to grow up, hints of their maturity could first be heard in Paul's earlier "Things We Said Today," (released as the B-side to "A Hard Day's Night," while found in the States on the 1964 compilation album *Something New*). Beyond the lover's earnest pledge of everlasting union, no matter what the future held, there was a quality, an atmosphere to that song, more red wine than rum and coke. You had to take it seriously; after all, it was in a noirish minor key, and not many pop tunes were written in minor keys at the time, beyond the Rolling Stones' sullen "Heart of Stone."

According to Eric Burdon, Paul, wildly excited about his new song, delivered a demo of "Yesterday" to the blue-eyed soul singer Chris Farlowe's house "in the middle of the night" while he "was out doing a show." (Farlowe would top the British pop charts in 1966 with a cover of the Stones' "Out of Time" that sounded more Righteous Brothers than Glimmer Twins.) McCartney allegedly left the recording in the care of Chris's mom, but Farlowe passed on the song, complaining to Burdon, "I don't like it. It's not for me. It's too soft. I need a good rocker, you know, a shuffle or something."

After Paul recorded two takes of "Yesterday" solo on his Epiphone Texan acoustic, with none of the other Beatles contributing to the track, George Martin composed and recorded a string arrangement for two violins, viola, and cello. Brian Epstein and George Martin were then faced with the quandary over whether to release the song under the Beatles' name or as a McCartney solo project, but Epstein insisted that the single remain a group effort, at the risk of breaking up the band.

There's little doubt that the other Beatles felt somewhat irked by all the fuss over McCartney's first masterpiece. Known for his dry wit, George Harrison allegedly remarked, "You'd think he was Beethoven or somebody."

As long as the classical session players that George Martin hired laid off the heavy vibrato while they overdubbed the string section on his pristine ballad, Paul was content to be "Beethoven"—just as long as no one compared him to Annunzio Paolo Mantovani, the Italian conductor whose name in the 1960s became synonymous with schmaltzy easy-listening arrangements for large orchestras.

Backed by a string quartet, McCartney performed a tender rendition of "Yesterday" before a television audience of 73 million people for the Beatles' final appearance on *The Ed Sullivan Show*, on August 14, 1965. John Lennon then dashed up to the microphone as the girls shrieked like a swarm of locusts, to thank "Ringo." "That was wonderful!" he cheered.

The Beatles' version of "Yesterday"—or, more accurately, McCartney's solo performance of the song—held tight at number one from October 9 through the 30th only to finally get shoved out of the coveted top slot by the Stones' tight and funky "Get Off My Cloud." Thanks to the relentless prodding of their manager, Andrew Loog Oldham, Mick and Keith were finally convinced (much to Brian Jones' chagrin) that the London blues scene where they first made their name would be dead inside of six months and they'd be buried along with it if they didn't start writing their own songs. Oldham, who'd worked under Brian Epstein before producing the Stones, knew the real money was in songwriting. Encouraging Jagger and Richards to model themselves after the Lennon/McCartney partnership was not enough. So Andrew locked them in their kitchen to force the issue. Eventually they cobbled together a morose ballad called "As Tears Go By," which Keith felt was "very un-Stonelike." The band then handed it to Mick's girlfriend, Marianne Faithfull, to record, and within weeks the song had climbed to the Top Ten. "That's when Mick and I looked each other and said, 'Well maybe we can write songs,'" Richards told author Terry Southern.

Jagger and Richards cranked out a string of hits that stormed the radio throughout 1965 (beginning with "The Last Time," in February and ending the year with their own version of "As Tears Go By"), their tunes revealing the influence of all things American, from the Staple Singers (whose "This May Be the Last Time" was clearly the inspiration for their recent hit) to Hank Williams to Chicago blues to Stax soul and Motown grooves.

According to *The Guinness Book of World Records*, "Yesterday" is the most recorded song in history, covered by nearly three thousand artists. The list is both predictable and bizarre, ranging from Ray Charles (whose dirgelike version was reminiscent of "Old Man River," teeming with angst and regret) to Rowan Atkinson as Mr. Bean (complete with purple mai tai umbrellas in his hair) singing in drunken reverie as he and his buddy wobble down the street. Elvis Presley's live version of "Yesterday," from his 1970 release *On Stage*, was cucumber cool, his delivery completely natural, as the words seemed to roll effortlessly off his tongue. Marvin Gaye only hinted at the melody, leaving the well-worn tune to the strings while his soaring vocal brings all the soul, sorrow, and regret that few could muster. Allegedly McCartney has said that he prefers Marvin's version to the original.

Sadly, when Frank Sinatra, the "Chairman of the Board," got around to it, he sounded, frankly, bored. With "Yesterday," for once, Sinatra seemed as if he wasn't in control of the music. He didn't own the song, as he simply went through the motions, singing listlessly, adrift in a sea of syrupy strings. The lyric, filled with deep regret, sounds phony, put-on. While Sinatra could be sentimental, *vulnerable* was not in the man's vocabulary. Perhaps he would have been more at home with the tune's original lyrics: "Scrambled eggs . . . Oh baby how I love your legs."

Frank and the Fabs certainly made strange bedfellows. Sinatra loathed rock 'n' roll and was quick to say so. He hated Elvis, in particular, branding Presley's music "a rank aphrodisiac." "Old Blue Eyes" could barely contain his contempt for the Beatles, despite his new makeover on the cover of his 1969 album *My Way*, in which Frank appeared to have made the slightest concession to the decade's most prevalent trend, growing his hair a half an inch longer and combing it down in a Julius Caesar–like fringe.

Paul once called "Yesterday" the "most complete song I have ever written." No matter who sings it or what format it's sold in,

"Yesterday," like it or not, is here to stay. It is, in fact the most played song of all time, with approximately 6 million performances on American radio, about 2 million times more spins than any other record.

With the enormous revenue it generated, McCartney could have hung up his rock 'n' roll shoes right then and there and moved to Scotland, where he and the blonde American photographer Linda Eastman (whom he'd marry four years later, in March 1969) could live happily ever after off his eternal cash cow, on a big farm in the bucolic highlands, singing "silly little love songs" to their hearts' content.

6

"I've Just Seen a Face"

"When I first heard [Rubber Soul] I flipped.
I said, 'I want to make an album like that.'
The entire album seemed to be like a collection of folk songs.
We did Pet Sounds *after that."*
—Brian Wilson

Perhaps the most telling difference between the American and British versions of *Rubber Soul* was the choice of the album's lead-off song.

With the Byrds' "Mr. Tambourine Man," Simon and Garfunkel's "The Sound of Silence" and the Mamas and the Papas' "California Dreamin'" (which was released the same week as *Rubber Soul*) pouring out of every jukebox, transistor radio, and dashboard speaker from coast to coast, "folk rock" had become the new sound shaking the nation, albeit briefly. Its prime ingredient: the glistening jingle-jangle chime of the electric twelve-string guitar that the Byrds' Roger McGuinn first heard when George Harrison struck that stunning F9 chord on his Rickenbacker twelve-string to kick off "A Hard Day's Night." McGuinn helped make that ringing sound omnipresent with the Byrds' gorgeous arrangement of Bob Dylan's "Mr. Tambourine Man," which topped the charts in April 1965. McGuinn, not yet having blossomed as a skilled songwriter, possessed the keen instincts to rework Bob Dylan's stream-of-consciousness verses into something that resembled the acceptable two-and-a-half-minute format of the pop song. Sweetened by David Crosby's honey-coated harmonies and propelled by a solid 4/4 beat (laid down by the Wrecking Crew's Hal Blaine, in lieu of the Byrds' inexperienced drummer, Michael Clarke), the Byrds then fashioned Bob's "All I Really Want to Do" and "Chimes of Freedom" into shimmering radio-friendly anthems as well. With pristine remakes of Pete Seeger's "Turn, Turn, Turn" and "The Bells of Rhymney," along with "I'll Feel a Whole Lot Better" and "She Don't Care About Time," written and sung by the band's original front man, Gene Clark, the Byrds had forged a sonic imprint all their own. *Newsweek* christened them "Dylanized Beatles" and America suddenly had their answer to the all-pervading British Invasion.

Meanwhile, someone in Capitol Records' A&R department had the brilliant idea of using Paul's "I've Just Seen a Face" as the lead-off song for their new album.

Having returned from his triumphant 1964 tour of England, Dylan (who'd made a deep impression on everyone from the Beatles, to the Rolling Stones and the Animals) had traded in his torn and frayed rambling-troubadour image for something more hip and beatific. While his latest release, *Another Side of Bob Dylan*, still featured his raspy voice, barbed-wire harmonica, and brisk acoustic guitar strumming, gone were his poignant proletariat anthems of the people. Politics suddenly seemed like the farthest thing from Bob's restless mind. Weary of being labeled a protest singer, Dylan refused to go down with the sinking folk ship. Inspired by the unspeakable visions of French symbolist poet Arthur Rimbaud and the bearded Beat bard Allen Ginsberg, Bob began writing introspective ballads that bristled with emotion yet overflowed with surrealist imagery. He even looked different. Gone was the baby fat, thanks in part to a diet of amphetamines, which fueled his chaotic journey. Turtlenecks and Cuban heels had replaced work shirts and old scuffed-up work boots. Inspired by the Stones' jagged of brand of blues rock, and by the Animals' cover of his "House of the Rising Sun" (a tune Dylan first learned from the burly Greenwich Village folk-blues picker Dave Van Ronk, which had been previously recorded by both Lead Belly and Woody Guthrie), Bob soon returned to his original love, rock 'n' roll, adding electric guitar to his 1965 release *Bringing It All Back Home*.

The Beatles, it seemed, had apparently "gone potty" for Dylan. "You've Got to Hide Your Love Away" featured John strumming his acoustic Gibson guitar and singing in a husky voice. Whether inspired by his own extramarital affairs or their manager Brian Epstein's gay escapades, the song and Lennon's weary delivery went beyond a tip of his cap to America's leading songwriter; it was as close to a Bob Dylan imitation as he could pull off without parodying his hero.

As Paul McCartney later admitted, "John had listened to his stuff and had been very influenced" by Bob. "You've Got to Hide Your Love Away," in his partner's estimation, was "virtually a Dylan impression."

Originally known as "Auntie Gin's Theme," "I've Just Seen a Face" was dedicated to Paul's dear aunt, who adored the song when he debuted it on piano at a family gathering. Recorded at Abbey Road on June 14, 1965, during McCartney's famous marathon session, which also produced "Yesterday" and "I'm Down," the song was Paul's raving response to John's "Help!" and the perfect vehicle for his Little Richard imitation.

For the generation that had grown up with the outrageous Little Richard, seeing Paul McCartney shaking his hair and whooping in falsetto just didn't cut it. A vocal accent that can be traced back to the Delta bluesman Robert Johnson singing "Kind Hearted Woman," it was certainly nothing new. "I didn't give a shit about the Beatles when they were doing that cutesy early shit," Atlantic Records producer Joel Dorn (whose credits include Roberta Flack, Bette Midler, Aaron Neville, and the Allman Brothers) stated emphatically. "They had catchy melodies but I didn't want to hear Paul McCartney go 'whooo!' I'd put Little Richard on! But later on, with *Rubber Soul*, I got the joke."

Oddly there is no bass track on "I've Just Seen a Face," according to the studio log. Instead, McCartney and Lennon strummed acoustic guitars, while Ringo gently laid down a steady chugging beat with brushes. While George Harrison picked a Framus twelve-string acoustic guitar, the lead on the song's introduction may very well have been played by Paul, who was growing more frustrated with his bandmate's more pragmatic approach to the instrument and (now thanks to the freedom offered by four-track recording) began to stay later to overdub his own parts after George left the studio.

Originally written while McCartney was living on Wimpole Street, "I've Just Seen a Face" remained a favorite song of his over the years. It was one of the few Beatle tunes he'd pull out of mothballs years later to perform while on tour with Wings. "It was a strange up-tempo thing . . . slightly country and western from my point of view," Paul explained. "The lyric works, it keeps dragging you forward, it keeps pulling you to the next line. There's an insistent quality to it that I liked."

The buoyant country-rock feel of "I've Just Seen a Face" could be heard a year later echoing throughout Stephen Stills's "Go and Say Goodbye" (sung by Richie Furay on Buffalo Springfield's 1966 self-titled debut album), which slyly worked the classic bluegrass riff from "Salt Creek" into its bridge. Both of these tracks went a long way in warming rock fans up to the notion that country music (at least in small doses) might be something they'd enjoy, and eventually opened the door for the Byrds' flight to Nashville, where they recorded *Sweetheart of the Rodeo* with a slew of Music City's best pickers.

The Beatles, like Shakespeare and Frank Sinatra before them, defined love for their generation. Lennon and McCartney's early songs, which were essentially adolescent passion plays, explored every imaginable nuance of how the game was played. Their close harmonies taught us what "words of love" should sound like. They coached us in what to search for in the ideal girlfriend: Michelle was demure, while the heroine of "Girl" was *cool*. Listening to Beatles records taught us what to say and how to feel if she wasn't true (as in "No Reply"), or how we might gallantly come to her rescue when she was mistreated by some jerk who was unworthy of her affection (as in "You're Going to Lose That Girl"). As Dylan later sang, "Love is all there is, it makes the world go 'round" (from "I Threw It All Away," a song from *Nashville Skyline* that many felt was too corny for their righteous bard but that would have easily been right at home on an album like *Beatles for Sale*).

In the not-so-distant past, the very idea of romantic love was deemed nothing more than a ridiculous notion, a malady that could be cured with the application of blood-sucking leeches. Marriage was a business deal, a contract, plain and simple. Weddings were agreed upon based on the size of the young lady's dowry. The potential for more cattle or greater acreage decided who was worthy of matrimony, not flowers, poetry, or pheromones. The idea that one day Prince Charming would suddenly appear and carry a young girl off to live happily ever after was only a fairy tale that, more often than not, became a sad joke, a rigged yardstick by which many beautiful, intelligent females over the years judged their happiness and lack of self-worth. Dare we forget Romeo and Juliet were a couple of self-absorbed adolescents whose unhealthy obsession with each other only wrought death and destruction? Nonetheless, of the Beatles' love songs scattered among their first batch of albums, "I've Just Seen a Face" is arguably the most romantic. No matter how experimental the Beatles albums became, Paul always managed to balance the band's wilder moments with a gentle, melodic love ballad. While *Revolver* was a truly revolutionary album, which featured Harrison's exotic raga pop and Lennon's hallucinatory opus, "Tomorrow Never Knows," McCartney offered the delicate "Here, There and Everywhere," a throwback to early-period Beatles songs like "And I Love Her," which assured anxious fans whenever the yellow submarine suddenly plunged into unknown territory.

"I've Just Seen a Face" begins in a minor key. The melody ascends quickly with a sense of yearning, practically bursting with urgency as Paul gingerly strums his acoustic guitar, relating a tale of the rarest and most coveted of all human emotions— love at first sight.

Not since "World Without Love" (an early Lennon & McCartney knockoff that Paul gave to Jane Asher's brother Peter, who, along with his partner, Gordon Waller, hit number one with it in 1964) had he employed such overtly romantic sentiments. In that song the protagonist pleads: "Please lock me away and don't allow the day, here inside, where I hide with my loneliness." The song, which was reminiscent of the melodramatic teen love ballads sung by Roy Orbison, was deemed too corny by Lennon and McCartney for the Beatles' repertoire, even in their cute matching-suit days, or they undoubtedly would have recorded it themselves.

With "I've Just Seen a Face," Paul revisited the image of the romantic recluse once more, singing wistfully, "I have never known the like of this, been alone and missed things and kept out of sight." How he managed to sound credible in the role of an emotional shut-in while in the throes of Beatlemania is a testimony to McCartney's integrity as a singer. And for a former teddy boy with a Liverpool scouse to keep a straight face when pronouncing "been" as "bean" shows just how much Jane's acting career must have rubbed off on him, whether he realized it or not.

A long way (in a short time) from the celebratory bump-and-grind and feral hoots and howls of "She's a Woman," McCartney digs into the olde English grammar bag for a scholarly adverb, singing, "Thus it is I'll dream of her tonight." At the end of each verse he is reduced to a refrain of syllables in order to express his overwhelmed heart, sighing, "Li di di da da di," as if any moment he might transform into a bard and break into a couple of bars of "Hey nonny nonny!" from Shakespeare's *Much Ado About Nothing*.

"I've Just Seen a Face" has been (and will continue to be for years to come) sung at thousands of weddings. It remains a timeless ode to that decisive moment when love, like a bolt of lightning, unexpectedly strikes a weary, jaded heart, rekindling in it hope and the will to blindly endure. Its deep wooden timbre could be heard resonating for years to come in records by Crosby, Stills and Nash, James Taylor, and Jackson Browne, among others.

RUBBER COVERS: "I'VE JUST SEEN A FACE"

With its driving rhythm and country feel, "I've Just Seen a Face" quickly found its way into the repertoire of bluegrass bands like Boston's Charles River Valley Boys, who cut the song in 1966 for their obscure album *Beatle Country*. Two years later, progressive bluegrassers the Dillards recorded Paul's wistful tune for their 1968 release *Wheatstraw Suite*. Along with their high lonesome harmonies, the Dillards mixed elements of traditional mountain music (banjo) with modern country (pedal steel guitar) that not only appealed to a new generation of longhairs but also inspired bands like the Byrds, the Grateful Dead, and the Eagles to dig deeper into American roots music.

Taking the song in a surprisingly different direction was Ray Charles' former alto saxophonist Hank Crawford, who laid down a funky version of "I've Just Seen a Face" over a percolating reggae beat for his 1976 album *Tico Rico*.

In 1997 Canadian jazz chanteuse Holly Cole covered Paul's song for her album *Dark Dear Heart*. McCartney's rambling romantic verse effortlessly rolls off her tongue in a husky whisper as the band lays down a solid groove and Cole's sultry eyes make love to the camera in a noir-style video that accompanied the song's release.

Ten years later, a younger generation would discover the tune by way of the 2007 soundtrack to *Across the Universe*, a film whose characters and plot were loosely based on Beatles songs. "I've Just Seen a Face" inspires leading man Jude (Jim Sturgess) to wax poetic over the fair Lucy (Evan Rachel Wood) in a somewhat bizarre love-fantasy scene staged in a bowling alley.

Over the last decade, Brandi Carlile has sung McCartney's tune as part of her live shows, with plenty of fine mandolin and guitar picking from her band. While there's nothing particularly different or innovative about Carlile's cover of "I've Just Seen a Face," she emphasizes the good-time country hoedown that always lay within its rhythm and chord changes.

Unquestionably the most bizarre take of Paul's song (retitled "I'll Just Bleed Your Face") goes to Beatallica. Milwaukee's fearsome foursome cleverly mashed up Beatle and Metallica songs to gratifying ends on their 2009 release *Masterful Mystery Tour*.

7

"It's Only Love"

"There is no remedy for love but to love more."
—Henry David Thoreau, 1839

Listening to McCartney wax so poetically about love might have been the catalyst for Lennon to compose some purple verse of his own, arguably the most embarrassing lyric of his career, "It's Only Love."

Coming into the studio to record this throwaway on June 15, the day after McCartney's triumphant session that yielded "I've Just Seen a Face," "I'm Down," and "Yesterday," John Lennon undoubtedly must have felt at a loss. "It's Only Love" was the last in a series of melodramatic love ballads by Lennon that began with the pleading "This Boy" and was followed by "Yes It Is," in which the protagonist, who is desperately trying to get over the pain of losing his girlfriend, seems to have developed a phobia of the color red. But for all his sensitivity, Lennon comes off sounding rather psychotic. Whether he wrote "It's Only Love" for his then wife Cynthia (perhaps out of guilt over his many extramarital affairs) or as a vehicle for revealing his well-guarded tenderness, Lennon ultimately loathed the song, as it sounded unconvincing.

The British critic Ian MacDonald (brilliant and harsh as he could be) rightfully slammed "It's Only Love" as "the hollowest lyric Lennon ever perpetuated." Unsatisfied with an earlier bare-bones take (later released on *The Beatles Anthology*), the band tried their best to save this turkey with Lennon double-tracking his voice and adding no fewer than five guitar overdubs. George's wobbly guitar lead was played on his 1963 Gretsch Tennessean through a Leslie cabinet, whose rotating speaker was most commonly heard, up to this point, with Hammond organs. Its shimmering sound soon became Harrison's trademark. Over the years no instrument was safe from this ethereal effect. The Beatles even used it to enhance John's otherworldly vocal on *Revolver*'s kaleidoscopic raga "Tomorrow Never Knows."

While "It's Only Love" has a feel as smooth and warm as the suede jacket that John wore on the cover of *Rubber Soul*, the words, unfortunately, are another story. Chock-full of cheap sentiments about butterflies in his tummy and nervous schoolboy poetry like "Why am I so shy when I'm beside you?" the lyrics resemble the kind of sexless pap that actors like David Niven and Rex Harrison were required to deliver in cornball musicals. Originally titled "That's a Nice Hat" (which gives some clear indication of the indifference John initially felt about the song), "It's Only Love" might have fared better had he stayed with his original inspiration.

Although the song was originally released as side-two filler on the British pressing of *Help!*, it didn't see the light of day in the States until four months later, when it appeared on side two of the American pressing of *Rubber Soul*.

"It's Only Love" was recorded between "Wait" and "Run for Your Life": together, these three songs represent something of a temporary artistic ebb for John. He had been the musical juggernaut behind *A Hard Day's Night*, providing the bulk of the material for the film's soundtrack with the exception of McCartney's hard-swinging "Can't Buy Me Love."

Though the song was originally Lennon's idea, McCartney helped John finish off "It's Only Love" at a writing session at his house in Weybridge. Paul considered the tune a 60/40 collaboration, with the lion's share of the credit going to his partner. While *Rubber Soul* was the first attempt by the Beatles to create an album of "all good stuff" (as Brian Wilson put it), "It's Only Love," along with "What Goes On" and "12-Bar Original" (if it had made the final cut) could only be considered filler at best on what otherwise amounted to a set of well-crafted, innovative songs. As John later confessed in *Hit Parader*, regarding "It's Only Love": "That's the one song I really hate of mine. Terrible lyric."

"Sometimes we didn't fight it if the lyric came out rather bland on some of those filler songs like 'It's Only Love,'" McCartney confessed, shrugging off the song's obvious short-comings. "If a lyric was really bad we'd edit it, but we weren't that fussy about it, because it's only a rock 'n' roll song. I mean, this is not literature."

As the shortest song on *Rubber Soul*, clocking in at 1:55, "It's Only Love" can be easily forgiven, if not forgotten.

RUBBER COVERS: "IT'S ONLY LOVE"

Bryan Ferry's high-polish, brassy cover of "It's Only Love" from his 1976 album *Let's Stick Together* strongly resembles the slinky disco hustle of David Bowie's *Young Americans* era. Ferry's fey vocal delivery only heightens the insecurity within the lyric that John seemed most uncomfortable with.

On the other hand, Gary US Bonds' version of "It's Only Love" packs a punch that Lennon never imagined the tune possessed. The song begins with a lightly strummed acoustic, the familiar wobbly guitar lead, and a wailing sax, and Bonds's soulful rasp loans John's verse some genuine credibility. He sounds like he means business when he begs, "Haven't I the right to make it up, girl?" Perhaps it's the voice of experience talking, as Gary was in his forties when he cut "It's Only Love" for his 1981 album *Dedication*. Bonds had already been around the block a few times, while John was in his early twenties when he wrote the song. Gary was one of the rare artists who managed to improve a Beatles song, and his cover of "It's Only Love" climbed to number forty-three on the UK charts, an amazing feat, considering he salvaged a tune that both Lennon and McCartney deemed no more than a throwaway.

Indie folk singer Russian Red (a sometimes blonde, some-times redheaded chanteuse from Madrid known to her mother as Lourdes Hernández) covered "It's Only Love" at a club date in Buenos Aires in 2013, giving the tune a sexy, lackadaisical feel. Between her loopy, nonchalant delivery and clunky drum fills (which she occasionally thumped on a floor tom) Russian Red transformed John's syrupy ballad into a slightly off-kilter tango.

8
"Wait"

"If you are not too long, I will wait here for you all my life."
—Oscar Wilde

The last song recorded for the *Help!* sessions, "Wait," was said to be the first full Lennon/McCartney collaboration since they'd written "Baby's in Black" together, "eyeball to eyeball," in a hotel room during their 1964 tour. McCartney would later dispute this, claiming he wrote the song by himself in the Bahamas while shooting *Help!*, with only the actor Brandon de Wilde (best known for his role as the little boy, Joey, in the western *Shane*) hanging around. Needing one final song to complete *Rubber Soul*, for a total of fourteen in all, the band dusted off "Wait," adding a few fresh overdubs, including tambourine, maraca, and some "tone pedal guitar" to the original bass, drum, and guitar tracks recorded on June 17. The descending guitar riff at the end of the song evokes the laughing/crying sound of trombone (when played with a plunger), commonly heard on early jazz records. Created by playing a guitar through a volume pedal, which both George and John had been experimenting with at the time, the riff's wavering tone predated the Vox wah-wah pedal, which first appeared in February 1967 (although guitar ace Chet Atkins had built himself a similar pedal while recording the shimmering "Slinky" in 1959).

The song's title was another one-word catchphrase that seems like a perfect bookend to "Help!" "Wait" addresses a pair of lovers hoping to reconcile the past, and "forget the tears [they] cried," while tenderly pledging to give love a second try. The tune is a formulaic exercise, drawing inspiration from previous soul tunes like Martha Reeves and the Vandellas' 1967 classic "Jimmy Mack," where the singer, uncertain what the future will bring if her steady doesn't come home soon, worries about a new "guy [who] keeps coming around, trying to wear [her] resistance down."

Ringo's drum fills steals the show, pumping passion into the lover's promises, building the song's dynamic, shifting gears, propelling the chorus, giving the song a sense of urgency. Both Harrison and Lennon employ their new volume pedals, to create weeping, bowed cello–like passages. (The Beatles would soon employ cellos on many of their psychedelic opuses, including "Strawberry Fields Forever," "Blue Jay Way," and "I Am the Walrus.")

Beginning with "All My Loving," the Beatles (Paul in particular) often wrote chivalrous verse promising to remain faithful to the girls they left behind. Although known to have had plenty of girls on the side while engaged to Jane Asher, Paul convincingly sang, "I've been good, as good as I can be." But, as Muddy Waters put it, "Who can you trust? I don't trust nobody!"

RUBBER COVERS: "WAIT"

With his voice soaked in reverb, and an army of strings, backup singers, and booming tympani, Liverpool-born Frankie Vaughan's 1965 rococo cover of "Wait" perfectly embodies the over-the-top commercial pop of the era, à la Tom Jones and Shirley Bassey.

In 2005 singer/songwriter Ben Kweller teamed up with Albert Hammond Jr. of the Strokes for a straight-ahead interpretation of "Wait," which appeared on *This Bird Has Flown: A 40th Anniversary Tribute to the Beatles' Rubber Soul*. While their arrangement was both unimaginative and lacking in emotion, they manage to do the song justice as a piece of catchy pop.

As part of their project *Acoustic Rubber Soul*, the Austin-based ensemble Will Taylor and Strings Attached recorded a smart arrangement of "Wait" that features violin, cello, muted trumpet, and Taylor's nimble guitar work over a sultry Latin groove that's sure to inspire a bit of close dancing. Jayme Ivison's husky vocal loans a certain weariness to McCartney's lyrics, which illustrate the ongoing frustrations of a faltering love affair.

Arguably the best cover of "Wait" appeared on the 2006 *Rubber Folk* compilation, courtesy of Irish folk singer Cara Dillon and her husband, pianist Sam Lakeman. As Lakeman's piano builds in intensity, Dillon's sweet, reedy voice surges, illuminating the hope and desperation at the core of Paul's lyric.

9

"Run for Your Life"

"There is always some madness in love.
But there is also always some reason in madness."
—Friedrich Nietzsche

A bit of a macho song," as Paul McCartney described John Lennon's "Run for Your Life," the first number to be cut for *Rubber Soul* during a five-and-a-half-hour session (from start to finish, including overdubs) on Tuesday, October 12, 1965. The Beatles finally nailed "Run for Your Life" on the fifth take. "Make it heavy!" Lennon implored his bandmates (years before anyone had heard the term *heavy metal*, or used the term *heavy* in lieu of *profound*).

John had unabashedly nicked the song's refrain "I'd rather see you dead, little girl, than to be with another man," from Elvis Presley's 1955 rockabilly hit "Baby Let's Play House," written by Nashville bluesman Arthur Gunter. Sung in Presley's trademark nervous herky-jerky style (which strongly resembled Professor Longhair's feral yowl), the lyric evoked twisted romantic dependency rather than a jealousy-fueled homicidal threat. But it was Lennon who really put teeth into Gunter's words.

"John was always on the run, running for his life," Paul surmised. "He was married; whereas none of my songs would have 'catch you with another man.' It was never a concern of mine, at all, because I had a girlfriend and I would go with other girls, it was a perfectly open relationship so I wasn't as worried about that as John was."

Lennon's dark side had surfaced previously in a handful of "stalker songs" he'd written in the past, including "I'll Cry Instead," "You Can't Do That," and, most recently, "No Reply," from *Beatles '65*, in which the singer's insecurity and obsession over his girlfriend lead him to spy through her curtains, after discovering her "walking hand in hand, with another man." In "Run for Your Life," John's ongoing anxiety spirals out of control as he threatens his lover, bitterly spitting out the lyric, "I'd rather see you dead."

Tired of being trivialized by their cute image, Lennon was hoping, perhaps, to gain some credibility by shocking his fans with an overtly harsh sentiment. Once again, John took a cue from Dylan, whose targets in his wrathful "finger-pointing songs," once aimed at the morally corrupt politicians and warmongers whom he singled out in "Masters of War" and "Only a Pawn in Their Game," were now old friends and hangers-on from the Greenwich Village folk scene whom he accused of stabbing him in the back during his meteoric rise to stardom. Dylan would record the vitriolic "Positively 4th Street" just four days after his controversial appearance at the 1965 Newport Folk Festival.

Bounding to number two on the *Billboard* charts, Bob's first Top Ten hit, "Like a Rolling Stone" had featured Mike Bloomfield and session guitarist turned organist in a pinch Al Kooper, who, with a few well-placed notes from a Hammond B-3, accidentally forged "the new Dylan sound," and overnight became one of the most in-demand session musicians of the 1960s. The song, a devastating portrait of a poor little rich girl (said to be the tragic model/actor Edie Sedgwick) who found herself living on the street with "no direction home," was unusual not just for the presence of electric instruments on a Dylan track (although Bob's previous album *Subterranean Homesick Blues* had featured a ramshackle electric jug band) but for its length, an unheard of 6:13 at a time when the standard pop hit was rarely over three minutes.

Released on September 7, Dylan's "Positively 4th Street" once again stretched our basic understanding of what a pop song was capable of.

The song bristled with devastating lyrics, which Bob crowed from the spleen. Lines like "What a drag it is to see you" and "You'd rather see me paralyzed" had never been heard on pop radio before. On top of that, the song didn't even bother with the formality of having a chorus! Contrary to popular assumption, Bob claimed "Positively 4th Street" was not a brusque retort to the critics who denounced him for turning his back on the folk scene. Notoriously impossible to peg, Dylan explained that "Positively 4th Street" was actually a song "about friendship" (or, more accurately, the downside of friendship. Many have speculated that the song's inspiration was Joan Baez, the raven-haired goddess of the Cambridge folk scene who helped launch Dylan's rise to stardom, and whom he would dump after a brief affair). Bob wasn't simply burning bridges; he seemed to be deliberately razing his past, along with everyone in it.

Bob's influence at his point on Lennon as an artist was both enormous and obvious, although Lennon probably didn't need much help with the macho bravado, the kind that can be traced back throughout traditional blues songs, like Robert Johnson's "32-20," in which the "King of the Delta Blues Singers" sends for his "baby" and when "she don't come, all the doctors in Hot Springs sure can't help her none." And if that's not enough, Johnson adds that he will "cut her half in two" if she fails to listen to his command.

"I gave her the gun!" Jimi Hendrix cried in his version of Scottish folksinger Billy Roberts's popular murder ballad, "Hey Joe." It's a tale we seem to enjoy hearing over and over again, as the song (whether it was a traditional, as some claim, or written in the mid-fifties) was passed on to a handful of sixties bands, from the Leaves, to Love, and the Byrds (whose groovy version was sung by David Crosby), to folksinger Tim Rose, to soul shouter Wilson Pickett. In the following decade, punk poetess Patti Smith would put her special twist on "Hey Joe" before the song wound up in the repertoires of Willy DeVille and Nick Cave.

No matter who wrote or sang it, "Hey Joe" is an age-old morality play in which justice, harsh as it is, is meted out for infidelity—the protagonist's promiscuous partner is murdered "for messin' round with another man." It makes one wonder how many people have ever stopped to think what the lyrics were really about as they sang along.

With "Down by the River," Neil Young took things a step further: after gunning down his ex, the killer flees, grasping the hand of his new lover, hoping she will understand and even sympathize with what he's done while she drags him "over the rainbow" to a new life. No matter what the deed, apparently anything, it seems, is forgiven for a good song.

John's apology for "Run for Your Life" was not for the song's severe sentiment but for cranking it out under pressure to meet the deadline for the new album. "It was just a song I knocked off," Lennon confessed, attempting to shrug off his overtly sexist verse. "I didn't think it was that important." Instrumentally, the tune was a solid midtempo rocker with a great guitar hook, reminiscent of "Day Tripper" and "Drive My Car." Arguably the album's weakest track, it was tacked on to the end of the record, stashed behind a second Harrison number (on the UK version).

"Run for Your Life" might have seemed more apropos coming from a well-known misogynist like Brian Jones (if he ever managed to finish and record any of the songs he was rumored to have written), considering his notoriously stormy relationship with the German actor Anita Pallenberg. Although the Stones' charismatic flaxen-haired multi-instrumentalist was famous for his colorful wardrobe, mixing women's blouses with exotic Indian and Moroccan togs, he was hardly all peace and love, particularly behind closed doors. Jones was known to beat women from time to time and once wound up missing a Stones recording session after he'd broken his wrist when he allegedly tried to slug Anita while they were on vacation in Tangier.

Whether or not he meant to shock fans with such dark sentiments, Lennon later confessed he "used to be cruel" in the bridge to McCartney's optimistic Summer of Love anthem "It's Getting Better." John clearly had a different relationship with women before he transformed into a "feminist" under Yoko Ono's tutelage. In contrast to Paul cheerfully chirping, "It's getting better all the time," Lennon admitted to having beaten his girlfriends in the past.

"It is a diary form of writing," John told *Playboy* in 1980. "All that 'I used to be cruel to my woman, I beat her and kept her apart from the things that she loved' was me. I used to be cruel to my woman. . . . I was a hitter. I couldn't express myself and I hit. I fought men and I hit women. That is why I am always on about peace, you see."

Rubber Soul ends with John chanting, "Nah nah no, Nah nah no," as "Run for Your Life" fades away, a far cry from the ebullient "yeah, yeah, yeah" from "She Loves You," just two short years before.

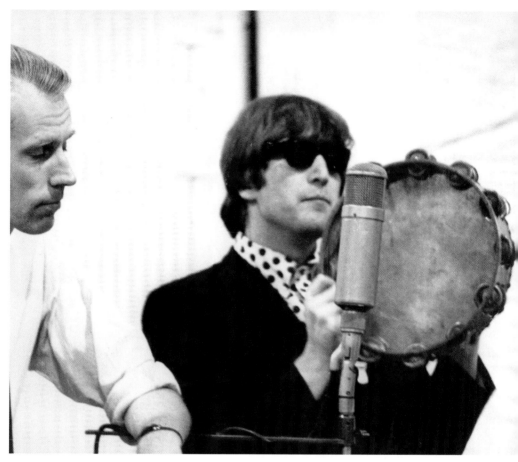

Hey, Mister Tambourine Man . . .
John adds some shake to the mix,
while producer George Martin
loans a discerning ear.
Photo by The Manchester Daily Express/
Getty Images

Released on December 15, 1964,
Beatles '65 set the benchmark for
every band for the following year.
Mitch Blank Collection

Released on August 6, 1965, Paul's solo performance of "Yesterday," backed by Ringo's country-rock cover of Buck Owens's "Act Naturally," showed the Beatles' burgeoning diversity.
Mitch Blank Collection

George in the studio playing his Rickenbacker 12-string, which inadvertently gave birth to the Byrds' jingle-jangle folk-rock sound.
Photo from the Michael Ochs Archives/Getty Images

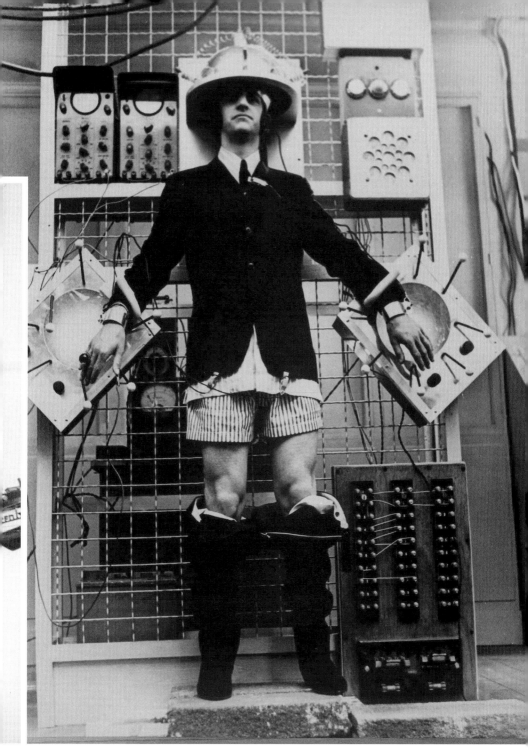

Ringo trying everything to get that cursed ring off his
finger while filming *Help* in the winter/spring of 1965.
Photo by Keystone—France/Getty Images

The Beatles looking none-too-pleased at meeting the Saturday morning cartoon versions of themselves. Although they originally detested the show, both John and George eventually admitted to liking it.
Photo by Mark and Colleen Hayward/Getty Images

Following in the footsteps of "I'm a Loser," John's "Nowhere Man," released on December 3, 1965, featured superb three part harmonies and an excellent lead guitar break from George. The B-side featured "What Goes On," a left-over Lennon/McCartney ditty from the old days, delivered by Ringo in his best country warble.
Mitch Blank Collection

Brian Epstein—man on the go. April 2, 1965.
Photo by Larry Ellis/Getty Images

Dylan recording *Bringing It All Back Home*, sporting sunglasses and Beatle boots. That July, Bob would plug in his Fender Stratocaster at the Newport Folk Festival and shock the crowd with his new look and sound.

Photo from the Michael Ochs Archives/Getty Images

Paul McCartney and Jane Asher arrive in London,
after vacationing together in Portugal, June 11,1965.
Getty Images

The Beatles, while on their European tour, line up for the
lens at the Negresco Hotel in Nice, France, June 30, 1965.
Photo by Reporters Associates/Getty Images

Although Lennon considered the song "a throwaway" he maintained "Run for Your Life" was "a favorite of George's," most likely for its bluesy guitar riff. Although its thin, wiry tone ensures that it was most likely Harrison, Ian MacDonald wasn't certain who played the lead, as its rough, slightly out-of-tune quality evoked Lennon's style more than Harrison's typically meticulous approach.

RUBBER COVERS: "RUN FOR YOUR LIFE"

Although framed by a wicked fuzz guitar riff, Gary Lewis and the Playboys' version of "Run for Your Life" is predictably light. The great jazz bassist Charles Mingus once remarked that the Beatles, to his ears, sounded like "little marching men." The son of the great comedian Jerry Lewis managed to confirm Mingus's jaded opinion within the first thirty seconds of his tepid 1966 cover.

That same year, Johnny Rivers released a live version of the song on his album . . . *And I Know You Wanna Dance.* Driven by a belching bullfrog bass and plenty of rockabilly twang, Rivers's rendition blends the easy groove of Presley's original "Baby Let's Play House" with Lennon's macho rocker.

Nancy Sinatra also cut John's sexist "sermon" for her popular 1966 album *Boots* (produced by Lee Hazlewood), which also included a hot take of "Day Tripper" as well. "Run for Your Life," Nancy told *Mojo* magazine, allowed her to "stay right in character" with her trashy alter ego, Nasty Jones. "I loved turning this song around," she said, referring to her fashioning the original lyric into "I'd rather see you dead, little boy, than to be with another girl." "It was a very powerful statement for a white woman in the '60s [along] with the pill and women finally having some freedom to express themselves sexually. I'd love to know what they thought of my versions of their songs," she added.

While Sinatra's cover failed to graze the *Billboard* charts, it briefly became a regional favorite in New York State, and was played in heavy rotation on radio station WTPR in Albany.

The Beatles' recording of "Run for Your Life" not only garnered little airplay at the time of its release but was actually banned many years later, in the 1990s, by radio station CFRA in Ottawa, Canada, for its chauvinist lyric. When the programmers were asked about Presley's "Baby Let's Play House," they had to admit they were unfamiliar with it but subsequently banned the song as well. The impetus for this decision may well have been the increased awareness of domestic violence brought to light by the O. J. Simpson trials of 1995.

Sinister from beginning to end, with a demented strip-tease beat and fun-house guitars howling like disembodied spirits, Canadian alt-country rockers the Cowboy Junkies' take of "Run for Your Life" is seriously dark and unforgiving. Lead singer Margo Timmins twists Lennon's misogynist lyric, threatening her "little boy" with the end if she ever catches him with "another woman."

On their 1991 *Girlsville* album, Thee Headcoatees sing, "You know that I'm a wicked chick" over a slapping snare and a growling fuzz-tone bass riff. The raw, menacing quality of this track embodies just about everything that John Lennon loved about rock 'n' roll.

"Run for Your Life" was a natural choice for punkabilly Robert Gordon, whose grinding guitar and vocals, soaked in Sun Records–style slapback, help make his 1998 *The Lost Album* a rare gem.

10

"Norwegian Wood"

"Sometimes before I go to sleep I think about what it would be like to be inside Ravi's sitar."
—George Harrison

Whether you owned the English or American version, the diversity of musical styles heard throughout *Rubber Soul* was striking from the first listen. The album's second song (on both releases), "Norwegian Wood," began with John strumming his Gibson acoustic on a lilting folk waltz. The Beatles had sung a few waltzes in the past, including "This Boy" and "Yes It Is," a pair of melodramatic love songs torched by John, as well as the Everly Brothers–inspired dual-harmony attack of "Baby's in Black," a rather morbid tune about a hot widow who only cares for her dead lover, no matter how the protagonist tries to console her. But just eight bars into "Norwegian Wood," a whole new world suddenly began to emerge. As Roy Harper, the legendary British guitarist celebrated by Led Zeppelin, put it, "After a few times on the turntable, you realized the goalposts had been moved, forever."

"We went through many different sort of versions of the song," Lennon told *Rolling Stone*. "It was never right and I was getting very angry about it." Frustrated, John began playing his guitar "very loudly into the mike [as he] sang it at the same time. And then George had the sitar and I asked him could he play the piece that I'd written, you know the dee diddley dee, diddley dee, that bit and he was not sure whether he could play it yet because he hadn't done much on the sitar but he was willing to have a go. He learned the bit and dubbed it in after. I think we did it in sections."

"When we were working on 'Norwegian Wood,' it just needed something," Harrison explained. "It was quite spontaneous from what I remember. I just picked up the sitar and kind of found the notes and I just kind of played it. We miked it up and put it on and it just seemed to hit the spot."

While the transcendental twang of George's sitar evoked the pungent atmosphere of the Indian subcontinent, the song's title transported Beatles fans north to the pristine forests of Scandinavia. But John Lennon's tune (which Harrison likened to an old Irish folk song) actually has its roots in a skiing holiday the singer and his producer, George Martin, took with their wives in Saint Moritz, in the Swiss Alps. The trip was cut short after Martin broke a toe on his first day on the slopes, and the group soon returned to London.

John's murky verses, a cleverly veiled jumble of images, were designed to keep his wife, Cynthia, in the dark about his string of ongoing extramarital affairs. "I wrote obscurely à la Dylan, I suppose, never saying what ya mean, but giving the impression of something. You know, you just stick a few images together, thread 'em together and you call it poetry," Lennon said flippantly. "[Dylan] just did his job as a poet . . . which is [writing] poetry of the day."

"It was all very gobbledygook," John said of the song's vague lyrics, claiming the inspiration came "from my experiences, girls, flats, things like that."

While George Martin considered the words to Lennon's hypnotic ballad "slightly sick," Paul believed his inspiration was "completely imaginary," pointing to the true source of his partner's song: "Peter Asher had this room done out in wood," he said. "It was pine, really cheap pine. But it's not a good title, 'Cheap Pine.'"

No matter what took place between John and the song's mysterious girl —whether it was photographer Robert Freeman's then wife, the model Sonny Spielhagen (aka Sonny Freeman Drane), who in recent years has claimed to have been John's secret muse—or, as others have suggested, the journalist Maureen Cleave, a friend of Lennon's whose March '66 interview in the London Evening Standard contained John's "more popular than Jesus" quip—the whole affair seems rather cold. But after too much talk and too much wine, the decisive moment is lost and the singer skulks off "to sleep in the bath." The only solace he finds follows the next morning, when he strikes a match and stands contentedly in the glow of her blazing love nest.

While McCartney claimed the song's punch line was his idea, Lennon said he had no clue how or where he came up with the notion of "Norwegian Wood," other than possibly the current popularity of sleek Scandinavian furniture in the 1960s. John either couldn't or wouldn't recall whether the song was about a particular woman. Pete Shotton claimed that "back in his poverty-stricken art school days" Lennon and Stu Sutcliffe had burned furniture in order to stay warm during long cold winter nights.

John's sultry waltz helped trigger a massive trend of all things Indian after George Harrison picked up the sitar, whose mesmerizing sound he'd discovered earlier that year, during the making of *Help!*. With this new mysterious instrument, George turned the world on to the exotic charm of the subcontinent. As went the Beatles in 1965, so followed most of world (at the very least nearly every rock band of the day, along with all of their devoted fans). With George's newfound obsession with Indian music came a passion for Hindu culture, from its vibrant fashions—the Fabs donned matching Nehru jackets when they rocked Shea Stadium on August 15, 1965—to a myriad of archaic spiritual practices.

Beyond Jack Kerouac's 1958 novel *The Dharma Bums* and Alan Watts's illuminating writings and lectures on Zen, Buddhism and Hindu consciousness, the West had previously been the exclusive domain of academics and peculiar aunts who found Ouija boards, séances, and paintings of blue multi-armed and elephant-headed gods a welcome relief from the doldrums of their daily lives. Now, thanks to the "quiet Beatle," as he was portrayed by the media, meditation, mantras, yoga, and burning incense had suddenly became all "the raj" with a younger generation.

Harrison and later McCartney (inspired by his wife Linda) soon became more mindful and outspoken about their diets, adopting vegetarianism not solely for the sake of personal health and as a way to keep their karma clean, but to demonstrate their compassion for all sentient beings. Keep in mind that most folks claiming to be vegetarian in the early sixties were generally looked upon with pity. It was just assumed they must have a serious health condition and couldn't eat or digest a proper meal, which at that time centered around a large portion of meat.

"We were growing very quickly," George explained "and there were a lot of influences. We were listening to all kinds of music." But nothing spoke more profoundly to him than the spiraling notes of Ravi Shankar's sitar. "It seemed very familiar to me. The pure sound just called on me," he mused. Enthralled with the sitar's majestic murmur, Harrison had to get his hands on the instrument as quickly as possible. He soon found "a very cheap sitar" for sale at a London import shop called India Craft.

Although most people became aware of the instrument through the simple melodic phrase he fashioned for "Norwegian Wood," George later confessed that he played the sitar "very badly." As fate would have it, sitar virtuoso Ravi Shankar would soon return to London to perform at the Asian Music Circle. George hoped to arrange a private meeting with the master musician without attracting any unwanted attention from the press. In lieu of creating a public spectacle, plans were made to spirit Shankar to Harrison's Essex estate, where, accompanied by tabla virtuoso Alla Rakha, he played a private concert for George, John, and Ringo. Ravi would also give George his first sitar lesson, instructing him on how to sit and hold the instrument properly, balancing it between his right thumb and the sole of his left foot, and teaching him some basic fingering technique, while introducing him to the intricacies of the Indian classical music form known as the raga.

While McCartney later admitted that he found Indian music "boring," Lennon, on the other hand was charmed by its mystical qualities, although he possessed a healthy disrespect for any formal method or tradition. While John might have found certain aspects of the Indian musical system poetic, he couldn't have cared less about what time of day or year a certain scale was meant to be played, or what color or emotion was associated with each note. He simply resonated with the sound of the sitar and was open to the possibilities the exotic instrument had to offer.

According to George, Ringo, while completely mystified by the tabla, had absolutely no intention of learning the Indian hand drum, as it was "so far out to him." Why complicate matters with all that fancy technique, mathematics, and intricate rhythms when two drumsticks had done the trick for him thus far? Meanwhile Harrison was so completely enthralled by the twenty-string Persian lute that he claimed he was ready, if necessary, to abandon his home and lovely wife, Pattie, and buy "a one-way ticket to Calcutta" to fully immerse himself in Indian music and culture.

Up to this point, Ravi Shankar had remained blissfully ignorant of the Beatles' music—until his niece and nephew played "Norwegian Wood" for him. While thoroughly unimpressed with Harrison's neophyte noodling, Shankar immediately recognized the tremendous "effect [the song had] on the young people. They were lapping it up," he enthused. "They loved it so much!"

Despite having grown a wispy moustache, Harrison was immediately recognized by a bellhop at the grand Taj Mahal hotel in Bombay when he went to India to study the sitar with Shankar. Suddenly the word was out, and "there was such a big flash all around the world," as Ravi recalled in his autobiography *Raga Mala*. "It was like wildfire, creating such a big explosion of fascination with the sitar that there was a tremendous demand for my concerts. I had become a superstar."

"The impact of George Harrison's life and times has been enormous," wrote the minimalist composer Philip Glass in his December 2001 *New York Times* elegy for the "quiet" Beatle. "He played a major role in bringing several generations of young musicians out of the parched and dying desert of Eurocentric music into a new world."

Glass recalled meeting Shankar in Paris in '65. "It was as powerful, and as important for my musical development, as it was for George," he said. Ravi "was a great mentor for me as he was for George."

Suddenly every band now had to include the sitar in their music or risk seeming hopelessly square, whether they simply posed with the instrument (as in the case of the Byrds and the Strawberry Alarm Clock) or tactually had to figure out how to finger the lugubrious lute, like Brian Jones of the Rolling Stones, Dave Mason of Traffic, John Renbourn of Pentangle, and Mike Heron of the Incredible String Band (arguably the finest and most dedicated sitarist of all the Brit rockers to adopt the instrument). For the less nimble and dedicated, an electric sitar/guitar hybrid soon became available on the market thanks to the clever folks at Danelectro Guitars. Better known as the Coral sitar, the six-string Masonite solidbody was customized with thirteen sympathetic strings whose electric insect drone could soon be heard all over the Top 40, on everything from the Boxtops' "The Letter" to Joe South's "Games People Play," even infiltrating Motown on Stevie Wonder's "Signed, Sealed, Delivered." Tacky advertisements claiming, "You don't have to be Hindu to play the Coral Electric Sitar" appeared in music magazines, featuring session guitarist Vinnie Bell (who designed the instrument) wearing a bejeweled turban.

"Sitars," as author and Gita scholar Joshua M. Greene pointed out, "were not entertainment instruments originally. They were part of sacred ritual music, intended to inspire listeners to go deeper into their eternal identity. The sitar's appeal in large measure is its microtones and fretless transitions, which are meant to mirror the heart's yearning for God . . . . Eric Clapton's solo in 'While My Guitar Gently Weeps' does this to a degree."

The sitar's modal majesty started to inform nearly every rock guitarist's approach to crafting his solos. Its linear, lyrical phrasing inspired an entirely new vocabulary for lead guitarists, catapulting the music beyond the well-worn country and blues riffs that everyone played up until that point. After Ravi Shankar drove the flower children into a frenzy at the Monterey International Pop Festival in June 1967 (amongst the mesmerized crowd sat two of America's greatest guitarists, Mike Bloomfield and Jimi Hendrix, who studied the master's every move with their mouths agape), blues rock string benders like Jorma Kaukonen of Jefferson Airplane and Carlos Santana began mixing quasi-raga riffs into their usual bag of tricks.

In his unpublished memoir, Shiv Dayal Batish (father of popular sitarist Ashwin Batish), who played the sitar on the soundtrack of *Help!*, wrote about working with the Beatles and their involvement in Indian music and culture: "Having had a good deal of experience with the Indian movie studios," Pandit Batish claimed he was "quite impressed" by the working conditions and the atmosphere on the set while providing the soundtrack to a few scenes in *Help!*

"The studio session lasted for the whole day, during which [Batish performed] vichitra veena [a droning four-stringed instrument common in Hindustani music] pieces of Beatles songs [in addition to various] background pieces of some ragas, which were used in the sequences of the goddess Kali. Working with the Beatles had not only earned us fame and popularity in the West," Pandit Batish stressed, "it had also brought us respect within our own Indian community."

The Beatles' office would soon phone again. This time it was George Harrison, inquiring to see if Pandit Batish was available to give George's wife, Pattie, lessons on the dilruba. A bowed instrument from northern India with no fewer than thirty sympathetic strings, the dilruba (in the Pandit's words) produces "a deep, lush, and dreamy sound." Its fretboard is like that of a sitar while its body, covered with goatskin, is similar to that of the sarangi. Two weeks later the dilrubas that Batish ordered from Bombay arrived. Chauffeured to the Harrisons' house in Sussex County, South London, Batish discovered Lennon's psychedelic Rolls-Royce parked in the driveway when he arrived, "fully painted with a sort of graffiti." Pandit Batish confessed to being "quite amazed with the art work on its huge body."

According to Pandit Batish, "peace was prevalent," at the Harrison home. "On seeing me entering from the door, Mr. Harrison stood up and came forward with folded hands, observing the Indian style of Namaste and then shook hands with me. A very beautiful young lady who was standing close behind him was introduced as Mrs. Pattie Harrison. She was the one who was to become my future pupil in learning the dilrubha." Pandit Batish was then introduced to John, Paul, and Ringo, whom he recalled as "real nice," and said they "waved their friendly hands as they smiled and then again went on in their serious discussion. I sat with the Harrisons and took out the dilrubha from the cover. Pattie was so filled with awe and wonder to behold the instrument. As soon as they had finished patting the instrument and getting acquainted with it, I took it in my hands and started playing a few notes to show how it sounded. Pattie was simply amazed with the tone, and Mr. Harrison happily thanked me for bringing it in time, saying that she was so anxious to get it and start learning on it." Apparently Pattie was a "smart student" who lost no time in learning the rudiments of the instrument. "I found the beautiful couple extremely good-natured and respectful. I cannot forget the kind of welcome which used to be given to me in their house, and shall cherish it always."

In the meantime, John Lennon confessed he'd become "very paranoid" after hearing Dylan's "4th Time Around," (the surrealist waltz from his 1966 double album *Blonde on Blonde*), a song that upon first listen seemed like a scathing parody of "Norwegian Wood." "I didn't like it," John told Jonathan Cott in *Rolling Stone* in September 1968. "I thought it was an out and out skit, but it wasn't. It was great. I mean, he wasn't playing any tricks on me. I was just going through the bit (paranoia)." In the end it was, as George was fond of saying, all in his mind . . . or was it?

Dylan, who had an uncanny explanation for nearly everything, told author Robert Shelton that the flowing guitar figure on which he hung his absurdist lyric was influenced by neither George's sitar nor Lennon's convoluted verse, but by Tex-Mex music.

Dylan's influence on John was apparent in *Help!* as Lennon sat on the sofa serenading a pink-clad Eleanor Bron with "You've Got to Hide Your Love Away." From the rasp of his world-weary voice, to the choice of an acoustic guitar over his usual Rickenbacker, to his wailing harmonica on "I'm a Loser" to a very familiar sailor's cap (similar to the one that Bob sported on the cover of his 1962 self-titled debut album), it was plain to see that John Lennon had fallen heavily under Bob Dylan's spell.

Famously, the two were filmed by D. A. Pennebaker in the back of a limo for Pennebaker's aggravatingly chaotic film, *Eat the Document.* Behind their dark sunglasses and between endless cigarettes and awkward silences, their dangling conversation nervously bounced from Johnny Cash, to the Silkies, to Barry McGuire and the "folker-rocker" boom of the day.

"I come from the land of paradise," Dylan joked, trying to keep the conversation lively, "baseball games" and "all-night

TV." But his usual sharp wit only seemed to fall flat until Bob, nauseous (reportedly sick on junk) and holding his head in his hands, contemplated whether or not he should make the ultimate statement and "vomit into the camera."

"Real life! Real life!" Lennon crowed.

The first take of "This Bird Has Flown," as the song was initially called, was recorded on the evening of Tuesday, October 12, during a four-and-a-half-hour session. It's easy to see why Harrison compared it to an Irish drinking song, as John sang "I once had a girl" to a slightly clunky bowlegged waltz.

"Norwegian Wood" began with a sly eye-winking boast of sexual conquest, but the situation quickly reversed on the singer. "Or should I say she once had me," Lennon admits, suddenly sounding vulnerable and awkward.

On take one, George's sinewy sitar answers John and Paul's voices, harmonizing on the line "She asked me to stay and she told me to sit anywhere." The first take ends with Harrison twanging a brief blues riff on the sitar, which was later omitted.

Recorded on October 21, take two began with John counting off the tune as Harrison picks a weepy sitar riff over the song's B section, which had been used previously as an introduction. John talk-sings the lyrics, sounding somewhat bored. Ringo now lays down a floppy backbeat while Paul's bass line plods along until the track ends with a loud, abrupt cymbal crash.

Take four, the "keeper" of the batch, begins with John flubbing his guitar part twice. George, on the other hand, seems to have gained better control of the sitar with each take.

It wasn't the first time George Martin had seen or heard the instrument, having first recorded it six years earlier, in 1959, along with the traditional tabla accompaniment for Peter Sellers's "Wouldn't It Be Loverly" on his album *Songs for Swingin' Sellers*. Ultimately, though, it was up to engineer Norman Smith (or "Normal," as John dubbed him) to get the levels right and make it all work. Although Smith found the sitar challenging to record, claiming it "has a lot of nasty peaks and a very complex wave form," he refused to use any sort of compression or limiter on the strange signal, as it risked "losing the sonorous quality." The solution was to double-track George's part, which gave the instrument a fuller presence.

GEORGE HARRISON'S WIDE WORLD OF STRINGS

"NORWEGIAN WOOD" was written and originally performed on acoustic guitar by John, in the key of D, before he capoed it up to E for its final version. It's interesting to note that the twenty strings of the sitar (including its thirteen resonating strings) are usually tuned to an open, droning C chord, with the lead string pitched at F. But according to *Record* magazine, George's instrument was tuned to "Western notes." Whether this refers to Harrison tuning his sitar like a guitar or is due to writer's ignorance is unclear, as each note of the Indian scale has a direct correlation in Western music: i.e., Sa = C, Ma = F, Pa = G, etc. But playing in D—or in E, for that matter—certainly would have been a challenge for George, as he'd only recently begun to explore the possibilities of the instrument.

"It was such a mind-blower that we had this strange instrument on a record," Ringo remarked following the release of *Rubber Soul*. "We were all open to anything when George introduced the sitar—you could walk in with an elephant, as long as it was going to make a musical note."

Starr was definitely onto something with his amusing analogy. Like the pachyderm, the sitar, with its long neck and bulbous pumpkin gourd body is both awkward and exotic nearly everywhere, except to natives of the subcontinent.

Originally a court instrument played for Persian royalty, the sitar was quickly adopted by Hindu culture following the Mughal conquest in the fifteenth century. A couple centuries later it suddenly leapt from the obscure realm of Indian classical music onto the world's stage, and, along with long hair, miniskirts, the Mini Cooper, and Nehru jackets, became synonymous with that brief magical moment of the sixties known as "Swinging London."

Before George discovered the sitar on the set of *Help!* the glistening chords of his Rickenbacker twelve-string had inspired the Byrds and the Mamas and the Papas to forge the new folk-rock sound that pervaded pop music in the mid-sixties.

With everyone jumping on the Indian bandwagon, Harrison, not wanting to trivialize Hindu culture and tradition, eventually quit playing the instrument he'd recently fallen so deeply in love with—but not before composing a series of modal pop tunes (including "Love You To," "Within and Without You," and the "Inner Light") that not only made the sonic spice of the subcontinent an integral part of sixties rock, but offered nuggets of Eastern spiritual wisdom within the lyrics.

By 1969 George had begun playing slide guitar, freely mixing riffs he'd picked up off old records by American bluesmen Robert Johnson and Elmore James with slippery ostinatos inspired by the great sarod player Ali Akbar Khan. Although lacking the virtuosity of Ry Cooder, Harrison created a distinctive voice with the slide guitar, using its sad, sweeping notes to embroider his finest solo work, from "My Sweet Lord" and "Give Me Love" to "Marwa Blues."

George's final contribution to rock was no mean feat. No matter how Tiny Tim intrigued and puzzled audiences with his ukulele-driven remake of the 1929 hit "Tiptoe Through the Tulips," the man formerly known as Herbert Khaury inspired very few guitarists to pick up the uke. But George's last album, *Brainwashed*, features the much-maligned instrument on a number of songs to tremendous effect, from a cheeky cover of Cab Calloway's "Between the Devil and the Deep Blue Sea" to the driving rhythm of Harrison's own "Any Road." Whether Harrison sparked the unforeseen ukulele fad of the early 2000s is debatable, but uke master Jake Shimabukuro's version of "While My Guitar Gently Weeps" stands as a testament to the man and his love for the instrument.

Gone on the final version of "Norwegian Wood" was McCartney's bumpy bass part, while Ringo, now off the drum kit, can be heard adding various light percussion, including maraca, finger cymbals, and tambourine. This time Lennon coaxed the melody, more than half-speaking, half singing his part as in the earlier version. "I showed ya!" John quips as the song ends.

While George attempted to record his sitar along with John on the first two tracks, they agreed it would be best to overdub it later. Harrison then switched to an acoustic twelve-string guitar before double-tracking his sitar onto take four, which ultimately yielded a better performance while giving the instrument greater presence in the song. The mono mix of "Norwegian Wood" as it appears on the American release of *Rubber Soul* reveals a number of blunders, including George coughing at one point, while somebody enthuses, "Sounds good!" as the sitar part ends.

Despite the Beatles' adventurous approach to adding new sounds to *Rubber Soul*, the Yardbirds were actually the first group to use the sitar in rock. According to their manager/ producer Giorgio Gomelsky, they brought an Indian sitarist in to overdub the exotic lead on their new single "Heart Full of Soul" in the spring of '65. Dissatisfied with its thin, buzzing tone (few engineers at the time knew how to get a good level on the instrument), Jeff Beck picked the classic riff on a fuzz-drenched Telecaster, sending the song rocketing up the British charts to number two that June. A month later the Kinks released "See My Friends," written and sung by Ray Davies, who claimed the song's ethereal melody (written for his sister who died suddenly from an undetected hole in her heart) was inspired after hearing a group of fishermen chanting together on a beach in Bombay during a stopover on the Kinks' first tour of Asia. Davies later imitated the droning effect of a sitar with the help of feedback from his Framus electric twelve-string guitar. From Pete Townshend's perspective, "See My Friends," was "the first reasonable use of the drone [in pop music], far, far better than anything the Beatles did and far, far earlier."

Gomelsky pointed out that Jimmy Page, having bought a sitar from the session musician who played it on "Heart Full of Soul," first turned George Harrison on to the instrument, not David Crosby and Roger McGuinn (as the story is most often told), with whom the Beatles would later spend the afternoon of August 24, at a rented house on Mulholland Drive, in L.A., tripping their heads off on LSD while listening to Ravi Shankar records and trading raga riffs on twelve-string guitars.

"What happened in those days; there was a great period of time where everybody was waiting for the next record somebody else would make, because everybody was discovering new sounds and new ways of doing things," Ray Davies explained. "And they [the Beatles] were waiting for my new single to come out and asking how I got the sounds on it."

Whether inspired by the Yardbirds, the Kinks, or the Byrds (most likely by all three), one thing is certain: Harrison first encountered the exotic instrument on the set of *Help!* Following the overwhelming response to "Norwegian Wood," the BBC's Brian Matthew told George, "You can't use the sitar again because everybody's using it," to which Harrison replied, "I don't care if everybody's using 'em, you know, I just play it because I *like* it!" But by early June of 1966, George, who never suffered fools gently, told the press that he was "fed up with the way the sitar has become just another bandwagon gimmick with everybody leaping aboard it just to be 'in.' A lot of people will probably be saying that I'm to blame anyway for making the sitar commercial and popular but I'm sick and tired of the whole thing now, because I really started doing it because I want to learn the music properly and take it seriously. The audience at Ravi's show [at Royal Festival Hall in London, June 1, 1966] was full of mods and rockers who, more likely than not, just want to be seen at the Ravi Shankar show."

"I've been listening more and more to [classical] Indian music," the great jazz saxophonist John Coltrane told a Dutch journalist back in 1961. Wanting to employ a drone to constantly reverberate throughout his music, similar to the way a tambura helps to lay the foundation in a raga, Coltrane began using two bowed acoustic basses weaving in and out of each other to achieve a similar sound.

As fate would have it, the great multi-instrumentalist Eric Dolphy (who joined John Coltrane's group in1961, adding his bass clarinet and flute to 'Trane's spiritually fueled improvisations) met Ravi Shankar while on his first American tour. It was a great opportunity for the jazzman to learn about ragas, talas, and other intricacies of Indian music directly from the master of the form.

As Dolphy later explained it: "Classical Indian music is the music of [Indian] people and jazz is the music of the American people, especially the American Negro. Quite naturally, there's something of a connection there, of people expressing themselves in the same way [both are ancient blues of various hues]. To the listener that doesn't pay close attention to the notes, the sound will get monotonous. But to the person that listens to the actual notes and the creation that's going on and the building within the players and within themselves, they'll notice that something is actually happening."

So enormous was Shankar's impact on Coltrane both musically and spiritually that Coltrane named his son (who also became an accomplished tenor saxophonist) Ravi in honor of the master sitarist.

While George's use of the sitar had a profound influence on the burgeoning counterculture, ultimately introducing the mysticism and exotic charm of the subcontinent to the West, it happened quite by accident, without any intent on his part. Journalist Palash Ghosh of the *International Business Times* felt that George Harrison was "handsome, smart, and charming, an ideal 'P.R. man' for [popularizing] something as remote and incomprehensible as Indian/Hindu culture."

Although they shared a mutual appreciation for bright clothes, vegetarian food, and bangles, traditional Hindus abhorred such hippie values as casual drug use and the notion of free sex (although the carvings of people copulating in every possible, way, shape, or form at the temples of Khajuraho might cause you to wonder). While Westerners were intrigued by India's unusual fashions and food, Ghosh suspected that "for many Westerners, India and Hinduism was nothing more than a fad, a temporary [and superficial] infatuation that led nowhere."

McCartney was only being honest when he claimed that he never cared for Indian music. Paul, in fact, confessed that he "always used to turn it off" whenever he heard it on the radio. "George got on this big Indian kick and he's dead keen on it. We've been round to his house a couple of times and he plays it and it's so boring," Paul groused. Ever the charming diplomat, and never wanting to insult anyone, McCartney quickly covered his tracks, adding, "No, no, it's good, you know, and you sort of hear millions of things in it that I never realized were in it." Despite his stringent opinion, Paul quickly absorbed everything he needed to know from Indian music. The most driven and competitive member of the Beatles, Paul would soon beat George at his own game, replacing Harrison's original guitar break on "Taxman," the opening track of *Revolver*, with a brilliant edgy riff infused with raga motifs. McCartney often played with a more emotional, spontaneous feel than his bandmate. Paul's searing, stinging lead on the title track to *Sgt. Pepper's Lonely Hearts Club Band* would rival the work of nearly any electric guitarist of his day.

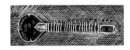

According to Norman Smith, the stylistic clash between Lennon and McCartney "was [first] becoming obvious" during the *Rubber Soul* sessions. At the same time, "George was having to put up with an awful lot from Paul," who tended to harangue him over his slow, methodical musical process. Despite writing and playing well-conceived melodic riffs, McCartney, believing he was capable of playing guitar just as well as, if not better than George, would, according to Smith, say, "'No, no, no,' and then reference American records he wanted Harrison to copy." Paul seemed incapable of complimenting George, offering a luke-warm response at best. He'd often wait until his bandmate had left the studio, then pull out a left-handed guitar and overdub the part himself. Starr would temporarily quit the band after McCartney had taken to tracking drums during the "White Album" sessions. Rather than suffer further humiliation, George chose to invite his friend Eric Clapton into the studio in order to take "While My Guitar Gently Weeps" to a higher plane.

Having seen the Beatles' effervescent camaraderie in *A Hard Day's Night*, and having watched them all living happily together in a big mod London town house in *Help!* and sing along to the all-for-one, one-for-all chorus of "Yellow Subma-rine," fans had a hard time fathoming this sort of resentment brewing within the band. Norman Smith was surprised when he "discovered that George Harrison had been hating Paul's bloody guts." But much to George's credit, temperament, and the good of the band, he managed to stuff his emotions away for the time being and keep a stiff upper lip. As Smith recalled, "It didn't show itself," at least not until the dreadful *Let It Be* sessions, in the spring of 1969, when George famously told Paul, who'd been hassling him over a particular passage, that he would play whatever he wished or "not play anything at all."

"Paul would never give you the opportunity to come out with something, having come into the studio already knowing all the parts of whatever song he was working on" Harrison told *Crawdaddy* in 1977.

Of all the Beatles, "Paul was the main musical force," Norman Smith opined. Beyond playing each instrument as well as, if not better than his bandmates, McCartney, in their former engineer's estimation, "didn't need George Martin to produce their records. He could have done them equally [as] well." Paul's only musical shortcoming in Smith's estimation was that "he couldn't write music, yet [he] was capable of telling an arranger [as with both 'Yesterday' and 'Eleanor Rigby'] how to do it by singing a part. . . . Most musical ideas," he told journalist Chris Salewicz, "came from Paul."

Differences in personal taste and artistic vision within the Beatles would became apparent over the next two albums (*Revolver* and *Sgt. Pepper's*), with Paul delivering the tender ballad "Here, There and Everywhere" while Harrison, who no longer needed the help of his bandmates on his latest Indian-inspired composition "Love You To," would replace the lead guitar with the sitar and employ the tabla in lieu of a drum set. George's stunning "Within You and Without You," which opened side two of *Pepper*, stood in stark contrast to McCartney's vaudevillian valentine, "When I'm Sixty Four." A complex composition with a soul-searching sermon on karma, "Within You and Without You" was deemed too serious by the rest of the band. The solution was to tag a laughter track on to the end of the song, in hopes of making George's sonic sermon seem like a big cosmic joke.

While Harrison's immersion in and devotion to Indian culture and consciousness deepened, it was actually Pattie who first introduced him to the benefits of Transcendental Meditation, as taught by the Maharishi Mahesh Yogi. The Beatles would soon board a train for Wales to meet the Maharishi, but just as they sat at the feet of the giggling guru, they received news that their manager (and father figure) Brian Epstein had been found dead in his apartment at age thirty-two from an overdose of sleeping pills.

Stumbling along the spiritual path, the Beatles soon arrived at the Maharishi's meditation camp in Rishikesh, India, for a three-week retreat (along with Donovan, Mia Farrow, and the Beach Boys' Mike Love). But their satori would end abruptly after Lennon (wrongly) accused the Hindu holy man of philandering.

Back in England, the Beatles (despite some of the worst bickering of their career) got down to the long, arduous process of recording thirty songs for the new "White Album." Disillusioned with "Sexy Sadie" (as he immortalized the Maharishi in song), John soon grew a heavy beard, dressed all in white, and declared himself his own guru. According to Lennon's old pal Pete Shotton, one day John, obviously stoned off his head, called an emergency meeting at the offices of Apple Records in May 1968 to inform his bandmates and press secretary Derek Taylor that he'd experienced a profound realization. He was the reincarnation of Christ. The meeting was quickly adjourned.

At a London press conference on June 15, 1968, the Beatles claimed they had made "a public mistake" in following the Hindu holy man. John then used the Maharishi as fodder for songs like "Sexie Sadie" and "I Found Out" (the latter from his first solo album, *Plastic Ono Band*, in which he howled, "There ain't no guru who can see through your eyes").

Years later, in 2009, Paul, hoping to take the sting out of his former bandmates' harsh accusations, claimed that "Transcendental Meditation was a gift the Beatles had received from the Maharishi at a time when they were looking for something to stabilize them." But it hardly mattered by then, as Lennon, Harrison, and the Maharishi had all since departed the earth plane.

By the late 1960s, England was faced with a serious crisis from the influx of immigrants from their former colonies, including India and Pakistan, as well as Jamaica. Although these foreigners were deemed "undesirables" by the British establishment, the younger generation was enthralled by many aspects of their lifestyle and culture. In this tense atmosphere, the Beatles, who'd probably done more to promote global peace and harmony through their music than any group of their day, were accused not only of misappropriating Indian culture, but of racism after Paul McCartney had sarcastically cried "Don't dig no Pakistanis," during an improvised passage in "Get Back," which was caught by the cameras during the shooting of their final movie, the rather dismal documentary *Let It Be*. Sung in a mock drunken Elvis-like drawl (while John gleefully punctuated his partner's satirical, free-form verse with shouts of "yeah!"), the phrase in no way reflected Paul's true feelings. McCartney, in fact, was responding to comments recently made by "Dirty Enoch Powell"—as he referred to the controversial conservative whose paranoid "River of Blood" speech (in which Powell laid direct blame on immigrants for destroying the quality of life in the UK) enraged much of the public and ultimately caused him to be ousted from his seat in Parliament.

While George Harrison would eventually abandon the sitar, feeling that he'd never attain a respectable level of virtuosity on the instrument, he never gave up on the beckoning call of his sweet Lord Krishna. Following the success of his number one hit song "My Sweet Lord"— in which George managed to subtly work the Maha Mantra into the chorus of a catchy pop song, leading a worldwide sing-along of "Hare Krishna"—he then joined with his friend and mentor Ravi Shankar in organizing the gala benefit Concert for Bangladesh, which featured Bob Dylan, making a return to the stage after his five-year retirement from performing, along with Eric Clapton, Leon Russell, and Ringo Starr, to raise money for millions of refugees fleeing civil war–torn Bangladesh (formerly known as East Pakistan). Palash Ghosh considered Harrison's act of charity "one of the greatest moments of post-war global cultural exchange." George not only talked the talk, but he walked the walk, right up to the end. Following George's death in November 2001, and cremation (his ashes were spread in the Ganges River in Varanasi), it was reported he'd left £20 million to ISKCON (the International Society for Krishna Consciousness).

RUBBER COVERS: "NORWEGIAN WOOD"

One of the most frequently covered songs in the Beatles' catalog, "Norwegian Wood" has been recorded by everyone from Tangerine Dream, who transformed it into a shimmering electronic raga, to legendary jazz drummer Buddy Rich, who delivered a brassy, hard-swinging, big-band arrangement, to Sergio Mendes and Brasil '66, whose version is an easy-listening sonic massage.

Complete with tubular bells and fake sitar riffs, the latter played on a fuzzed-out twelve-string guitar, and couched in mellifluous surf choir harmonies, Jan & Dean's 1966 cover of "Norwegian Wood" bordered on parody.

Country singers Waylon Jennings and Hank Williams Jr. favored the song for its inherent Irish quality, and for its bawdy lyrics that brimmed with sexual innuendo.

Jazz musicians from Count Basie to Herbie Hancock have included the lilting waltz in their repertoire not only for its association to the Fab Four but for its modal melody, which has sparked flighty improvisation for nearly half a century.

"This tune is known as the decline and fall of the British Empire," jazz flautist Herbie Mann quipped moments before his nonet launched into a soaring version of "Norwegian Wood," recorded live at the Village Theater in New York City on June 3, 1967. Propelled by a driving rhythm section that included John Coltrane's bassist Reggie Workman, Mann's flute and Roy Ayers's shimmering vibes wove intricate bright solos while a handful of exotic instruments including the oud, the zither, and the dumbek turned Lennon's waltz into a magic-carpet ride. (From Herbie Mann's 1967 album *The Wailing Dervishes/ Atlantic Records.*)

The British band Cornershop brought "Norwegian Wood" full circle when singer/songwriter/guitarist Tjinder Singh sang it in a Punjabi dialect for their 1997 album *When I Was Born for the 7th Time*. Gone is Cornershop's unique blend of exotic rock and electronica that the band is best known for. In its place is a simple reading of the tune on acoustic instruments, including a droning tambura, a sitar, and an acoustic guitar, which allows the strange cadence of a foreign language (at least to Western ears) to take center stage.

Victor Wooten, bassist with banjo ace Bela Fleck & the Flecktones, played "Norwegian Wood" as a vehicle for his fantastic instrumental chops. The fingers of his left hand effortlessly fly up and down the neck while Wooten's right hand taps the strings, creating an array of surprising tones and textures.

Dozens of guitarists have covered the tune over the years. After faithfully playing the melody, backed by a slew of strings, Puerto Rican guitarist supreme José Feliciano turned Lennon's ballad into a groovy/bluesy jam while Dutch prog-metal guitarist Arjen Anthony Lucassen (aka "Iron Anthony") deep-fried the famous guitar riff with gobs of snarling wah-wah to spare, his vocals, swimming in delay, resembled John's hazy ones from "Tomorrow Never Knows."

11

"Drive My Car"

*"I hear Wilson Pickett or a sound on a record and I want to make
one of those, with the cowbell goin' four in the bar."*
—John Lennon

*R*ubber Soul (whether the British or the American pressing)
was unlike any record of its day. Within the grooves of this
shiny black "licorice pizza" (a euphemism for albums amongst
the more poetically inclined) was a road map of styles and influences that took the listener on a sonic safari to new and unexpected territories, fresh frontiers that the Beatles themselves
were in the throes of discovering. But no one who was familiar
with their music at the time was too surprised by the unmistakable influence of Motown and Stax on the British edition's
opening track, "Drive My Car." John Lennon had already sung
three Motown numbers on *The Beatles' Second Album*, including
a smoldering version of the Marvelettes' "Mr. Postman," Smokey
Robinson's "You Really Got a Hold on Me," and Barrett Strong's
R&B standard "Money."

Recorded on October 13, "Drive My Car" paid homage to
Stax Records, the chugging funk of Otis Redding in particular.
From the song's snarling guitar riff, which clearly bore the
influence of Booker T. and the MGs Telecaster master, Steve
Cropper, to its surging Donald "Duck" Dunn–style bass line and
a punchy backbeat, punctuated by the syncopated clank of a
cowbell (whether played by Ringo or, as some claim, Lennon),
the Beatles were starting to get genuinely funky.

There has been quite bit of confusion over who actually
played what on "Drive My Car." The lead guitar part, which
clearly bears Harrison's stamp on both its phrasing and sinewy
bends, was said to have been later doubled by Paul. As George
later recalled in a 1977 interview with *Crawdaddy*, Harrison
"helped out such a lot in all the arrangements. There were a lot
of tracks though where I played bass. Paul played lead guitar on

'Taxman' and he played guitar, a good part, on 'Drive My Car.'"
Harrison claimed that he originally "played that line on guitar
and Paul laid that with me on bass. We laid the track down
like that. [Either he was referring to doubling the McCartney's
bass line at one point with his Stratocaster or the overdubbing
session that followed.] "We [Harrison and Paul] then played the
lead part later on top of it."

Then there is the issue of who overdubbed the piano track.
Although the bluesy triplets sound like Paul, who was influenced by Fats Domino's rolling syncopated style, John is most
often credited. If it was McCartney, Lennon did little on this
track, other than shake a tambourine or thwack a cowbell (if
Ringo didn't!), as there is no rhythm guitar part on the song.
A track sheet kept at the time of this historic recording would
have gone a long way toward clearing up this ongoing mystery.

McCartney's remarkable voice, a diverse instrument capable of
leaping from an intimate coo to a manic blues wail, now bore a
husky growl as he sized up the object of his desire. Paul's sultry
insinuation "You can do something in between" revealed there
was something more on his mind beyond holding hands. `

While Lennon and McCartney's double entendre was pretty
sexy stuff, it was nowhere as hot as Memphis Minnie's 1929 "Me
and My Chauffeur Blues," in which the bodacious blues singer
blatantly begged, "Won't you be my chauffeur, I want you to ride
me, I want you to ride me . . . downtown." A more likely source
of the Beatles' inspiration for "Drive My Car" was Chuck Berry's
1965 release "I Want to Be Your Driver," an obvious knockoff
of "Me and My Chauffeur Blues" that borrowed heavily from
Memphis Minnie's sassy lyric and groove.

Unlike their American counterparts, the Beach Boys, the
Beatles did not grow up in a car culture. Long before they could
afford Aston Martins, Rolls-Royces, and Ferraris, the Fabs got
around by train. Convertibles were seldom seen on the streets
of rain-gray Liverpool. Brian Wilson and his brothers first built
their reputation singing catchy ditties about girls, surfing, and

automobiles. When they were not employing their vaulted harmonies in praising the many virtues of California Girls, they gleefully sang of the glories of dragging little deuce coupes "up and down the same old strip." In the late fifties and early sixties, custom cars and hot rods were as much a part of the California landscape as bikini-clad blondes, surfboards, and neon-lit hamburger joints.

Following World War II, a new market suddenly exploded across America, catering to the whims of teenagers with plenty of extra time and cash on their hands. Parents rightfully feared their borrowed Chevys and Fords, parked down at the shady end of the street, would instantly be transformed into rolling boudoirs, complete with a dashboard radio to provide the necessary mood music.

McCartney would revisit the popular car/sex metaphor again with "The Back Seat of My Car," when he and his wife Linda sang of the joys of making love in a plush limo, on their 1971 album *Ram*. Saturated with a schmaltzy string and brass arrangement, whatever edge "Drive My Car" once held had turned to marshmallow fluff as the happy couple crowed, "We know that we can't be wrong," in the song's triumphant coda.

The esthetics and limitations that each Beatle possessed individually quickly became apparent following the band's breakup in 1970. There is little doubt of McCartney's brilliance in writing, playing, and arranging music, but his lyrics were often another story. "Fucking hell," was all Lennon managed to mutter upon hearing Paul's second solo effort. "I just feel he lets me down," Ringo concurred. It was clear that without the scrutinizing gaze of his longtime partner keeping him from his worst excesses, McCartney, now happily married and living in the country, was finally free to sing whatever ditty came into his head. He soon began releasing material that by comparison made "Maxwell's Silver Hammer" (a song as responsible for breaking up the Beatles as the constant presence of Yoko Ono in the recording studio) sound profound.

McCartney confessed that the original lyrics to "Drive My Car" were "crappy" at best. The song began as a follow up to "Can't Buy Me Love," with more trite rhymes about buying golden rings until, after "a cup of tea and a ciggie," Lennon got straight to the heart of the matter, tossing in a line that brimmed with sexual innuendo: "Baby you can drive my car. . . ." Images of "L.A. chicks" began to flash in Paul's mind. He thought the song would pack more punch, he explained years later, if the girl was "a bitch." It was McCartney who provided the song's punch line, when the wannabe chauffeur finally confessed to having no such automobile.

"We've written some funny songs," Paul told *NME* on October 22, 1965. "Comedy numbers are the next thing after protest songs," McCartney declared. Apparently Paul never gave up on the idea of chuckleheaded music over the years, going on to write the likes of "Yellow Submarine," "Rocky Raccoon," and "Maxwell's Silver Hammer."

RUBBER COVERS: "DRIVE MY CAR"

While Wilson Pickett never covered "Drive My Car" (he did shred "Hey Jude" after Duane Allman dared him), the band Black Heat certainly funked it up nicely as the lead-off track to their 1974 Atlantic album, *Keep On Runnin'*.

The airtight eighties production of the Breakfast Club's version of "Drive My Car" sucked every trace of soul from the Beatles' original, while the band's accompanying video made the Monkees look like geniuses.

On the other hand, Bobby McFerrin's a cappella version of "Drive My Car," from his 1988 release *Simple Pleasures*, is pure joy. From the opening bass groove, Bobby builds a vocal arrangement that is at once stunning and infectious.

12

"Day Tripper"

"I wish I could talk in Technicolor."
—*California housewife under the influence of LSD*
during the Veterans' Administration Hospital Study for
Mental Health Issues, 1956

Following their concert at the Forest Hills Stadium in Queens, on August 28, 1964, Bob Dylan and Al Aronowitz, a pop culture writer from the *New York Post* (and original manager of the Velvet Underground) headed to Manhattan on a mission to turn on the Beatles. Armed with an ounce of pot, carried by Bob's faithful tour manager, Victor Maymudes, Dylan and Aronowitz made their way through the tightly knit police barricades that blocked approximately three thousand fans who'd gathered outside the Hotel Delmonico, waiting, hoping to get a glimpse of their favorite band.

Once inside the Fab Four's inner sanctum, they were promptly offered a garden variety of top-shelf intoxicants. The enigmatic Dylan preferred "cheap wine" to the expensive French vintage the Beatles had been enjoying with their dinner. Bob also declined the electric zing of the purple hearts the Beatles regularly popped to keep up with the mad pace of touring. Instead, Dylan favored "jazz cigarettes," and was sure the boys from Liverpool were hip to its sweet musky smoke— after all, hadn't he heard them gleefully chant, "I get high, I get high, I get high" before breaking into the mellifluous chorus of "I Want to Hold Your Hand"? Apparently not. It seems that Bob, who was always on the cutting edge of hip culture and consciousness, was also ahead of his time when it came to deciphering the Beatles' lyrics. After discovering the Fabs had been singing, "I can't hide," Bob proceeded to twist a skinny joint to initiate his naive pals from across the pond. Everybody watched, waiting, as Ringo, John's "official taster," as Lennon ceremoniously dubbed him, gulped the sweet smoke deeply into his lungs. Gently choking as he exhaled, he broke into a big grin, and the gathering spontaneously transformed into "a jolly party," as Pattie Harrison later described the scene. Meanwhile, down the hall, New York's finest stood by, on guard, while everyone proceeded to get "very high indeed."

"We were kind of proud to have been introduced to pot by Dylan, that was rather a coup," McCartney later told Barry Miles. "It was like being introduced to meditation and given your mantra by Maharishi. There was a certain status to it."

The Beatles' newfound love affair with marijuana certainly helped ease the tedium of shooting repetitive takes for *Help!*, which John claimed was "too Disney" for his taste. "The best stuff is on the cutting room floor," Lennon complained. "He [director Richard Lester] really didn't utilize us in that film. It was like having clowns in a movie about frogs."

As with everything they did, when the Beatles discovered something new, they became obsessed, diving headfirst into the deep end to explore all it had to offer before abandoning it (whether marijuana, meditation, or a new studio effect) and moving on to the next thing. Although they claimed smoking pot was nothing more than a giggle, it in fact caused them to blow their lines as actors. Director Richard Lester could only watch in dismay as the band would crack up laughing hysterically at each other's smallest provocation. Yet getting high clearly enhanced their creativity and inquisitiveness when it came to the recording studio. Years later, Ringo chalked up many of the Beatles' greatest innovations to the ethereal effects of marijuana.

"Grass was influential," Ringo observed in the 1995 documentary *The Beatles Anthology.* "We were all expanding in all areas, opening up to a lot of different attitudes."

Previously the domain of jazz musicians, poets, and a variety of urban "degenerates," pot, as our parents, teachers, and preachers routinely warned us, turned out to be "the gateway drug." If smoking herb had thrown open the funhouse door to the Fab Four's minds, the warping effects of LSD would soon send them soaring to unimagined corners of their consciousness, "where newspaper taxis appear[ed] on the shore, waiting to take [them] away," as Lennon later sang in "Lucy in the Sky with Diamonds."

LSD (better known in the scientific community as lysergic acid diethylamide) was discovered by the Swiss scientist Dr. Albert Hofmann, after he accidentally absorbed the drug he'd been researching through his fingertips. Heralded as a medicine for the soul by Aldous Huxley in his book *The Doors of Perception*, the unruly hallucinogen soon blossomed in the consciousness of the baby boomers and spread worldwide.

At the dawn of the sixties, Dr. Timothy Leary and Dr. Richard Alpert (the latter would later be known as Ram Dass, and his 1971 best-selling book *Be Here Now* would introduce an entire generation of spiritual seekers to Hindu mysticism) were a pair of cavalier professors from Harvard University who became world famous after conducting a series of controlled experiments in which they administered LSD to more than three hundred students, professors, artists, and writers. Despite testimony from three-quarters of the participants involved who felt the drug had had a positive effect on them and was, if taken with respect and under the right circumstances, a powerful educational and spiritual tool, the United States government begged to differ. Acid, it seemed, had quite the opposite effect in their experiments in mind control. In fact, they found the unruly substance absolutely useless when trying to coerce captured North Vietnamese POWs into handing over strategic information.

Oddly, it was the Beatles' dentist, John Riley, who first turned them on to LSD at a posh dinner party at his flat on Edgeware Road in the Bayswater neighborhood of London. "[He] laid it on George, me and our wives without telling us. He just put [acid-laced sugar cubes] in our coffee," Lennon later told Jann Wenner in his two-part marathon interview with *Rolling Stone* in December 1970.

Harrison recalled that he'd "heard vaguely about it, but [he] didn't really know what it was."

Stunned, Cynthia Lennon watched in dismay as "the room seemed to get bigger and bigger. . . . The bottom was falling out of my world," she later recalled. "We suddenly found ourselves in the middle of a horror film [and] he [Riley] seemed to change into a demon," she said of their diabolical host, who, with his Playboy bunny girlfriend, Cindy Bury, abstained from the hellish concoction himself.

Both Lennon and Harrison immediately grew suspicious of Riley's motivations (having heard a rumor that he was a swinger and fond of orgies) and quickly left despite his warnings. Heading over to the Ad Lib, they soon discovered "incredible things going on." "Screaming . . . hot and hysterical," as John recalled, they all believed they "were going crackers," hallucinating "a fire on the lift" as they entered the club, only to realize "it was just a little red light" inside the elevator. Overwhelmed and in no state to socialize, they all piled back into George's Mini Cooper and motored home slowly, with their senses fully lit.

Following the life-altering experience, Lennon confessed to have been "pretty stunned for a month or two."

"We didn't ask for it," George said of his maiden voyage into the unknown, "but we did say thank you."

The next time the Beatles (John and George, along with Ringo) took another ride on Dr. Albert Hofmann's swirling lysergic carousel was in Los Angeles, with Roger McGuinn and David Crosby of the Byrds. This time they found the experience far more enriching and enlightening, although tainted by the presence of pesky reporters as well as actor Peter Fonda, who freaked John out by recalling how he'd accidentally shot himself as a ten-year-old, after which he slipped into a coma and discovered "what it's like to be dead." Aggravating as the actor was, he did manage to inspire Lennon's song "She Said, She Said," which appeared on the Beatles' following album, *Revolver.*

While their initial trip had been a bonding experience for George and John, Paul remained reluctant to indulge in "them devil drugs" (as he referred to LSD). Although McCartney habitually smoked pot, he feared losing total control of his reality and possibly becoming irreparably altered, having heard people claim, "You never think the same way again," after experiencing LSD's warping effect. In contrast to Paul, John claimed to be "rather excited by that prospect."

By his own estimate, Lennon must have taken "a thousand trips. . . . I used to eat it all the time," he boasted. Much to the chagrin of his bandmates, McCartney would soon sing the praises of LSD to the press, causing a seismic shift in public opinion about just how "Fab" the Beatles really were.

The life-altering experience of smoking grass and dropping acid directly affected the Beatles' music. With their vanishing innocence came a new, unexpectedly bold direction, which some of their old fans found strange and alienating. The Fabs had clearly changed. They were no longer "cute," as Dylan observed, and had begun to openly embrace the unknown and surreal.

As author/acid avatar Ken Kesey observed, "People don't want other people to get high, because if you get high, you might see the falsity of the fabric of the society we live in."

"All our ideas are different now," Paul explained. "If someone saw a picture of you taken two years ago and said that was you, you'd say it was a load of rubbish and show them a new picture. That's how we feel about the early stuff. People always wanted us to stay the same, but we can't stay in a rut. No one else expects to hit a peak at twenty-three, so why should we? *Rubber Soul* for me is the beginning of my adult life."

John put it flatly: "You don't know us if you don't know *Rubber Soul*."

Recorded on October 13, "Day Tripper," (originally Lennon's brainchild) was built on a killer guitar riff inspired by the Beatles' old friend Roy Orbison's "Oh, Pretty Woman," which had spent three weeks at the top of the UK charts in August of '64.

"'Day Tripper' is one of the great riffs of the day," said Lenny Kaye (author and guitarist with Patti Smith). "I was a beginner guitar player back then and had just learned my first rock chords. It was easier to play the Stones or the Yardbirds. The Beatles stuff was always more difficult. By then their sonic palette was really starting to expand. In a weird way, they weren't part of their time. They transcend their era and stand apart from everyone."

A writer at *Time* magazine theorized that "Day Tripper" was inspired by a prostitute, while "Norwegian Wood" portrayed a difficult relationship with a lesbian. Queried by a journalist as to what his intent was behind their new songs, Paul quipped, "We're just trying to write songs about prostitutes and lesbians, that's all." Incidentally, there was a last-minute change made to the song's original lyric, after John and Paul were admonished that "prick teaser" was absolutely unacceptable. "Big teaser" it was unanimously agreed, was more suitable for radio play.

"Day Tripper" followed in the funky footsteps of "She's a Woman" (released November 1964 as the B-side of "I Feel Fine") and "Drive My Car." But despite its infectious lead riff (that every kid in the UK and the States who played guitar at the time *had* to learn), Lennon and McCartney considered it a "forced" composition, as they were under the gun to produce fourteen tunes for the new album within a one-month period. They nailed "Day Tripper" on the third take, on October 16, a couple days after "Drive My Car."

"Day Tripper," as it turned out, was more popular in Britain, topping the charts at number one while it peaked at number five in the U.S., where "We Can Work It Out" held the top slot. The song took dead aim at "weekend hippies." "Day Trippers," Lennon pointed out, "are people who go on a day trip, right? Usually on a ferry boat or something."

Georgia soul shouter Otis Redding was so moved by "Day Tripper" that within the year he recorded it with his backup band Booker T. and the MGs for his album *Dictionary of Soul*. Redding's rendition featured a slinky organ part and punchy horns and was peppered with plenty of Otis's trademark "gotta, gotta, gottas" to make sure you knew he meant business.

Lennon routinely dismissed most other artists' recordings of Beatle songs, although they helped increase his newfound wealth. Surprisingly, he didn't care much for Otis Redding's sweat-busting cover of "Day Tripper," while he was very complimentary of Judy Collins's earnest reading of "In My Life."

Both *Rubber Soul* and the Beatles' new double A-sided single—"Day Tripper," backed with "We Can Work It Out" — were released on December 3, 1965 (the same day as *Rubber Soul* in the UK).

MEANWHILE, BACK IN THE USSR . . .

ON THE SAME DAY *RUBBER SOUL* WAS RELEASED, the Russians launched *Luna 8*, a robotic probe intended to land on the moon. But three days later, on December 6, 1965, the Soviet satellite came crashing down on the moon's cold, barren surface after its retro rockets failed to fire. Years later, conspiracy crackpots relished the idea that the Beatles' music played a major role in tearing down the Iron Curtain, but most likely the Communist regime collapsed due to plain old human ineptitude, not refrains of "yeah, yeah, yeah."

The highlight (or low point, depending on how you view it) of this sort of lunacy can be found in the hysterical paranoid rantings of David A. Noebel's *Communism, Hypnotism and the Beatles: An Analysis of the Communist Use of Music*, a now rare and highly collectible pamphlet written and published in January 1965. Noebel didn't stop there, writing two more books of half-baked theories over the next four years: 1966's *Rhythm, Riots and Revolution: An Analysis of the Communist Use of Music*; *The Communist Master Plan*; and *The Beatles: A Study in Drugs, Sex and Revolution*, which should easily convince the reader that while John Lennon claimed to have indulged in over "a thousand trips," it was Mr. Noebel who was clearly out of his mind.

Although the Beatles' records were once sold in the USSR on the black market, and though the band had been officially banned behind the Iron Curtain, Sir Paul and his group would eventually rock Russia in May 2003, when he performed at Palace Square in St. Petersburg (where he was awarded an honorary doctorate from the city's distinguished conservatory N. A. Rimsky Korsakov, alma mater to legendary Russian composers Tchaikovsky and Stravinsky), and in Moscow's Red Square for a crowd of thirty-five thousand (including a late-arriving Vladimir Putin). Beyond the thrill of singing tunes like "Back in the USSR" and "It's Getting Better" in the former Soviet Union, Paul was delighted to learn that many Russian officials had learned to speak English by singing along to his songs.

Braving foul weather, the Fabs performed that night at the Odeon Cinema in Glasgow, kicking off what turned out to be their final UK tour. As Beatle biographer Philip Norman observed, "After creating an album like *Rubber Soul*, it was galling to run back onstage with their same old matching suits and hair and blast the same old thirty-minute repertoire into the same vortex of mindless screams."

"Beatles concerts," as Lennon rightfully complained, had "nothing to do with music anymore. They're just bloody tribal rites."

It was apparent to anyone who hadn't succumbed to madness of Beatlemania that the band was sick and tired of the nonsense. While their albums were quickly becoming rather sophisticated affairs, their live shows had seemed like nightmarish scenes from the theater of the absurd. The Beatles' old friend from Hamburg, bassist/artist Klaus Voormann, believed that by 1965, John had had enough of the madness and that he now "hated the audience."

RUBBER COVERS: "DAY TRIPPER"

Recorded live by the BBC in 1967, Jimi Hendrix ripped through a red-hot "Day Tripper" driven by Noel Redding's growling bass and Mitch Mitchell's polyrhythmic drums. It's some pretty sexy stuff until you hear Mae West's take on the song, as she delivers the lines "I'm a big teaser, I took him half the way there" in her trademark husky hush of a voice. "Oh, give me some more," West moans while the guitarist wields a nasty fuzz-drenched lead and the band busts into a sizzling striptease groove. The cover was originally released on her 1966 album *Way Out West* (which also included a cover of "Shaking All Over" that made everyone who played the song, from Johnny Kidd & the Pirates to the Who, sound like a bunch of nervous schoolboys). The Fabs would return the favor a year later when they included Mae amongst the mélange of idols and icons who graced the cover of *Sgt. Pepper's Lonely Hearts Club Band.* An unexpected hassle arose after West discovered herself, a world-famous sex symbol, amongst such forlorn company. "What would *I* be doing in a lonely hearts club band?" she demanded. But Mae soon became amenable to the idea after receiving a personal note written and signed by those charming scoundrels.

Recorded live in 1979, Cheap Trick relentlessly rocked "Day Tripper" before an ecstatic throng (cleverly ending the tune with a quote from the chorus of "She Loves You"). Unhappy with the sound quality, but hoping to maintain the energy of their kickass performance, the band allegedly returned to the studio and overdubbed their parts, one at a time, until virtually nothing of the original recording remained except for the enthusiastic crowd response. Nonetheless, Cheap Trick's "Day Tripper" remains a standout track from their 1980 release *Found All the Parts.*

Ten years later, the Bad Brains whipped up their own punky reggae version of "Day Tripper" on their live album *The Youth Are Getting Restless* (1990). Lead singer H.R. (also known as Human Rights) added some lyrics of his own before unexpectedly throwing a couple verses from the Stones' "She's a Rainbow" into the mix, creating a rather quirky medley.

13

"If I Needed Someone"

"If you move your finger about. You get various little melodies
(and sometimes you get various little maladies)."
—George Harrison, 1980

Recorded on October 16 and 18, in Abbey Road's Studio Two, "If I Needed Someone" was George's mellifluous bookend to "I Need You," his number from *Help!* that the band lip-synched in the film with a handful of tanks surrounding them on the deep green fields of Salisbury Plain. It was as if the heavy artillery was sent to protect England's number one cultural export from the bizarre rituals of some slapstick Indian cult. "If I Needed Someone" contained one of *Rubber Soul's* most enigmatic lyrics: "Carve your number on my wall," evoking the imagery of "Norwegian Wood" once more on side two of the album.

The mad pace of George Harrison's life had become, as he later sang, "All Too Much." The overwhelming hysteria and his desperate search for peace of mind was a theme that George would revisit throughout his career, from his first song, "Don't Bother Me," from *Meet the Beatles*, through *Revolver's* "Love You To," in which he exclaimed, "You don't get time to hang a sign on me."

"The only place he got any peace was locked into the bathroom in his hotel suite," Pattie Boyd wrote in her autobiography *Wonderful Tonight*. "I think the Beatles were quite frightened of their fans," she surmised.

While Harrison claimed to have written "If I Needed Someone" for his girlfriend and soon-to-be wife, British model Pattie Boyd, the lyric addressed the quandary a young man of such enormous fame and influence constantly found himself in when surrounded by an overabundance of beautiful girls. As he and Pattie soon became an item after meeting on the set of *A Hard Day's Night*, one has to wonder if George wasn't still playing his options, albeit gently, as he imbues a sense of hope in the girl who has come too late when he sings, "Maybe you will get a call from me." A trace of regret lingers in his voice as George explains his current situation: "But now you see that I'm too much in love."

While the Beach Boys stoked the great California myth singing, "Two girls for every boy," they never honestly addressed the reality of such awkward situations. John Sebastian of the Lovin' Spoonful (one of many bands heralded at the time as "America's answer to the Beatles") wrote a pair of songs addressing the perplexing moment when you must choose and "say yes to one and leave the other behind," as he sang in his tongue in cheek "Did You Ever Have to Make Up Your Mind?" the follow-up to "Younger Girl," a lilting ballad which came to Sebastian after finding himself attracted to two beautiful sisters at summer camp. Only the Byrds' outspoken and outrageous harmony singer David Crosby was wild enough to beg the taboo-breaking question: "Why don't we go on as three?" Crosby's sultry ballad "Triad" had caused his fellow Byrds such great consternation that they refused to release the song on their 1968 album *The Notorious Byrd Brothers*, lovely as the melody was. Soon after recording "Triad" with the Byrds, Crosby was unceremoniously booted from the band for mouthing off about the Kennedy assassination between songs while onstage at the Monterey International Pop Festival. Once on his own, he delivered his flowing anthem of sexual liberation to Grace Slick of the Jefferson Airplane to sing. Suddenly the tale of a three-way relationship became even more risqué—Slick turned the tables on Brian Wilson's fantasy and sang about the delightful confusion of loving two men simultaneously in an open relationship.

The Byrds' influence on "If I Needed Someone" was clear from the first chime of George's Rickenbacker twelve-string. But without Harrison and that gorgeous G7sus4 chord that kicked off *A Hard Days' Night*, the Byrds as a group might never have happened in the first place.

Roger (still known as Jim in those days) McGuinn, Gene Clark, and David Crosby were a trio of fledgling folksingers barely known around L.A. at the time as the Jet Set when they strolled into a Hollywood theater in the summer of '64. Ninety minutes later, the band had been transformed by the zany optimism and warmhearted harmonies of a pack of madcap mop-tops from Liverpool.

It certainly wasn't the first time that McGuinn had seen or heard a twelve-string guitar. A veteran of the folk scene from New York's Greenwich Village to Chicago's Gate of Horn to L.A.'s Ash Grove, McGuinn had backed up the likes of Bobby Darin, Judy Collins, and Hoyt Axton and was familiar with the recordings of Lead Belly's thunderous old Stella punching out songs like "House of the Rising Sun," "Gallows Pole," and "The Midnight Special." Pete Seeger, best known for popularizing the five-string banjo and employing the sing-along as a tool for social change, was also a fine twelve-string picker himself. McGuinn would soon fashion the left-wing troubadour's adaption from the Book of Ecclesiastes, first known as "To Everything There Is a Season," into the classic antiwar anthem now called "Turn! Turn! Turn!," which topped the charts in December of 1965.

Trading in their banjos and acoustic guitars, which suddenly seemed old hat, McGuinn chose a Rickenbacker twelve-string while Crosby fancied the Gretsch Country Gentleman (both favorite guitars of George Harrison). While doing everything humanly possible to make their hair grow faster, the Byrds, as they now called themselves in honor of the great explorer Richard Byrd (famous for his explorations of both the North Pole and Antarctica), drove down to the barrio in search of shiny black Cuban heels, which overnight had become famous as "Beatle boots" and were flying off shoe store shelves from coast to coast.

In his 1980 memoir *I Me Mine*, Harrison likened "If I Needed Someone" to "a million other songs written around the D chord." George, like McGuinn (in the Byrds' anthemic arrange-ment of Dylan's "Mr. Tambourine Man") and the Who's Pete Townshend (most notably in "Pinball Wizard"), found a variety of "little melodies" by fishing around with his pinkie finger to augment the basic chord structure. (George played the song in D, with a capo at the fifth fret of his Rickenbacker twelve-string. Four years later he would return to the same motif while writing "Here Comes the Sun.")

What soon became celebrated as the "jingle-jangle sound," an essential component of folk rock as popularized by the Byrds, had actually been a Beatles innovation. Given an early prototype of the new instrument, George first used the semi-hollowbody Rickenbacker 360 twelve-string on "I Call Your Name" in March 1964.

Inspired by the Byrds' "The Bells of Rhymney" (another great arrangement of a Pete Seeger number based on the 1938 book *Gwalia Deserta* by Welsh poet Idris Davies), Harrison fashioned the opening riff to "If I Needed Someone" and promptly sent a promo copy to McGuinn with his compliments. Soon after that, Brian Jones could be seen posing for the camera on the Stones' greatest-hits album *High Tide and Green Grass* holding an identical model (right down to its red "Fireglo" finish). Although Jones used the instrument sporadically to add color to the Stones' sound, the Rickenbacker twelve-string (along with their flowing harmonies) had become the sonic trademark of the Byrds' early records, immediately identifiable and integral to shaping their initial string of hits. "That's a sound that will never go away," the smoky-voiced folk troubadour Richie Havens predicted, and he was right. The Rick's glistening chime has continued to echo across the decades on songs by everyone from Tom Petty to REM to Jeff Buckley and, most recently, Ed O'Brien of Radiohead.

Released in England on December 3, 1965 (on the same day as *Rubber Soul*), the Hollies' latest single, a cover of George's "If I Needed Someone," climbed to number twenty on the UK charts (while remaining unreleased in America until November 1967). George Harrison was far from impressed. "I didn't write it for the Hollies," he bristled. "Their version is not my kind of music. I think it's rubbish the way they've done it. They spoiled it," George complained.

With Lennon and McCartney garnering the lion's share of attention, it's surprising that Harrison appreciated neither the recognition as a burgeoning songwriter nor the extra income from royalties from the Hollies recording of his song. Perhaps George was aggravated by the Hollies' release garnering so much attention when he knew full well that one of his songs had no chance being released as a single by his own band (at least until the fall of 1969, when "Something" topped the charts).

"They are alright musically, but the way they do their records, they sound like session men who just got together in a studio without ever seeing each other before. Technically they're good, but that's all," George chided.

Harrison's dour critique of the Hollies immediately kicked up a row between himself and the usually mellow Graham Nash: "It's that bit about the session men that really annoyed us," Nash replied. Graham was peeved, as his band had gone out on a limb with their decision to cover George's new tune against the advice of both friends and their record company. "You can't please everyone you know, but if it's a hit, it'll mean two or three thousand pounds for George," Nash said, adding, "I'd back any of us boys against the Beatles musically any time."

Perhaps George's objection to the Hollies rendition of "If I Needed Someone" was due to its complete lack of originality in replicating his chiming twelve-string guitar sound and using a similar vocal harmony arrangement, although their cover features some strong drum fills by Bobby Elliott and some tight rhythmic guitar accents that give the tune a slight ska feel. Overall, the Hollies' version was bit more bubblegum, but "nothing to get hung about," as Lennon later sang.

Or maybe George took a shot at the Hollies as he felt they were not a "real" band. It had taken a few years before they'd developed their craft as songwriters, relying on outside tune-smiths for many of their hits and employing the likes of Jimmy Page to play lead and everyone from Jack Bruce to Klaus Voormann to John Paul Jones to fill their ever-revolving bass chair.

"I thought we made a damn good record of it," Graham Nash countered. "It was perfectly suited to our voices, with a smart three-part harmony that gave the song a soaring melodic virtuosity."

Sick and tired of the Beatles' "holy status," Graham shot back: "Sometimes, even Saint George didn't know when to keep his snarky views to himself. He felt as though he owned the fucking song and no one else had the right to interpret it."

After the press got wind of George and Pattie's secret nuptials on January 21, 1966, one reporter jokingly asked Harrison, "Did the Hollies go to the wedding?" to which he laughed and brushed off the row, saying, "All the papers took it up and it just got out of hand."

Although Graham and George eventually became "great friends," Nash claimed that Harrison's grousing "kind of cursed the record."

George was beginning to establish himself as a respectable tunesmith. For the second time in a year, a Beatles album would feature two Harrison compositions. Both "Think for Yourself" and "If I Needed Someone" were a cut above his previous efforts, "You Like Me Too Much" and "I Need You," from the UK edition of *Help!*

"Songwriting for me, at the time of *Rubber Soul* was a bit frightening because John and Paul had been writing since they were three years old," he explained. "It was hard to come in suddenly and write songs. They'd had a lot of practice. They'd written most of their bad songs before we'd even got into the recording studio. I had to come from nowhere and start writing, and have something with at least enough quality to put on the record alongside all the wondrous hits. It was," he humbly confessed, "very hard."

While "If I Needed Someone," appeared on the British pressing of *Rubber Soul*, it was one of the four original tracks cut by Capitol Records in the States and saved for *Yesterday . . . and Today*. The song was George's moment in the spotlight on both the 1965 and '66 tours.

RUBBER COVERS: "IF I NEEDED SOMEONE"

Regardless of George Harrison's snide remarks about the Hollies' covering his song, Nash and company's was arguably the best version of "If I Needed Someone," recorded by no fewer than three American bands in 1966, including the Kingsmen (of "Louie Louie" fame), the Cryan' Shames ("Sugar and Spice"), and an obscure San Jose band named Stained Glass.

George's indignation at the Hollies is puzzling. Thanks to Graham's band, "If I Needed Someone" was Harrison's first song to make the UK charts, climbing to number twenty on December 9, 1965. Whether spurred on by jealousy, or feeling like the Hollies had crossed some invisible line (after all, they'd recorded the song at EMI, in the same studio as the Beatles, and released their new single on the same day as *Rubber Soul*— December 3, 1965), George remained disgruntled.

Recorded for a live broadcast by the BBC in 1970, James Taylor's solo reading of the tune featured his trademark mellow vocal style and plenty of his pristine fingerpicking. Taylor's career had taken off two years earlier, in 1968, when he became the first American signed to the Beatles' new label, Apple. His self-titled debut, produced by Peter Asher, featured Paul McCartney on bass (and a noncredited George Harrison on guitar) on "Carolina in My Mind." The album also included a song whose title, "Something in the Way She Moves," became the inspiration and opening line to George's most popular song, "Something."

Whether performing solo or backed by a band, Taylor would pay tribute to the Beatles throughout his career, with tasty covers of "In My Life," "Day Tripper," and "Here Comes the Sun."

The Brooklyn-based goth band Type O Negative (aka "the Drab Four") recorded a skull-crushing seven-minute Beatle medley on their 1999 album *World Coming Down*. Kicking off with an ominous "Day Tripper," in which the band demonically chants the song's title, they break into a soaring (surprisingly) melodic version of George's "If I Needed Someone," complete with cawing crows in the mix, before falling into a massive, plodding groove of "She's So Heavy."

For his cameo at the Concert for George (a celebration of Harrison's life and music held at the Royal Albert Hall on November 29, 2002, one year after George's death), Eric Clapton was joined by an army of all-star guitar strummers, including George's son Dhani chopping chords on an acoustic, while Marc Mann (a bloody Yank!) nimbly picked Harrison's lead part on a Fender twelve-string. Clapton's choice of "If I Needed Someone" seemed odd considering George had written it at the peak of his love affair with Pattie Boyd, whom Eric would later wrest away from his best friend, by writing "Layla" in her honor. Nonetheless, George and Eric managed to remain good friends despite the ensuing drama over a woman they would both lose in the end.

In 2004 Roger McGuinn, master of the Rickenbacker twelve-string chime, released a supersonic reading of George's tune on his album *Limited Edition*. McGuinn's version spelled out loud and clear the Byrds' influence on Harrison as both a songwriter and guitarist.

The most interesting take on "If I Needed Someone" in recent years comes from the eight-piece Argentine reggae band Kameleba, whose rock-steady groove of George's tune appears on the 2013 compilation *Hemp! Tributo Reggae a the Beatles Vol. 2.* (The album cover, a hilarious knockoff of *Help!*, portrays the Fab Four floating above a large marijuana plant.) The accompanying video follows the band as they happily wander around in the sunshine handing out flyers to pretty girls for their gig. The horn section blows like a cool breeze through the palm trees until the band breaks into a grungy "Day Tripper" on the song's tag.

14

"In My Life"

(Including the Mystery of the Fifth Beatle)

*"I like first-person music. It's real, y'know? It's about me and I
don't know about anything else, really."*
—John Lennon, December 1970

Recorded on October 18 and 22, 1965, "In My Life" was one of the first songs written and sung by John Lennon (along with "Nowhere Man") that was not solely about love. Rather, the song was said to be inspired after BBC reporter Kenneth Allsop suggested that Lennon compose an ode to his hometown of Liverpool; an early failed draft of "In My Life," according to John, read like an overtly sentimental list of "happy hours" that he'd once known. Lennon felt the song was initially "glib," "a throwaway." Although "In My Life" was buried halfway through side two of *Rubber Soul*, John later recalled it as "my first real major piece of work."

"Before we were just writing songs à la Everly Brothers, Buddy Holly, pop songs with no more thought to them than that," Lennon confessed. "The words were almost irrelevant."

The original inspiration behind "In My Life" was a bus trip that began at John's house at 251 Menlove Avenue in Liverpool. As he rode into town, Lennon listed all of the places along the way that held any significance or sentimental meaning for him. John soon deemed both the idea for the song and its outcome "boring." As with "Nowhere Man," the moment he gave up trying to write the lyrics they suddenly began to flow naturally. As Lennon explained, "these lyrics started coming to me about friends and lovers of the past."

Like Dickens's Ghost of Christmas Past, John takes the listener on a tour of what once was and will never be again, "down the foggy ruins of time" (as Dylan sang just a few months earlier in his surrealistic ballad "Mr. Tambourine Man"). While

Lennon tenderly evokes visions of his Liverpool youth, "In My Life" gently unfolds with a nod to friends and lovers he's left behind. The lyric "some are dead and some are living" refer to John's old pals Stu Sutcliffe (deceased) and Pete Shotton (still among us as of this writing).

In the song's first draft, Lennon mentioned both the avenue of dreams the Beatles would soon immortalize as Penny Lane, along with Strawberry Field, a looming Victorian orphanage near John's house, favorite places that he and Paul would revisit a year later while in the early stages of creating their masterpiece, *Sgt. Pepper's Lonely Hearts Club Band*.

"Strawberry Fields Forever" and "Penny Lane," a double-sided single (both sides were labeled *A*) was released in February 1967, while *Pepper* appeared that June, containing Lennon's rousing "Good Morning, Good Morning," which returns to the original concept for "In My Life," as Lennon takes another walk into town, observing the rhythm and rhyme of life as it transpires all around him.

Melodically, "In My Life" revealed the influence of Roy Orbison's lilting "Blue Bayou." But it's George Martin's "harpsichord" solo (first played on an electric piano and then sped up to recall an Elizabethan-era keyboard) that helped forge a new hybrid of "baroquedelic" sound that would inspire the Rolling Stones' Brian Jones to employ such exotic instruments as the Appalachian dulcimer on "Lady Jane" and the recorder on "Ruby Tuesday."

"There was a gap in the song," Martin said, explaining his contribution to "In My Life." "And I said, 'We need a solo here. They went away and had their tea, so while they were out, I wrote something like a Bach inversion, and played it, then recorded it. I played it back to them when they returned and they said, 'That's great!' So we left it like that."

Once more, George Martin went uncredited for his role in the Beatles' music. Martin, considered by many to be worthy of the title "the Fifth Beatle," was in truth a salaried employee at EMI, a staff producer who was never given any extras in terms of writing or publishing credits, or money for his integral input to the band's music.

THE MYSTERY OF THE FIFTH BEATLE

ONE TITLE THE BEATLES KICKED AROUND for their seventh album, *Revolver*, was *The Magic Circle*. The name was voted down, perhaps because it evoked images of hooded druids carrying out cryptic pagan rites at Stonehenge—or at the very least a coven of witches chanting incantations in the dark forest. *The Magic Circle* conjures the sort of "Middle Earth" imagery that soon became popular with songs like "Ride a White Swan" by T. Rex and Led Zeppelin's "Stairway to Heaven." But what the title really referred to was the tightly knit group that no one outside of Lennon, McCartney, Harrison, and Starr could ever penetrate.

"A lot of what we, the Beatles, did was very much in an enclosed scene. Other people found it difficult, even John's wife, Cynthia, found it very difficult to penetrate the screen that we had around us," Paul explained. "As a kind of safety barrier we had a lot of 'in' jokes, little signs, references to music; we had a common bond in that and it was very difficult for any 'outsider' to penetrate. That possibly wasn't good for relationships back then."

In an essay for *Rolling Stone*, critic Greil Marcus compared each Beatle to the leg of a chair, and then defended his clever metaphor by explaining how each member was essential if the furniture (which supported a generation in style and comfort for nearly a decade) was to function. No matter who tried to enter the magic circle, they would always remain a fifth leg.

The liner notes to the Beatles' second album of 1967, *Magical Mystery Tour*, began: "Long ago there were four or five magicians," hinting at the ongoing presence of a fifth Beatle. Since the void created after the death of Stu Sutcliffe, who actually *was* the fifth Beatle for a short time, the band always seemed to be attracting a phantom member.

The original bassist for the Silver Beatles, as they were known before they became "Fab," Stu was John's drinking buddy and showed great artistic promise, but he had very little, if any, musical ability. With his clip-on shades and slicked-back hair, he was the embodiment of James Dean cool. Sutcliffe's myth has only continued to grow since his death in April 1962 from a brain aneurysm. Inspired by Buddy Holly and the Crickets, Stu suggested the name the Beetles, which Lennon then cleverly morphed into the Beatles. It was Stu's beautiful leather-clad German photographer/model girlfriend, Astrid Kirchherr, whom he met in Hamburg in the Reeperbahn, who asked why the band looked like a bunch of Elvis throwbacks. After she combed his hair down, the rest of the band laughed, before quickly falling in line.

It was Pete Best, their drummer at the time, who told them to keep their mitts off his pompadour. Best was actually the *fourth* Beatle until the lads conspired to replace him with the guy with the big nose and all those rings, who was actually the sixth Beatle who (after Stu died and Best was booted) then became the fourth Beatle. Some would argue that no one deserves the title more than Brian Epstein, the band's doomed, debonair manager/impresario, who cleaned up the Beatles' image, groomed them like a new breed of hip bankers, persuaded them to stop swearing and smoking onstage, and coached them to bow in unison. No matter how fruity their flower-power threads got, Brian, to his credit, stuck to his hand-tailored suits. If the sleeping pills hadn't done him in, John and Yoko posing au naturel on the cover of their *Two Virgins* album would have certainly done the trick.

The first inkling the public had of a fifth Beatle came in *A Hard Day's Night* with Wilfrid Brambell, Paul McCartney's "very clean" grandfather. Paul was supposedly looking after the wrinkly old codger, who repeatedly sneaked off to play cards and carouse with showgirls. With Brambell as their mascot, the Fabs retained their cuteness level. After all, how much trouble could they manage to get into with the old man around?

Initially, the concept of the fifth Beatle came from Murray the K, the New York DJ from 1010 AM WINS (aka "the Good Guys") who called himself "the Fifth Beatle" in hopes that the band's enormous popularity might rub off on him while he fanned the flames of Beatlemania. But this was nothing more than an obvious attempt at self-promotion.

With the death of Brian Epstein, the boys lost their father figure. Who better than the master of Transcendental Meditation, the Maharishi Mahesh Yogi, to fill the aching void? But after a quick trip to his North India ashram, John realized he could grow his own beard, dress in white, and become his own messianic figure (see the cover of *Abbey Road*). He no longer needed "Sexy Sadie" to show him the way and was rather brusque about it.

If anyone deserves the title of "the Fifth Beatle," it is Sir George Martin. From his Elizabethan piano break on "In My Life" to his gentle stirring of the psychedelic soup of "Tomorrow Never Knows," the Beatles were lucky to have him at the board. Martin was savvy. He had no illusions about his relationship to the band: "It was a brotherhood," Sir George explained. "It was like a fort really, with four corners that was impregnable. Nobody got inside that fort once they were together, not even Brian Epstein or I."

Perhaps the only one to make it over that moat was Yoko Ono, about whom John had no qualms bringing into the studio during recording sessions for their last three albums, insisting she constantly be at his side and even in band photographs. Lennon's collaborator after Paul was someone he could both protest wars and create art happenings with. The pair snorted heroin, did primal scream therapy, and made love for the camera. John seemed surprised and became indignant when the public failed to share his obsession with Ono.

Synthesizer wizard Magic Alex (aka John Alexis Mardas) was also a leading candidate for Fifth Beatle status for a brief moment in 1967. Mardas, who Lennon proclaimed "a genius" was given carte blanche to build the Beatles a state-of-the-art studio (which remained unfinished). Magic Alex traveled with the Beatles to Greece when they considered buying Leso, an island in the Aegean Sea, where they hoped to move, to flee fame and find paradise.

With a little bit of Fender Rhodes and a whole lotta soul, Billy Preston arrived just in time to help keep the Fabs together long enough to finish the basic tracks for the *Let It Be* sessions. Preston and the Beatles "were old friends" (Billy's words), having met when they toured together in the early sixties when he played with Little Richard's band. Although hardly featured in the film, Billy spent two weeks playing with the Beatles. (That's his electric piano on "Get Back.") Perhaps they had to behave themselves somewhat with an illustrious guest in the studio. After the fort collapsed, Billy played on several of George and John's solo projects.

The list of potential "Fifth Beatles" is long and odd and includes everybody from Bernard Purdie, the seasoned session drummer who claims to have filled in for Ringo on nearly every song since "Love Me Do," to Mal Evans, the band's faithful roadie, who, when not out buying socks for John, helped Paul write "I'm Fixing a Hole" and "Magical Mystery Tour," among others.

"George Martin had just finished working with the Beatles in 1969 when he decided to produce the first Seatrain album," their onetime lead singer/guitarist Peter Rowan recalled. (Seatrain were a California-based roots rock group.) "George liked our demos and got us a deal with Capitol. He was totally at home with what we were doing, particularly with Richard Greene, our violinist and pulled good performances out of the band. We went to London to record at Air Studios. There they were, George and the engineer, Chris Thomas, in their long white medical coats that they used to wear, pushing recording equipment into the studio on a dolly. George was always very punctual," Peter said, shedding a little light on the Beatles' enigmatic producer. "We'd work from 11 to 6 and come back in the evening for overdubs. He'd have a glass of scotch while all the boys toked up."

There's little doubt that Paul had taken the lead in getting away from the simple Leiber and Stoller "playlets" of teen love and angst they'd been crafting, and had begun to compose based on personal experience. Dylan, of course, had already been there for a few years, along with Leonard Cohen, who was a published poet before becoming a songwriter (his first collection, *Let Us Compare Mythologies*, appeared in 1956), while the Beatles were a bunch of young punks in the process of emerging from a dank basement in Liverpool. So it's understandable how they might have been behind the ball as far as lyrics were concerned.

As Dylan later pointed out to musician/photographer/author John Cohen in an interview with *Sing Out!*, "You can't say they've carried on with their [British] poetic legacy." Perhaps not in song initially, but John's books of curious doodles and nonsense verse, *In His Own Write* (published in 1964), along with his follow-up, *A Spaniard in the Works* (1965), bore traces of both Lewis Carroll and nineteenth-century British poet and illustrator Edward Lear, whom John claimed to have never read. (Oddly, after donning round wire-rimmed glasses and growing a bushy beard, Lennon resembled Lear.) There's little doubt that Lennon's literary success spurred Bob into finally finishing his tangled mess of a manuscript called *Tarantula* in 1966.

Although great songwriters, neither Dylan nor Lennon was foolish enough to consider himself a poet, a somewhat narcissistic trap that Jim Morrison would later fall into. Allen Ginsberg, an inspiration to both John and Bob (the Beat laureate appeared on the back of Dylan's 1965 album *Bringing It All Back Home* as well as in the video to Bob's "Subterranean Homesick Blues"), could rest easy for the time being—that is, as long as his acid-fueled apocalyptic visions would allow.

By the mid-sixties Dylan had begun composing his songs at the typewriter, with a cigarette perpetually dangling from his lips . . . and "the ghost of electricity howling through the bones of [his] face," to paraphrase his "Visions of Johanna." Originally written as a poem, "Like a Rolling Stone" was hammered out in a marathon of linguistic "vomit," as Dylan later explained.

Initially, Lennon preferred to keep the two disciplines of songwriting and poetry separate. While his early songs chronicled the foibles of teenage love, his whimsy and social satire were reserved for the pages his first two books. Eventually the two styles merged. The influence of Lewis Carroll was obvious within the lyrics of many of his later songs like "Lucy in the Sky with Diamonds," and "I Am the Walrus," and "Glass Onion."

It's strange that a song based on the power of memory should be one of the few Lennon and McCartney compositions about which they could never agree regarding their individual creative contributions. The dispute over songwriting credit continues to this day—McCartney claims to have written the perfect melodic vehicle for his partner's lyrics, while Lennon always maintained that Paul only added the harmony part and the song's "middle eight."

McCartney recalled arriving at Kenwood, where John had already written "the very nice opening stanzas of the song." The rough draft, as Paul explained, contained "the first pangs of nostalgia for Liverpool. Not that we longed to return there but, like everyone, you look at your youth, as Maharishi used to say, through a golden glass, and it looks much better than it was. . . . But as I recall, he didn't have a tune to it," Paul said. "And I went down to the half-landing, where John had a Mellotron, and I sat there and put together a tune based in my mind on Smokey Robinson and the Miracles. Songs like 'You've Really Got a Hold on Me' and 'Tears of a Clown' had really been a big influence. You refer back to something you've loved and try and take the spirit of that and write something new."

The change in the Beatles' songwriting, according to Paul, came after his Auntie Lil asked him one day: "Why do you always write songs about love all the time? Can't you ever write a song about a horse, or the summit conference or something interesting?"

"So I thought, 'Alright Auntie Lil.' and recently," he said in a 1965 interview, "we've not been writing all our songs about love."

McCartney claimed he composed "the whole melody [to "In My Life"]. And it actually does sound very like me, if you analyze it," he pointed out. "My recollection is going back up into the room and saying, 'Got it, great! Good tune, I think. What do you think?' John said, 'Nice,' and we continued working with it from then, using that melody and filling out the rest of the verses. As usual, for these co-written things, he often just had the first verse, which was always enough. It was the direction, it was the signpost and it was the inspiration for the whole song. I hate the word but it was the template. We wrote it, and in my memory we tagged on the introduction, which I think I thought up. I was imagining the intro of a Miracles record, and to my mind the [lazy Hawaiian-style] phrases on guitar are very much Smokey and the Miracles. So it was John's original inspiration, I think my melody, I think my guitar riff."

"Paul," according to Lennon's interview with *Playboy*, "helped me write the middle-eight melody. The whole lyrics were already written before Paul even heard it. In 'In My Life' his contribution melodically was the harmony and the middle-eight itself." As for "the middle eight" that Lennon refers to, there isn't one. The song alternated between the verse and chorus, without a bridge, or, as the Beatles often referred to it, "the middle eight."

"I find it very gratifying that out of everything we wrote, we only appear to disagree over two songs," Paul said years later. "'Eleanor Rigby' was the other."

The song made an unlikely return to the Beatles universe in 1974. As if George Harrison's solo tour that year wasn't fraught with enough problems, after he lost his voice during the rehearsals and had to croak his way through the opening night, George ran into further trouble when he refused to play any hits from the old days with the Fabs. The good vibes of the Dark Horse tour (aka "the Dark Hoarse tour") quickly began to sour. Harrison finally relented to his fans' demands at the urging of his friend and mentor Ravi Shankar, who convinced him that he should make the effort to please his crowd with a couple of oldies, which he then performed, but not without a twist. George relented with "In My Life," replacing the word *you* with *God*, singing, "In my life, I love God more," which must have seriously irked John Lennon, who had recently summed up his belief (or lack thereof) in the almighty in his song "God," claiming he, or it, was nothing more than "a concept by which we measure our pain."

RUBBER COVERS: "IN MY LIFE"

It's easy to hear why John was moved by Judy Collins's 1966 interpretation of "In My Life." Collins's simple arrangement (sans the song's languid guitar riff and Ringo's cool high-hat accents) frames her lilting voice, which hangs in the air like a warm breeze.

Although no one expected such tenderness from the Who's lunatic drummer, Keith Moon's recording of "In My Life" is oddly touching. Spoken in a halted, nearly choked cadence over a simple piano accompaniment with a soaring angelic choir doing their best to make up for the fact that Moonie can barely sing, this version, recorded in 1975 for his solo effort *Two Sides of the Moon*, is more than a mere lapse into nostalgia, and exudes a sense of deep regret.

In a powerful scene from the 1991 film *For the Boys*, Bette Midler is portrayed entertaining the troops in Vietnam at Christmastime. Clad in fatigues, crudely sucking on a cigarette, she tells a mob of catcalling soldiers to "shut the fuck up!" before pulverizing them with a heartfelt version of "In My Life." As the tune ends, the teary-eyed homesick GIs are suddenly pummeled by rockets and a shower of bullets.

While Stephen Stills recorded the song on his 1991 solo album, employing his husky voice and fine guitar chops, "In My Life" was better suited to the full Crosby, Stills and Nash vocal complement. Their flowing harmonies were tailor-made for John's gentle melody and sentimental lyric. Having recorded the tune for their album *After the Storm*, CSN (who initially failed an audition for Apple Records) performed it at Woodstock in August 1994, with the strains of Graham Nash's simple harmonica riff evoking "Love Me Do."

James Bond finally met the Beatles in 1998 when George Martin recorded an album of florid Beatle arrangements for his own album, not surprisingly titled *In My Life*. In a thick Scottish brogue, Sean Connery whispered Lennon's poem against Martin's sweeping strings without the slightest trace of irony.

On his final recording, released in 2002, *American IV: The Man Comes Around*, Johnny Cash brought a gripping wisdom and maturity to "In My Life." Although his voice is ragged to the point where he is barely reciting the lyric, the tenderness and sincerity of Cash's delivery is nothing short of heartbreaking. Three years later, in 2005, Ozzy Osbourne (whose similarities to the song's author end with his hairstyle and round glasses) offered a dull and forgettable version of "In My Life."

Despite Randy Jackson's airtight production, Boyz II Men's rich harmonies are on the flow in their glossy cover of "In My Life" from their 2009 release, *Love*. The sudden cliffhanger ending gives the song a clever twist.

Guitarists of every stripe (from jazzers Joe Pass to Al Di Meola, to the gods of shred, Metallica) have covered "In My Life," but the genre-bending Bill Frisell's take, complete with a weeping pedal steel guitar on his 2011 release *All We Are Saying*, is truly singular. While his unique chord voicings loan the song a dreamy atmosphere, Frisell's interpretation of George Martin's original baroque keyboard solo on the song's bridge is exceptional without being flashy.

15

"We Can Work It Out"

*"The secret was to just be cool,
stay in God's graces, and work it out."*
—Solomon Burke

The 1967 film *Guess Who's Coming to Dinner* boldly addressed the issue of biracial relationships at a time when civil rights had come to a head. The lovely and rather innocent Joanna Drayton (played by Katharine Houghton) is perplexed when her liberal parents (Katharine Hepburn and Spencer Tracy) are shocked over her impulsive decision to marry a black man (a very handsome doctor named John Prentice, played by Sidney Poitier). Prentice, who is on his way to Geneva, has come to ask the Draytons for their daughter's hand. Meanwhile, his parents fly in to meet the Draytons. All hell soon busts loose and a tipsy Catholic priest, Monsignor Ryan (played by Cecil Kellaway), is called in to be the objective party. He doesn't quote from scripture, instead relying on a popular phrase of the day: "What was that the Beatles sang?" he asks, "'We Can Work It Out,' yeah, yeah, yeah, yeah."

An argument with a girlfriend is hardly a fresh idea when a songwriter is in need of inspiration, but Paul and Jane's problematic relationship would become a gold mine for McCartney's art. Recorded on October 20, 1965, "We Can Work It Out" was triggered by Paul's troubles with controlling Jane Asher, a very independent woman with a solid career as an actress, who was far from content to quietly follow her cute Beatle boyfriend to the ends of the earth.

While "Things We Said Today" was arguably McCartney's first "serious" song (after all, it was sung in a minor key) "We Can Work It Out" revealed a new level of maturity in both its sentiments and musicality. Although Paul appears to be holding out the olive branch to his lover in hopes of reconciliation before their differences once and for all destroy their relationship, he is painfully one-sided in his approach, doing all of the talking and none of the listening. At the time, Jane had temporarily left London to appear in a production titled (ironically enough) *The Happiest Days of Our Lives* at the Old Vic in Bristol.

Paul in many ways seems to have a lot in common here with the protagonist of Paul Simon's "The Boxer," who bides his time until he "hears what he wants to hear and disregards the rest." Beyond his gentle coaxing, McCartney is waiting for his sweetheart to acquiesce and "get it straight," so they can "say good night." He remains optimistic that they can work everything out, just as long as he gets his way. In the end, Paul comes off rather patronizing and insincere.

"We Can Work It Out" seems to perfectly illustrate the differences in Paul's and John's psyches. While McCartney brims with optimism and self-confidence, Lennon's moods were far more reaching. From one song to the next he could be tender, whimsical to the point of ethereality (particularly after a steady diet of LSD), or skeptical, filled with angst, self-doubting, jealous, and paranoid, depending on which way the winds of his emotions were blowing. After meeting Yoko Ono, John began to open up in a myriad of ways, suddenly becoming more conscious and outspoken over issues of war, hunger, and feminism. While he sympathized with humanity on a larger scale, composing gentle utopian anthems like "Across the Universe" and "Imagine," Lennon, like Dylan with his finger-pointing songs, would frequently take aim at those around him. Like Holden Caulfield, the protagonist of *Catcher in the Rye*, John was intolerant of phonies. Everyone was fair game for his acerbic tongue, from Peter Fonda in "She Said, She Said" to the Maharishi Mahesh Yogi, at whom John took a nasty swipe with "Sexy Sadie," to Tricky Dick Nixon in "Just Gimme Some Truth" from Lennon's second solo album, *Imagine*.

In hindsight, it seems ironic that Lennon, who spewed such vitriol on his first solo album (1970's *Plastic Ono Band*, which was at least in part inspired by Arthur Janov's primal scream therapy), had been the one to remind us that "life is very short and there's no time for fussing and fighting my friend." John's eerie chant about the preciousness of life would later seem all the more profound following his assassination in December 1980.

No one suffered Lennon's wrath more than Paul McCartney. Besides giving a gut-spilling interview to *Rolling Stone*, in which he repeatedly skewered his former partner, John recorded the scathing "How Do You Sleep?" from his second solo album, 1971's *Imagine*, in which he called out Paul for surrounding himself with "straights who tell you, you was king." George Harrison (who, along with John and Ringo, was at the time battling Paul in court) also joined the fray, adding his bitter-sweet slide guitar riffs to the mix.

While McCartney's cheerfulness was uplifting at times, it often bordered on knuckleheaded, as in his vaudevillian ditty "Honey Pie," or the country-western spoof "Rocky Raccoon." Then there was "Maxwell's Silver Hammer," a song that John Lennon royally detested and refused to have any part of.

Over the years, Paul has repeatedly appeared in photographs giving his trademark thumbs-up salute, to the point where it has become a meaningless gesture, like Ringo's peace sign, which he is known to flash at the drop of a hat. As George Harrison later sang, his old bandmates desperately needed to "Cheer Down."

The "old world" waltz time in the song's bridge, suggested by George Harrison and played by John on harmonium, evokes the sound of Kurt Weill and Bertolt Brecht's pre–World War II macabre cabaret, until the verse returns with Paul's desperate plea for compromise. The Beatles would soon return to this motif again with the mad swirling carnival music that makes Lennon's "Being for the Benefit of Mr. Kite" so beautifully surreal.

With *Rubber Soul*, the Beatles had begun to season each song with a new sound or instrument. The mystery ingredient on "We Can Work It Out" was the Indian harmonium, a small, hand-pumped organ with a reedy tone, most commonly used for kirtan—group devotional singing.

While the broadening of the Beatles' sonic palette had an enormous influence on every band of its day, it impacted Brian Jones most profoundly. As the Rolling Stones' original leader, Jones had envisioned his group as a rough-and-tumble electric blues unit; he was eventually forced to reinvent himself in order to endure the humiliation he suffered in having to perform a repertoire mostly comprised of Jagger/Richards originals. One of the first British guitarists to play slide guitar in the style of Elmore James, Brian, like his hero Howlin' Wolf, also blew a pretty mean blues harp (which Jagger would soon play equally as well). Beginning with the Appalachian mountain dulcimer that he'd heard on records by Richard and Mimi Fariña, Brian would embroider "Lady Jane" with its gossamer tone. His intuitive use of the sitar on "Paint It Black," the funky clunk of the marimba on "Under My Thumb," and the strains of Renaissance recorder on "Ruby Tuesday" were not only integral to the respective songs' arrangements but reflected his brilliant musicianship as well. Where his big bowl of blonde hair and sinister grin once drew the limelight away from his nemesis, Mick Jagger, his unbound creativity and flair for exotic sonic touches made every new Stones album an adventure.

"That wonderful harmonium sound [gave 'We Can Work It Out'] a sort of religious quality," the Kinks' visionary front man Ray Davies opined. Davies also believed the song's lyric was insightful, reflecting not only Paul and Jane's troubled relationship but the disunity that had been brewing within the Lennon and McCartney partnership. "Maybe it's a subtext to where the band was," he mused.

With "Getting Better," which would appear on *Sgt. Pepper*, Lennon and McCartney created a lyrical dynamic similar to the one they'd used earlier in "We Can Work It Out." Composed by Paul, the song was initially inspired by a favorite phrase repeated by drummer Jimmie Nicol of the Shubdubs, who had been substituting for Ringo after Starr had suddenly taken ill and wound up in the hospital with tonsillitis in the midst of the band's 1964 world tour, which took them from Scandinavia to Australia. After each set, Nicol kept reassuring his famous employers, "It's getting better all the time." The song perfectly embodied the optimistic spirit that permeated 1967's Summer of Love. It's not difficult to imagine American soldiers fighting in the jungles of Vietnam, chanting the chorus like a nervous mantra as villages burned around them, shells exploded, and bullets whizzed by their heads, hoping that maybe one day soon the lyrics would magically transport them back home again (like Dorothy after clicking her ruby slippers in *The Wizard of Oz*) to the life they once knew.

Once more, Lennon threw a monkey wrench into McCartney's mirth when he alluded to beating his woman and keeping her "apart from the things that she loved." John balances out his madness by acknowledging his faults as he sings: "Man I was mean, but I'm changing my scene and I'm doing the best that I can." Nonetheless, the sentiment comes as something of a shock in the midst of another cheerful McCartney ditty.

While upbeat, the lyrics to "Fixing a Hole," the following song on *Pepper*, come off as rather arrogant, yet no one at the time seemed to give them a second thought. With its bouncy bass and irrepressible spirit, "Fixing a Hole" gently chugs along as McCartney makes a variety of home improvements. But you've got to wonder where he's coming from when he declares, "It doesn't really matter if I'm wrong, I'm right."

McCartney's hubris would fulminate with "Back Seat of My Car" from his 1971 album *Ram*, as he and Linda merrily sang, "We believe that we can't be wrong."

In a four-part newspaper interview, Denny Laine, a former member of the Moody Blues and key musical component in McCartney's Wings, later revealed that Paul's self-confidence bordered on arrogance when he recalled how Paul and Linda repeatedly found themselves in trouble with the law for smuggling pot, but felt assured that the authorities would be so charmed by their celebrity they would conveniently wave them through without a hassle. But it didn't work out that way in Japan—on January 16, 1980, Paul was busted for a little over seven and a half ounces of marijuana at the Narita airport in Tokyo. Not only did the arrest lead to McCartney (Prisoner 22, as he was known while incarcerated) doing ten days behind bars, but Wings's tour of Japan was immediately canceled and their music banned from Japanese radio.

RUBBER COVERS: "WE CAN WORK IT OUT"

While Petula Clark's version of "We Can Work It Out" from her 1966 album *My Love* is too perky for its own good, nearly everything excessive about sixties rock can be found within the mind-bending grooves of Deep Purple's 1968 album *Book of Taliesyn*. The album's fourth track, the seven-minute "Exposition," begins with a medley inspired by Beethoven's "Allegrettto," from the composer's Seventh Symphony, before the band breaks into a heady version of "We Can Work It Out," which features some furious guitar riffing from Ritchie Blackmore. "Life is very short," John Lennon once sang. Perhaps too short to sit through this overblown production, which all these years later resembles parody.

For their 1975 album *Street Rats* (produced by the Stones' enfant terrible Andrew Loog Oldham), Humble Pie boldly dropped the song's familiar melody and fashioned "We Can Work It Out" into a worried blues (revealing an influence more Sonny Boy Williamson than Fab Four) that featured Steve Marriott's raspy, soulful vocals, and slinky guitar riffs.

Stevie Wonder's rave-up of "We Can Work It Out" molds the song into a great dance groove, over which he blows a dynamite harmonica solo. Wonder performed the song (backed by McCartney's band) live at the White House on June 3, 2010, for a crowd that included Sir Paul sitting beside Barack and Michelle Obama. Stevie's version, not surprisingly, packed a funky punch, turning Paul's breakup tune into a jubilant prayer for world peace.

16

"Nowhere Man"

"I can't remember anything without a sadness so deep
that it hardly becomes known to me, so deep that its tears leave me
a spectator of my own STUPIDITY. And so
I go on rambling on with a hey nonny nonny no."
—John Lennon, in a letter to Stuart Sutcliffe, summer 1961

While Dylan was the gleaming hub on which the spoked wheel of the sixties whirled, Lennon, before meeting Yoko Ono, had remained aloof. Ensconced in his Kenwood home, a mock Tudor mansion in the sedate stockbroker suburb of Weybridge, along with his wife, Cynthia, and young son, Julian, John was unhappily married and a reluctant father—"fat and depressed and crying out for help."

If "Help!" had been a desperate plea from a man slowly drowning in boredom, "Nowhere Man" went beyond the realm of self-criticism to the brink of self-loathing. "That was John after a night out, with the dawn coming up," Paul McCartney told *Playboy* in December 1984. "I think at that point in his life, he was a bit . . . wondering where he was going."

As with "I'm a Loser," the leader of the world's most popular band, who most people assumed was at the top of his game at the time, was "not what [he] appear[ed] to be." Frustrated and disappointed with himself following a fruitless five-hour songwriting session, Lennon, feeling like a "Nowhere Man," composed a tune about a guy who seemed to be aimlessly drifting on a rudderless ship. His subject wasn't merely "a bit like you or me," but a brutal self-portrait. "Nowhere Man" only began to take shape once John stopped forcing the issue and gave up trying to write. As an observer of the first order, Lennon turned his razor-sharp perception on his own inability to express himself, and suddenly the lyrics began to flow. As John later recalled the experience, he was "just going through this paranoia, trying to write something."

Another source of inspiration might easily have been John's suppressed feelings about his long-lost father, Alfred, aka "Alf," who, after going AWOL from the merchant marine during World War II, deserted his wife and young son and would suddenly appear one day out of the blue at John's doorstep. When Cynthia opened the door of their mansion, she found a shabby but familiar-looking "tramp," as she later recalled, standing there with John's eyes.

Suffice it to say that John was far from pleased by the prospect of such a reunion. "I didn't want to see him," Lennon said flatly, having lived for years with the emotional scars after "what he'd done to me and my mother." Alf, whom John considered "almost a Bowery bum," had garnered quite a reputation over the years. As an enlisted man, he was said to have done time in the brig on a number of occasions—once for the sorry crime of having stolen a single bottle of beer, while on another wild night, he danced drunk in the street with a mannequin in a wedding dress that he'd recently pilfered from a nearby department store window.

Alf's crazy escapades seemed to foreshadow the most famous and pitiful incident of John's "Lost Weekend," when, in 1974, he and his pal Harry Nilsson, drunk beyond repair, were ejected from the Troubadour in L.A. after Lennon heckled the Smothers Brothers with a tampon wrapped around his head.

Now, twenty-some-odd years after deserting his family, Alf, in his mid-fifties, was attempting to force a reunion with his rich and famous son. He had previously stopped by Brian Epstein's office, and once more reappeared at Kenwood, like a phantom, his hat in hand, hoping to find his pregnant teenage fiancée some sort of employment within the Beatles' organization. John's nineteen-year-old "stepmother" would wind up answering the band's fan mail with Julian.

After selling his side of the story to *Titbits* magazine for two hundred pounds, Alfred Lennon was immediately approached by manager Tony Cartwright, who secured him a deal with Pye Records (best known as home to the Kinks and the Who), whose earlier attempts on cashing in on Beatlemania included Rolf Harris's tacky novelty number "Ringo for President."

Apparently music ran deep in the Lennon family. John's grandfather Jack had been a British Music Hall performer who is said to have toured America in the 1890s, while Alf played the banjo and, much to John's chagrin, would try to ride his coat-tails by recording a single as "Freddie" Lennon, as he was now known. "That's My Life (My Love and My Home)," a lightly sung/spoken ballad (recited in a Liverpool scouse accent) evoked Alf's times in Liverpool and at sea, complete with sound effects of crashing waves.

Backed with a song titled "The Next Time You Feel Important," "That's My Life," was thought to be Freddie's reply to his famous son's poignant ballad from *Rubber Soul*. Freddie Lennon's recording debut was released on New Year's Eve 1965, despite John trying to do everything within his power to stop it.

While the public has always perceived John as the cutting-edge Beatle, (although his life-as-art collaborations and peace crusades with Yoko Ono would not begin for a few more years), it was actually Paul McCartney who routinely made the rounds of London at the time, hobnobbing with the likes of Beat writer William S. Burroughs and delving into the radical music of free-jazz saxophonist Albert Ayler as well as that of avant-garde composer Karlheinz Stockhausen.

While Bob Dylan spouted his consciousness-expanding lyrics in fits and starts that began to resemble dadaist slogans more than pop songs, Lennon turned his muse inward, revealing that the all-powerful wizard behind the curtain of the world's most popular band was nothing more than a lazy daydreamer riddled with self-doubt. Whether or not his fans cared to know it or not, John was singing about himself.

"Ordinary people need other people *not* to be ordinary," Pete Townshend told DJ Scott Muni in an interview following Lennon's tragic murder in December 1980. "Most of us know that people like me or John Lennon, people who've become famous, film stars, even politicians, presidents, it doesn't matter who they are—they're just ordinary guys. And if you fire a gun at them, they drop dead, and they suffer all the same things that everybody else suffers."

Lennon loathed the very idea of normalcy, often going to extremes as an artist to avoid appearing common at any cost. His home life in Kenwood had become increasingly mundane, despite all the accoutrements of his newfound wealth. John found himself isolated, gaining weight, watching the telly for hours on end, leafing through newspapers, which would eventually inspire songs like "A Day in the Life" and "Good Morning, Good Morning" on *Sgt. Pepper's Lonely Hearts Club Band.*

"He had everything money could buy," Maureen Cleave explained. "But [the suburban family life was] not what he wanted."

"Here I am in my Hansel and Gretel house, famous and loaded, and I can't go anywhere," John complained to Cleave. "There's something else I'm going to do," he said, as if divining the future, knowing he could barely hang on much longer in his current state. "Only I don't know what it is, but I do know this isn't it for me."

The last time Maureen saw Lennon, in 1966, the "Nowhere Man" was still living like a prisoner in a gilded cage. John's isolation was immediately obvious to Cleave (over the years, John would revisit the theme of personal alienation, writing such navel-gazing lyrics as "No one I think is in my tree," from 1967's "Strawberry Fields Forever" and confessing in 1970, in the riveting "Isolation," that he and Yoko were "afraid of the sun, afraid of everyone.") According to Maureen, John was "cut off from the rest of the world except for George and Ringo, who lived in stockbroker Tudor mansions nearby." John was so detached from day-to-day life that when he spoke to friends on the telephone, he often needed to ask, "What day of the week is it?"

Although coming with every imaginable perk, fame felt increasingly hollow to John. His bandmate had recently upstaged him, having written one of the most popular songs of the century, which he performed solo, strumming an acoustic guitar and batting his big round brown eyes at the millions who sat spellbound on the other side of the TV set, while the rest of the band waited, disgruntled, offstage. It is no wonder that John threw himself at the Japanese queen of mind games the moment he laid eyes on her. Lennon intuitively knew that Yoko was his only way out of the crazy paradox he'd found himself in, caught between the swirling cyclone of Beatlemania and living "down at the end of lonely street," as his fat, aging hero, Elvis, once sang.

Lennon originally paid £20,000 for his Kenwood mansion in July 1964, and then sank an additional £40,000, into creating its lush surrounding gardens, along with a swimming pool, which he rarely, if ever used, as well as a kitchen filled with state-of the art gadgetry that baffled Cynthia.

"I didn't particularly like the look of it, it was all a bit golf club for me," McCartney told Barry Miles. "But Cynthia wanted to settle John down . . . pipe and slippers. The minute she said that," Paul said he knew it was the "kiss of death" to their relationship. "I know my mate and that is not what he wants. She got a couple of years of that, but he finally had to break loose and because he couldn't tell her he didn't want it, he had to bring Yoko to breakfast."

Lennon, like the great American poet Walt Whitman (whose "Song of Myself" bore the lines "Do I contradict myself? Very well, then I contradict myself, I am large, I contain multitudes"), possessed a wildly diverse personality. The author of "All You Need Is Love" and "Imagine" would later confess to abusing his girlfriends as a young man. The millionaire rock star who wrote and sang such revolutionary agitprop anthems as "Woman Is Nigger of the World," and "Attica State" and led antiwar protests would become a reclusive househusband with the birth of his second son, Sean, in 1975. Following a handful of patchy solo albums, John felt the time was right to flee the limelight and begin a five-year hiatus from the music business. Friends and fans alike scratched their heads in wonder as the world-famous Beatle chose to retreat behind the indomitable walls of New York's Dakota apartment building to stay home and bake bread rather than continue to record and perform. But as Lennon put it simply in "Watching the Wheels," from his 1980 comeback album *Double Fantasy* (which drew some interesting parallels to both "Nowhere Man" and "I'm Only Sleeping,"), "I just had to let it go."

Recorded on October 21 and 22, 1965, "Nowhere Man" may actually have been John Lennon's first political song, a mournful hymn to the silent majority, who, even if they had "a point of view," were not willing to take a stand and voice it, whether due to apathy or to being "Comfortably Numb," as Pink Floyd later sang. The tune begins with a lilting a cappella, until the band kicks in, augmented by an economical guitar solo played in tandem by George and John on a pair of Sonic Blue Fender Stratocasters. The immediately identifiable riff is as melodic and catchy as the song itself, with not a note wasted. Despite the fact that Lennon deemed his own lyric somewhat "trite," "Nowhere Man" (which was included in the original UK release of *Rubber Soul*, while in the U.S. it appeared six months later on the compilation *Yesterday . . . and Today*) remained in the Beatles' repertoire for both their 1965 and '66 tours.

THE BUTCHER SLEEVE

DUBBED "THE ULTIMATE BUTCHERY"—not only for its slapdash production but for the original photograph portraying the Beatles in blood-smeared butcher smocks holding slabs of red meat and decapitated dolls—the American release *Yesterday . . . and Today*, released on June 20, 1966, was a compilation of singles and songs edited from previous albums. The LP included Paul's best-selling eponymous ballad, along with Ringo's "Act Naturally," and the single "We Can Work It Out" and "Day Tripper." Leftover tracks from *Rubber Soul* included "Drive My Car," "Nowhere Man," "What Goes On," and George's "If I Needed Someone."

The story behind the controversial cover began in the spring of 1966 when photographer Robert Whitaker invited the Beatles to his London studio to pose for a concept art piece he was working on at the time called *A Somnambulant Adventure*. "By then we were beginning to hate it," Lennon complained about having their picture taken, claiming that posing for photo shoots had become "a big ordeal [as] you had to look normal and you didn't feel it." According to Lennon, Whitaker "was a bit of a surrealist and he brought along all these babies and pieces of meat and doctor's coats." Alan Livingston, president of Capitol Records at the time, claimed it was Paul, in fact, who insisted on using "the dead baby picture" (as it soon became known) for the cover of *Yesterday . . . and Today*. McCartney believed the unsettling image would make a powerful commentary on the Vietnam War, without the band actually speaking out. Brian Epstein was undoubtedly on holiday when the decision was made.

While Lennon was in cahoots with McCartney, stating the image was "relevant as Vietnam," George Harrison, who would soon become a vegetarian, regretted leering at the camera with a psychotic grin while draped in slabs of red meat. Both the experience and the album cover in his estimate, were "gross. . . . Sometimes we all did stupid things, thinking it was cool and hip, when it was naïve and dumb, and that was one of them," Harrison later admitted.

Another likely inspiration for the lyrics to Lennon's "Nowhere Man" came after the Beatles finally met Elvis Presley on August 27, 1965, at his home in Bel Air, California. The band arrived late, at 11p.m, to find Elvis waiting for them in his sprawling living room, which featured a totally modern king-size color TV. Colonel Tom Parker and Brian Epstein, who'd engineered the much-anticipated meeting, stood off to the side, chatting, as their legendary clients sized each other up. The atmosphere apparently grew tense as the Beatles sat, gobsmacked, gawking at "the King." Presley soon became uncomfortable at their awkward silence, complaining that he was "gonna go to bed" as he said, if "you damn guys are gonna sit here and stare at me."

But after breaking out the guitars—Elvis thumped bass while Paul played piano, John and George strummed as usual, and Ringo provided some backbeat—everybody finally began to relax as they chatted about the grueling aspects of touring, the antics of their wild fans, and boring movie shoots. John, who didn't think much of Presley's films, finally got "real" with his onetime hero, pressing him, "Why don't you go back to making rock 'n' roll records?" Elvis blamed his "tight" filming schedule and promised to get back to the music one day soon. (And although it took several years, Presley's brief return to rock 'n' roll did not disappoint. Broadcast on December 3, 1968, *Elvis*— or "The Comeback Special," as the hour-long show has become known in pop music culture—was the King's first live performance since appearing at Pearl Harbor seven years earlier. The live portion of the show, recorded in the round with a handful of good-ole-boy guitar pickers, which included Scotty Moore and drummer D. J. Fontana from Elvis's original band, proved that Elvis, despite being drafted by the army and battered by the British Invasion, making scores of B-movies, and engaging, it was rumored, in ceaseless debauchery, still had it. "Suspicious Minds" (an anthem celebrating a dysfunctional relationship that rivaled Lennon's twisted "Run for Your Life") soon hit number one, and Presley, for the time being, was indisputably back on top. But despite his renewed passion and tight black leather suit, Elvis, as far as the sixties counterculture was concerned, was no more than a vanishing relic of the 1950s, like finned cars and neon-lit diners).

Three hours after the Beatles sat down with Elvis, their historic hangout came to an end. Presley politely invited the Fab Four to drop by Graceland the next time they were in Memphis.

Although Elvis generously loaded each of the Beatles up with armloads of souvenirs, which included a complete set of his LPs, hand-tooled gun holsters, and wagon-wheel lamps, just a few years later he would meet with Richard Nixon at the White House in Washington, DC, on December 21, 1970, to discuss the band's role in undermining the youth of America. As he reverently removed his sunglasses after entering the Oval Office, Presley solemnly asked the president to deputize him as a federal agent of the Bureau of Narcotics. While he had no expectation of an honorary title, the King desired a badge in order that he might better serve his country. Assuring Nixon that he was "on [his] side," Elvis then turned the topic of conversation to the Beatles. Despite having sung their songs for years as part of his stage show, Presley blamed the band for coming to the States and making and hauling large sums of money back to England, while instigating the degenerate hippie drug culture and antiwar protests that he felt was destroying the American way of life. After Elvis presented the leader of the free world with a spontaneous hug, which caught both Nixon and his aides off guard, the president thanked the King for his "willingness to help" and said goodbye, slightly bewildered by the whole affair. Years later McCartney confessed that he felt "a bit betrayed" by Elvis's trip to the White House. "The great joke," Paul pointed out, after Presley's death in August 1977, "was that we were taking drugs, and look what happened to him."

But as their Cadillac pulled out of the driveway into the warm California night, Lennon quipped, "Where's Elvis?" It had become apparent to the Beatles, that the King was definitely nowhere, man. Disillusioned, John compared Presley to Engelbert Humperdinck, although Lennon's caustic quip may have been inspired by the fact that the British schmaltz merchant's "Release Me" had blocked the Beatles' double-A-sided single "Strawberry Fields Forever" and "Penny Lane" from reaching number one, marking the first time a new release by the Fabs failed to occupy the top slot in the UK charts. John would later bitterly renounce Elvis amongst other singers, politicians, avatars, and holy books he'd lost faith in, in the gospel tinged "God" from his "primal scream" album *Plastic Ono Band* in 1970.

RUBBER COVERS: "NOWHERE MAN"

Everyone from the freaky, shrill-voiced, ukulele strummer Tiny Tim to synth-pop pioneer Gershon Kingsley, to glam-metal rockers Dokken and the New Age king of easy listening, Yiánnis Chryssomállis (aka Yanni) has felt compelled to take a whack at "Nowhere Man" at one point or another in their career. Back in 1967, the Carpenters cut a simple vocal/piano demo of the song, which lay dormant until 2001, when Richard Carpenter resurrected it for their final album, *As Time Goes By*, eighteen years after his sister's death. Unfortunately, her brother smothers Karen's pristine performance with a ludicrous string arrangement.

Delivered with a resonant voice and square-jawed earnestness, Randy Travis's down-home take of "Nowhere Man" (for the 1995 tribute album *Come Together: America Salutes the Beatles*) featured a sweet cascading pedal steel guitar riff.

You might expect the Replacements' front man Paul Westerberg to transform Lennon's navel-gazer into an all-out rocker, but instead he gently strums an acoustic guitar, delivering a touching reading of "Nowhere Man," turning the tune into a regretful lullaby on the soundtrack to the 2001 movie *I Am Sam*.

Leave it to Marky Ramone to kick out the jams on his balls-to-the wall version on his 1999 album *The Answer to Your Problems*. The Ramones' drummer spits and sprays Lennon's lyrics while guitars slash and grind. Yet no matter how loud, fast, and rude his band the Intruders play it, this interpretation of "Nowhere Man" brims with plenty of soul.

17

"I'm Looking Through You"

*"Never pretend to love which you do not actually feel,
for love is not ours to command."*
—*Alan Watts*

Paul's most bitter song to date, "I'm Looking Through You," was the second of three songs recorded by the Beatles in the fall of 1965 that openly addressed his faltering relationship with Jane Asher.

"I knew I was selfish," Paul confessed. "It caused a few rows. Jane went off [to Bristol to act in a production of John Dighton's *The Happiest Days of Your Life*] and I said, 'OK then, leave. I'll find someone else.'" Paul quickly came to the harsh realization that there was no one else quite like Jane. "It was shattering to be without her" he said. He wrote "I'm Looking Through You" to help bolster his waning spirits.

Following George and Pattie's secret nuptials on January 21, 1966, the press began to fixate on the last single Beatle. But according to Cynthia Lennon, Paul and Jane "were not ready for marriage. They had quite a few personal problems to iron out. Jane confided in me enough to say that Paul wanted her to become the little woman at home with the kiddies but Jane was not prepared to give up her flourishing career as an actress. It seemed that they had both reached a stalemate, so they carried on happily in their own way."

"Love has a nasty habit of disappearing overnight," McCartney sings with a gentle twist of the knife, a sentiment that conjures Billie Holiday's 1939 classic "Fine and Mellow," in which the jazz diva moaned, "Love is like a faucet, it turns off and on." As Billie had learned years ago, Paul too would eventually discover, "Sometimes when you think it's on, baby, it has turned off and gone." "Disillusioned over her commitment," McCartney seemed uncharacteristically harsh when he said "I'm Looking Through You" was about "getting rid of some emotional baggage. . . . 'I'm looking through you, and you're *not there!'*"

Paul claimed to have written the song on his own, alone in his room at the Ashers' London home with out any help from John. Engineer Norman Smith recalled that it was during the sessions for *Rubber Soul* when McCartney began to hang around the studio after the others had left to replace George's lead guitar tracks with his own, as he was frequently frustrated with Harrison's playing, which he felt was forced and often took up too much studio time to accomplish.

The theme of romantic disillusionment and the feeling of emptiness and alienation that follows would return a year later in Paul's icy ballad "For No One" from *Revolver.* Written in March 1966 in a Swiss chalet while Paul was on a skiing vacation with Jane, "For No One" was, as McCartney recalled, inspired by "another argument."

"I don't have easy relationships with women," Paul confessed. "I never have. I talk too much truth." Paul and Jane's relationship would finally come to an end in 1968.

Listening to the outtakes of "I'm Looking Through You" provides a good window to the Beatles' studio process at the time. Take one begins with handclaps and a snappy nylon guitar part reminiscent of Simon & Garfunkel. As McCartney chants, "You're not the same," the band explodes into a funky two-chord soul vamp that sounds like the inspiration for Neil Diamond's "I'm a Believer," which became a chart-topping hit for the Monkees a year later, in December 1966. Paul cries, "I'm a lookin' through you!" in what seems more like jubilation than a frightening realization.

Having attempted to record "I'm Looking Through You" during sessions on October 24 and November 6, the Beatles finally got it right on November 10. The fourth take was the keeper, featuring McCartney on bass, Lennon strumming his Gibson acoustic, and Harrison shaking a tambourine. Ringo is said to have played some Hammond organ (which for the most part is inaudible), and George overdubbed the lead guitar riff on his Epiphone Casino. The session ended that night at around four in the morning.

They finished up the tune the next evening (on November 11), with Paul laying down his lead vocals. Afterward, he and John added backup vocals and handclaps and plenty of adlibbing as the song faded out.

Recorded on November 11, 1965, during a session that ran from two-thirty until six that evening, the fourth take, as released on the American mono pressing of the album, revealed that Paul, on acoustic guitar, had played two false starts on the song's introduction.

While edited from both the British and the American stereo pressings of the album, it managed to slip through (for whatever reason—perhaps someone at Capitol Records thought it was cool) on the initial monaural copies. Not commonly heard at the time, false starts and studio chatter gave the listener the feeling of being an insider, a sense of intimacy with the artist. Earlier in 1965, Bob Dylan's absurd folk/rap number "Bob Dylan's 115th Dream" bravely began with producer Tom Wilson uncontrollably laughing after Bob fumbled the chords to the beginning of the song. It's curious to note that *Bringing It All Back Home* was the last LP of Dylan's that Wilson would record. . . .

The song at this point had more of a country feel on the verse, while the chorus's funky section was dropped. Gone is the jam, with its loose, bluesy improv that featured a stinging lead guitar break. Although cutting out a fun bit, the edit ultimately tightened up the tune.

Credited with playing an inaudible organ (listed as both a Hammond and a Vox Continental), Ringo also plays a funky conga drum—a sound of which, along with the acoustic guitar, would soon become a trademark of Marc Bolan's T. Rex. "I'm Looking Through You" also served as the inspiration for one of the weekly cartoons *The Beatles*, in which the band winds up practicing inside an Egyptian pyramid when the spirit of a mummy suddenly inhabits Ringo's body. The animators, confused over who sang the lead vocal on the song, never bothered to ask and portrayed John singing instead of Paul.

RUBBER COVERS: "I'M LOOKING THROUGH YOU"

Complete with twanging Dobro and mandolin, Steve Earle breathes new life into "I'm Looking Through You," giving the song a Southern twang as he sings, "You're not the sayme" and "Baby you chaynged."

"I was making the closest thing to a bluegrass record I could make at the time and I always thought that's what the Beatles were trying to do on 'I'm Looking Through You' and 'I've Just Seen a Face,'" Earle explained.

Framed by a grungy guitar riff and the steady thwack of a snare, the Wallflowers' rendition of "I'm Looking Through You" rocks righteously. Although echoes of his old man (*circa Blonde on Blonde*) can be heard in Jakob Dylan's husky vocals as he wails, "Luvvv has a nasty habit of disappearing overnight," Dylan Jr.'s Beatles cover from the 2002 *I Am Sam* soundtrack has feel all its own.

Ultimately, it's McCartney who offers the best version of his song, performing it forty-five years later at Philadelphia's Wells Fargo Center on August 14, 2010, as the crowd explodes into a joyous sing-along. Talk about staying power!

18

"Michelle"

The song that eventually became known as "Michelle" had been kicking around in one form or another for a few years until, under pressure to crank out the Beatles' second album of 1965, McCartney finally got around to finishing it off, at Lennon's prodding. The tune was originally inspired by Chet Atkins's trademark fingerpicking on a swing number called "Trambone," in which "Mr. Guitar" walked a loping bass line while picking its bluesy melody.

"This was an innovation for us," McCartney told biographer Barry Miles. "Even though classical guitarists had played it, no rock 'n' roll guitarists had played [this fingerpicking style]."

The Beatles' foray into "ham-fisted jazz" (as Paul described it) actually began with their cover of Meredith Willson's "Till There Was You" on *Meet the Beatles*. Following a couple of lessons from Jim Gretty at Frank Hessy's music shop in Liverpool, the lads soon began employing flat/minor/seventh chords in their sound. As Bob Dylan stressed, it wasn't the Beatles' hair or harmonies or cute matching collarless suits or even those cool Cuban-heeled boots that initially caught his attention—it was their chords.

"They were doing things nobody was doing. Their chords were outrageous, just outrageous, and their harmonies made it all valid," Dylan told biographer Robert Shelton. "Everybody else thought they were for the teenyboppers, that they were gonna pass right away. But it was obvious to me that they had staying power. I knew they were pointing to the direction where music had to go."

"The chord changes really had magic in them," the Byrds' Roger McGuinn concurred. McGuinn claimed that whenever he heard a new Beatles song for the first time it always made him spontaneously break out into "goose bumps."

"Michelle," was not, as many speculated, inspired by the blonde California beauty Michelle Phillips (singer/songwriter of the Mamas and Papas) but had actually begun years before as a parody of the "Exies," as Lennon and McCartney called the dour beret-clad, Gauloises-puffing French existentialists who sported goatees and black turtlenecks. McCartney never really gave the tune—a corny soft-shoe—much of a second thought until Lennon remarked one day, "That wasn't a bad song. . . . You should do that."

According to Paul, one of John's art-school teachers, Austin Mitchell, used to throw wild all-night parties where they could "get drinks" and "maybe pull girls." Trying his best to appear "enigmatic," McCartney would sit, alone in a corner, gently strumming his guitar while murmuring lyrics in fake French, because, as he told Barry Miles, "everyone wanted to be like [the popular French singers] Sacha Distel, or Juliette Gréco."

The refrain "Michelle, ma belle," was actually written by Jan Vaughan, the wife of Paul's old friend Ivan from Liverpool, the original bassist with the Quarrymen, who first introduced Paul to John. As McCartney spoke very little or no French, he "needed help in sorting out the actual words," Jan, a French teacher, recalled. She then translated Paul's line "these are words that go together well" into the famous phrase, "*sont des mots qui vont très bien ensemble.*"

The way Lennon remembered it, Paul hummed him "the first few bars with the words" and asked him, "Where do I go from here?" McCartney had begun to grow tired of his own lyrical clichés, hoping to get beyond the song's original lyrics "good night sweetheart," and "hello my dear." Inspired by Nina Simone's sultry, emotive phrasing on her rendition of Screamin' Jay Hawkins' "I Put a Spell on You," John spontaneously burst out singing, "I luvvv you, I luvvv you, I luvvv you," over the chord change to the song's bridge in imitation of the moody, broody jazz singer.

"My contribution to Paul's songs was always to add a little bluesy edge to them," John explained. "Otherwise, you know, 'Michelle' is a straight ballad, right?"

By this time, Abbey Road's Studio Two had become the exclusive domain of the Beatles. Recent leaps in technology had seen the advancement from two- to four-track recording, which allowed more freedom to overdub, creating an atmosphere of innovation, which permeated their new album. And perhaps even more importantly, George Martin had given up watching the clock. Always the gentleman, in nicely pressed shirt and tie, with every hair in place, no matter what season or time of day or night, Martin, who suffered in silence as Harrison slowly, methodically worked out his precise, economic guitar leads, would finally admit years later that he had been "rather beastly to George." Perhaps the two had gotten off on the wrong foot during the Beatles' first recording session with Martin, when the producer, hoping to put the boys at ease, said that if there was anything they were uncomfortable with or didn't like, they were to just let him know.

"Well, for a start, I don't like your tie," Harrison quipped. While everyone laughed, it may have rubbed the fastidious producer the wrong way.

In 1993, George Martin claimed in an interview that "the guitar solo in 'Michelle' is my composition, actually." According to the Beatles' producer, he "wrote down the notes and said, 'I'll play this; George, you can do these notes with me on guitar.'" Harrison, who was fed up with being bossed around by Paul in the studio, was somewhat reluctant at first. Martin then suggested they "play in unison," to make the recording process go a bit more smoothly. David Rybaczewski, who maintains the obsessive website beatlesebooks.com, suggests that "since no keyboards can be heard on the recording, the unison piano work of George Martin was most likely played off microphone."

"Michelle," as Paul recalled, was recorded "only on four little tracks," during a nine-hour session on November 3. McCartney was particularly fond of "Michelle," as "it was very easy to mix. There were no decisions to make, we'd made them all in the writing and in the recording," he said.

By McCartney's estimate, "Michelle" was mixed in about half an hour and has since garnered over four million airplays. Curiously, each mix made of the song came in at a slightly different length. The UK mono track is 2:33, while the stereo version comes in at 2:40, allowing for an extra guitar solo at the end. The US mono release was the longest of all, tracking at 2:43. The original recording actually ended with McCartney strumming a major 7th in lieu of a fadeout.

Two years following its release, "Michelle" was voted 1967's Song of the Year over such emotional geysers as "The Impossible Dream," "Somewhere My Love," and "Born Free." BMI's records claim that McCartney's little Gallic satire would become the forty-second most performed song of the twentieth century. The song's enormous success eventually prompted Paul, a notorious "skin-flint" (as he described himself), to write Jan Vaughn a check, as "she's virtually a co-writer on that," he confessed.

Beatle biographer Phillip Norman flatly dismissed "Michelle," as "bland," certain that McCartney's crooning in French was nothing short of "a plain act of social climbing."

Dylan prefaced his March 1966 dismissal of "Michelle" by stating, "I dig the Beatles," but he clearly loathed McCartney's latest pop confection. "A song like 'Yesterday' or 'Michelle,' hey God knows, it's such a cop-out man. Both of those songs . . . if you go to the Library of Congress you can find a lot better than that. There are millions of songs like 'Michelle' and 'Yesterday' written in Tin Pan Alley."

THE OVERLANDERS SCORE WITH "MICHELLE"

"'MICHELLE' WAS VERY LUCKY FOR US," recalled Terry Widlake, bassist with the Overlanders (and later Roy Orbison). "It was late November 1965," Widlake recalled. "The Overlanders were in Bradford, Yorkshire, appearing at the Alhambra Theatre for a week, and preparing to leave for Frankfurt, Germany, on the following Sunday to open at the Storyville Club for the entire month of December. On the Thursday afternoon of that week, we had a surprise visit from our manager, Harry Hammond, who was clutching an unlabeled bootlegged acetate in his hand. We were learning a lot of new material for the German club, so we had a record player on hand. Harry dropped it onto the turntable, and, before he activated the start button, turned to us and said, 'I want you all to listen to this record twice without commenting or saying anything, OK?' We all agreed and the soft, gentle guitar introduction to 'Michelle' filled the otherwise silent room.

"'That's Paul McCartney, isn't it?' I said, and was rebuked by Harry, who reminded me we were going to listen to it twice. He played it again as we all looked at each other in astonishment.

"'Did you like it?' Harry asked.

"'Ringo can't even keep a steady tempo,' pianist/singer Laurie Mason said. 'But I like it.'

"'Good,' Harry replied. 'Because it's your next record.'

"Harry had already arranged the recording session with Tony Hatch at Pye Records. We drove overnight to London after the show at the Alhambra on Saturday evening and had to be at Pye studios on Sunday morning. 'Michelle' was done with a single vocal take and was released on December 31, 1965. By January 22 it was number one on all the British charts."

"This was a subtler Beatles, where the ballad writing really started to shine," said Steve Katz, founding member of Blood Sweat & Tears. "The combination of the gentler material and the use of acoustic instruments marked a turn-around in their music and also in my life. The fact that you could do this kind of stuff with a rock band was liberating for a ballad writer like myself. It also helped me get laid a couple of times."

"*Rubber Soul* was beautiful but made me mad," said Howard Kaylan of the Turtles. "It wasn't rock enough for me. It was too sentimental and logical. I drifted toward the Stones for a while until *Revolver* came out and forced me to take acid and talk to the trees. 'Turn off your mind' ['Tomorrow Never Knows'] saved my life while *Rubber Soul* only got me laid. I had to wait 'til I found a girl named Michelle but it worked. Now I'm married to a girl named Michelle and she ain't buyin' it."

Perhaps one reason why the recording went so quickly was because Paul, as many have speculated over the years, was the only Beatle (other than Lennon, who added a harmony part) to appear on the track. McCartney, a top-notch multi-instrumentalist, was certainly capable of playing all the parts himself. His ability on drums was on par with Ringo's (though he lacked Starr's unique voice on the instrument) and on occasion he could (and did) outshine George on lead guitar.

The longer the Beatles spent in the recording studio, the more Paul McCartney became a control freak. With his first solo album, *McCartney*, released in the spring of 1970, Paul not only managed to aggravate John, George, and Ringo by arrogantly launching his debut disc within weeks of the Beatles' *Let It Be*, but he further alienated his former bandmates with a self-serving self-interview (inserted in the album's sleeve) in which he took issue with each of their songs as well as his bandmates' personalities and musicianship. Brilliant, with the technical prowess to back it up, Paul played all the instruments on *McCartney* himself, not solely for the experience or esthetic, but as an attempt to prove to the public once and for all who the musical genius behind the Beatles had been all along.

The track sheet for "Michelle" lists three guitarists on the song. As McCartney wrote "Michelle," it seems certain that he would have been one of them. Photographs taken during the session reveal John playing a nylon-string Spanish-style guitar and George picking his Gibson J-160E, which led Beatleologist David Rybaczewski to dispute Ian MacDonald's theory (from his authoritative book, *Revolution in the Head*) that "Michelle" was recorded entirely by Paul.

One thing we can be sure of: McCartney played his iconic 1963 Höfner 500 on the track. "I'll never forget putting the bass line in 'Michelle,'" McCartney later recalled. "It was a kind of a [French romantic composer Georges] Bizet thing. It really turned the song around. You could do that with bass, it was very exciting."

Another unusual production touch was the slowing of the song's tempo as it reached the end. "Paul asked for the music to be slowed on the last part of 'Michelle' to add more emphasis to it," said George Martin, who agreed that it "achieves the desired effect." Or, as McCartney simply put it, "We thought it sounded better that way."

RUBBER COVERS: "MICHELLE"

With "Yesterday" recently topping the charts in the States (oddly, it stalled at number eight in the UK), the Beatles passed on issuing "Michelle," another McCartney ballad, as the lead-off single from *Rubber Soul* (most likely due to John Lennon's objections). The song was immediately recorded and released by the Overlanders, as well as by David and Jonathan, whose innocuous cover climbed to number one in Canada, proving once again what a new Lennon and McCartney song could do for an otherwise mediocre group.

One of the most recorded songs in history, "Michelle" has taken on a life of its own over the years, no matter who inter-

The Beatles pause for a portrait while rehearsing for *The Ed Sullivan Show*, August 14, 1965.

Photo by John Pedin/NY Daily News/Getty Images

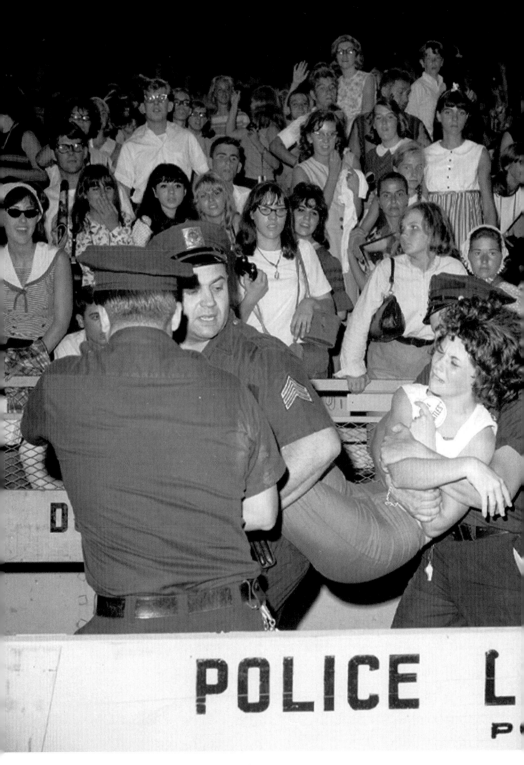

Pandemonium at Shea Stadium, August 15, 1965.
Photo by Jim Hughes/NY Daily News/Getty Images

A ticket to Shea.
Mitch Blank Collection

Beatle fan extraordinaire, Carol Dryden (holding the Beatles' latest release), who spent $8.40 trying to mail herself to the Beatles and nearly suffocated after forgetting to punch air holes in the package which held her.
Mitch Blank Collection

Showing off their M.B.E.'s (which either stands for Most Excellent Order of the British Empire or Mr. Brian Epstein, according to George Harrison), October 26, 1965, at Buckingham Palace.
Photo by Philippe LeTellier/Getty Images

Just in time for Christmas! *Rubber Soul*, the Beatles' sixth studio album, released December 3, 1965, in the UK, and December 6, in the US.
Mitch Blank Collection

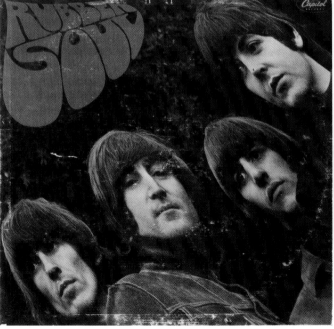

George introduces Paul to the mystical drone of
the tambura during the Beatles' first trip to India.
Photo by Mark and Colleen Hayward/Getty Images

БИТЛЗ · ПОМОГИ

Сторона 1
ПОМОГИ — 2.21
ВЧЕРА ВЕЧЕРОМ — 2.36
ТЫ ДОЛЖНА СКРЫВАТЬ СВОЮ ЛЮБОВЬ — 2.11
Я НУЖДАЮСЬ В ТЕБЕ — 2.31
ДРУГАЯ ДЕВУШКА — 2.08
ТЫ ПОТЕРЯЕШЬ ЭТУ ДЕВУШКУ — 1.53
БИЛЕТ НА ПОЕЗД — 3.12

Сторона 2
ИГРАТЬ ЕСТЕСТВЕННО — 2.33
ЭТО ПРОСТО ЛЮБОВЬ — 1.58
ТЫ НРАВИШЬСЯ МНЕ ТАК СИЛЬНО — 2.38
СКАЖИ МНЕ, ЧТО ТЫ ВИДИШЬ — 2.39
Я ВСЕГО ЛИШЬ УВИДЕЛ ЛИЦО — 2.06
ВЧЕРА — 2.07
ГОЛОВОКРУЖИТЕЛЬНАЯ МИСС ЛИЗЗИ — 2.54

Lennon (and company) in the land of Lenin. If the Beatles didn't tear down the Iron Curtain, they certainly helped rip a hole in it. The Russian release of *Help!* in 1992.
Mitch Blank Collection

EMI "factory girls" assembling *Rubber Soul*.
Photo by Keystone/Getty Images

prets its well-worn melody. Thousands of versions of the song, whether instrumental or vocal, attest to the durability and versatility of a Lennon/McCartney (mostly Paul in this case) composition.

The Ventures' effortless instrumental version of "Michelle" offers plenty of their trademark reverb and twang, and features a cool clavinet solo in the song's bridge. Years later, Booker T. and the MGs would transform "Michelle" into a breezy groove, with plenty of the band leader's trademark organ. The most elegant Muzak version of "Michelle" was recorded by the French mustachioed bandleader Paul Mauriat and his orchestra in 1967 for his album *A Taste of Mauriat*. The record jacket even featured a smiling nude on its cover, who must undoubtedly have been "Michelle."

Banjo ace Bela Fleck gently swings the melody, using the tune as a vehicle for his own stellar solos while harmonica wizard Howard Levy's plaintive reed work evokes the French cabaret where McCartney first envisioned himself singing to his dream belle.

The Brooklyn-based band Rubblebucket's cover of "Michelle" takes McCartney's ballad to a new indescribably delicious place where sultry vocals, electronica, and horns blend beautifully to give the listener something clever, innovative, and refreshing, while Ben Harper's interpretation of the song is well worth a listen, with his smoky vocals and righteous reggae groove.

Taking the song to the outskirts of freakazoid is the Milwaukee-based band Beatallica, whose love of the perverse forged a brilliant musical marriage of the Beatles' tune and Metallica's "For Whom the Bell Tolls" into the crunchy mash-up "For Whom Michelle Tolls," which simply must be heard to be believed.

19
"What Goes On"

"His Rolls-Royce is equipped with a cartridge player
which plays tapes by Ernest Tubb, Hank Snow
and other country artists."
—Pete Drake (pedal steel guitarist/producer),
on Ringo's tricked-out car, 1970

Reporter at a Beatles press conference, Los Angeles, August 27, 1966:

What type of music do you prefer?

George: Sort of honky-tonk and country-and-western and congo rhythms

Reporter: Out of all the country-and-western American stars, do you have a favorite?

George: Yeah, Buddy Holly, he was pretty good!

Reporter: What do you think of the number one country singer in this country, Buck Owens?

George: Ringo likes him a lot.

Ringo always loved both kinds of music—country *and* western. In 1959, he briefly played drums for a local Liverpool combo known as the Raving Texans. Although he wore plenty of jewelry, Ringo's handle was in part an homage to the legendary gunfighter Johnny Ringo (sometimes referred to as John B. Ringgold), said to have been tracked down and killed by Wyatt Earp in Turkey Creek Valley, Arizona, in 1882.

While history has christened the space cowboy Gram Parsons as the unequivocal "Father of Country Rock" for spiriting the Byrds to Nashville in 1968 to record their American roots opus *Sweetheart of the Rodeo*, the Beatles—and Ringo in particular—have long deserved some overdue respect for their cover of "Act Naturally." Recorded and released in September 1965, this catchy Buck Owens and the Buckaroos chart topper from 1963 was originally deemed a throwaway and tacked onto the B-side of "Yesterday. It was also the last cover song the Beatles would record until their marathon *Let It Be* sessions in 1969.

"Act Naturally" was written by Johnny Russell, who'd gotten a bit of traction in the music biz after "Gentleman" Jim Reeves recorded his "In a Mansion Stands My Love" in 1960 as the B-side to his classic heartbreaker "He'll Have to Go."

Allegedly knocked off in just a matter of minutes, the song was said to have been inspired after Russell canceled a date with his girlfriend in order to make a recording session in Hollywood. "They're gonna put me in the movies" was his cheap excuse. Three years later, Buck Owens cut "Act Naturally," which was cowritten with Voni Morrison, who first presented the song to a less-than-impressed Buck. But the Bakersfield cowboy eventually caught on and would soon ride "Act Naturally" straight to number one.

Then came Ringo warbling the lyrics to a song that seemed tailor-made for his carefully cultivated sad-sack persona. Starr, the band's beloved underdog, happened to be America's favorite Beatle. As Lennon once claimed at the height of Beatlemania, "When I feel my head start to swell, I just look at Ringo and know we're not supermen."

Starr's next foray into country rock came with an old Lennon/McCartney throwaway, a tune the Beatles first planned to record back in March 1963 as a follow-up to "Please Please Me." Previously rejected by producer George Martin, the song was suddenly revived two years later when the band found themselves pinched for more material to meet the impending deadline for their new album. "What Goes On" was also highly unusual as it bore Starkey's name in the writing credits, although he couldn't recall exactly what he'd contributed to the tune other than "about five words." After cutting the rhythm tracks in one take, in which Ringo played drums, he then over-dubbed his vocals while John and Paul smoothed the edges of Starr's wonky delivery with their cooing harmonies. The tune's rough production also proved to be a perfect vehicle for George Harrison, a devotee of Carl Perkins and Chet Atkins, who played his Gretsch Country Gentleman with ease and credibility.

Although an integral ingredient of rock 'n' roll, country music was generally disdained by most folks north of the Mason-

Dixon Line well into the early seventies, when the Allman Brothers' transcendental blues-rock jams and the egalitarian politics of a Georgia peanut farmer who moved into the White House in the winter of '77 would help the South to rise again. Television shows like *Hee Haw*, which featured the lightning-fast picking of Roy Clark and the fine rasp of the Grand Ole Opry's Roy Acuff, along with the show's host, Buck Owens, with his big honey-drippin' grin, went a long way in turning off snobbish Yankees to the joys of Southern culture—the cornpone humor, bountiful bustlines, and expertly coiffed bouffants had millions of city folk rolling their eyes.

Nobody took Ringo too seriously as a country rock innovator, and perhaps that's just what the music needed most to find a home with a broader audience. Who (other than perhaps Merle Haggard) could take offense at the Beatles' drummer having a little fun with a country number?

Although the Rolling Stones' sixth album, *Aftermath* (released in April 1966), revealed a bit of twang on "What to Do?," Jagger and Richards's first real shot at playing country wouldn't come until two years later, in 1968, with the bare-bones acoustic tracks "Dear Doctor" and "Factory Girl," from *Beggars Banquet*.

While country music came naturally to Ringo, the Stones' first foray into white Americana came off as a joke at best. Although both Gram Parsons and Ry Cooder had tutored Keith Richards in the nuances of American roots music, Mick's vocals evoked the hick warble of the freckle-faced, cowlicked Carl "Alfalfa" Switzer from old *Our Gang* comedies. Parody or not, the Stones regularly revisited the style over the years, recording a loose and boozy acoustic version of their number one hit "Honky-Tonk Women" (renamed "Country Honk") along with "Sweet Virginia" and "Far Away Eyes," to name but three. But no matter how close Keith Richards got to the source with his soulful guitar accompaniment, Mick's over-the-top delivery always had a way of making the song sound like a put-on. Always class-conscious, Jagger seemed somewhat embarrassed by his band's forays into the genre. "We still think of country as a bit of a joke," Mick confessed in a 1968 interview, yet by the early seventies a few of the Stones' finest songs revealed a strong country influence, "Wild Horses," "Dead Flowers," and "Let It Bleed" among them.

For Bob Dylan, country singers like Hank Williams and Hank Snow were both great inspirations. (As he once declared, "I like any singer named Hank.") Following his motorcycle accident in May 1966, in which he fractured several vertebrae in his neck, Bob managed to momentarily "get out of the rat race," as he put it, retreating to the bucolic Woodstock countryside in order to heal and raise his family. His hired guns, a clutch of Canadian roots rockers and a boozy, blues-belting drummer from Arkansas, together simply known as the Band, had recently backed him on his controversial tour of England in which crowds relentlessly heckled them night after night for the unforgivable crime of rocking joyously. Moving to the small, quaint upstate New York town to keep Dylan company, Robbie Robertson, Levon Helm, Richard Manuel, Rick Danko, and Garth Hudson holed up down in the basement of a split-level house in Saugerties, soon to become world famous as "Big Pink," and began working on a remarkable batch of new songs.

Dylan eventually emerged in Nashville the following fall with a portfolio of stark folk tunes and languid country numbers that he warbled in a strange new voice that sounded as if he'd been gargling mercury out of an old fruit jar. Although the bulk of the songs that comprised *The Basement Tapes* would remain unreleased until 1975, Dylan would make his comeback with the disquieting *John Wesley Harding*, a set of haunted hymns for the Aquarian age.

The Byrds, in the meantime, had been going through a myriad of changes as well, both in style and personnel. Having concocted the new genre of folk rock, they in short order would beat the Grateful Dead, Jefferson Airplane, and the Beatles to the punch, inventing psychedelic music by fusing aspects of John Coltrane's modal jazz with the hypnotic drone of the Indian raga that Crosby had picked up after attending a Ravi Shankar recording session at World Pacific Studios in L.A. "Eight Miles High," written to commemorate the band's disastrous tour of England in August 1965, was the first pop single of its day to feature a band freely improvising. Propelled by Chris Hillman's growling bass, Roger McGuinn's shimmering twelve-string guitar rose and fell around a set of cryptic lyrics that evoked London ("rain gray town") as well as the "stranger than known" visions conjured by LSD. Released in March 1966, "Eight Miles High" was quickly jumped on by censors, who banned the song from radio play for its flagrant drug reference, disregarding the protests of Roger McGuinn, who would soon become a born-again Christian. McGuinn, an aeronautic fanatic, unsuccessfully tried to explain that commercial airliners on intercontinental flights usually cruised at an altitude of six miles, but "six," being too sibilant, just didn't sing right, and so (inspired by the Beatles' latest single "Eight Days a Week") he changed the word to the easier to intone "eight." Crosby and Clark for the time being remained silent on the subject, smiling knowingly, betrayed only by a strange glint in their eyes.

But by 1968 both Gene Clark and David Crosby were out of the picture, replaced by Gram Parsons of the International Submarine Band. A country music fanatic posing as a jazz pianist when Chris Hillman first invited him to jam with his floundering band, Parsons soon persuaded the Byrds to trade in their trademark twelve-string Rickenbacker sound for a folksy fiddle, some banjo twang, and the sweet whine of a pedal steel guitar.

Recorded on November 4 and first released in the States on December 3, 1965, as the B-side to "Nowhere Man," "What Goes On?" managed to blur the hard and fast battle lines drawn between longhair and redneck. At that point in time you were either on one side or the other. There was no in-between. Outlaw country singers like Willie Nelson and Waylon Jennings had yet to let their "freak flags fly," while country music legend Ernest Tubb sang Jimmy Helms's knuckleheaded "patriotic" anthem, "It's America (Love It or Leave It)," and Merle Haggard extolled good-ole-boy values with his Grammy-winning "Okie from Muskogee," describing a place where apparently "even squares can have a ball."

Nonetheless, Ringo stuck to his guns, cutting country tracks from his first self-penned song, "Don't Pass Me By"—which appeared on the Beatles' "White Album," complete with scratchy fiddle riffs played by jazz bassist Jack Fallon—to his 1970 Nashville session, which produced the underrated *Beaucoups of Blues*, which featured Starr's excellent cover of Bobby Pierce's "Loser's Lounge." Ringo and his All Starr Band would perform at Nashville's legendary Ryman Auditorium in 2012, playing "Don't Pass Me By" along with "Act Naturally," for which he briefly donned a black ten-gallon hat for a verse before tossing it into the crowd. You had to wonder for a moment if the boot didn't fit as he gleefully sang, "the biggest fool that ever hit the big time."

Following "Don't Pass Me By," Ringo's second songwriting credit with the Beatles came with "Octopus's Garden" from *Abbey Road*, a reprise of sorts of "Yellow Submarine," which celebrated an idyllic life beneath the waves, a theme that Starr would revisit on his 1973 self-titled album *Ringo!* with "Sunshine Life for Me (Sail Away Raymond)," written for him by George Harrison and featuring members of the Band, along with Dylan session guitarist extraordinaire David Bromberg.

Starr's solo career began in March 1970 with the "horrendous" yet "classy" (in the words of critic Greil Marcus) *Sentimental Journey* as he warbled his way through a portfolio of old standards and lost melodies by everyone from Cole Porter to Hoagy Carmichael, beating his drinking buddy Harry Nilsson to the punch by three years (Harry would expertly croon *A Little Touch of Schmilsson in the Night* in 1973), while helping to trigger the brief nostalgia trend of the early seventies, which saw everyone from Dan Hicks and the Hot Licks and Commander Cody and His Lost Planet Airmen to California session guitarist Ry Cooder digging through secondhand shops in search of forgotten records and vintage clothes. Ringo also inadvertently opened the door for a gaggle of over-the-hill rock stars, from Rod Stewart to Glenn Frey, Brian Wilson, and Sir Paul, to sing standards as a last stab at respectability.

RUBBER COVERS: "WHAT GOES ON"

No longer just a vehicle for a simple country-rock tune, Sufjan Stevens's surprising interpretation of "What Goes On" (which appeared on the 2005 compilation *This Bird Has Flown: A 40th Anniversary Tribute to the Beatles' Rubber Soul*) sounds closer in spirit to the music the Beatles played circa 1968. Recalling late-sixties Kinks (perhaps a lost track from their obscure rock opera

Arthur?), Stevens's vocal on the verse evokes Ray Davies, while a marmalade of grinding guitars, flowing flutes, and organ, along with the haunting refrain of the chorus and sleigh bells, conjures the more sophisticated arrangements of Brian Wilson.

In recent years, Ringo has performed "What Goes On" with his All Starr Band on his 2006 and 2008 tours. While providing a dose of nostalgia for the audience, the song allows Ringo to momentarily don a Stetson and take a detour to the heart of the country.

20

"12-Bar Original"

"I mean, blues are like breathing. As long as you got it,
you're alive and when you ain't, you're dead."
—Keith Richards, 1987

While the Rolling Stones, Yardbirds, and Animals all began as blues bands, slugging it out in smoky London clubs, rocking covers of Lead Belly, Muddy Waters, and Howlin' Wolf songs, the Beatles cut their teeth on the old-school rock 'n' roll of Elvis, Little Richard, Chuck Berry, Buddy Holly, and Carl Perkins. Although Robert Johnson's *King of the Delta Blues Singers*, a compilation of sixteen recordings originally cut in a San Antonio, Texas, hotel room in 1936 and 1937 and released nearly twenty-five years later in 1961, would one day become the Rosetta stone to the likes of Eric Clapton, Keith Richards, Jeff Beck, and Jimmy Page, the tortured songs, Faustian mythology, and stinging slide guitar work of an obscure bluesman from Hazlehurst, Mississippi, meant little at the time to the lads from Liverpool.

Not that the Beatles didn't know their American roots music. John Lennon's first band, the Quarrymen, once covered "Rock Island Line" by the legendary Louisiana folk/blues gangsta Lead Belly, although they probably had never heard of Huddie Ledbetter and his thunderous Stella twelve-string guitar—John most likely learned the song from a record by the Scottish multi-instrumentalist Lonnie Donegan, whose chugging skiffle version of the tune was an enormous hit in 1955. But the British blues explosion (much like the American folk revival) would turn out to be a short-lived phenomenon, although its most passionate devotees—Clapton, Richards, Beck, and Page among them—continued to play the music over the next five decades.

As a singer and guitarist, John Lennon was a true primitive, perhaps the closest thing to a bluesman the Beatles would ever have, while George Harrison, early in his career, had been so obsessed with Carl Perkins that he spent nearly every waking moment perfecting rockabilly riffs on his trusty Gretsch Tennessean, while imploring his friends to call him "Carl." Popularized by Perkins in the 1950s, "Matchbox," had originally been a Blind Lemon Jefferson tune. Jefferson, considered by many to be the father of lead guitar, played for spare change on the streets of the Deep Ellum neighborhood of Dallas, where he was led around by his young protégé, Aaron Thibeaux (better known as T-Bone) Walker. In 1929 Blind Lemon would allegedly freeze to death in a Chicago blizzard at age thirty-six, never to know his song would one day become world famous thanks to Perkins, let alone four boys from Liverpool. Whether inspired by Brian Jones or Delta bluesmen like Robert Johnson and Bukka White, George Harrison soon shifted his focus to playing slide guitar and would write a few bluesy numbers of his own, including "Old Brown Shoe" and "For You Blue," in which he exclaimed, "Elmore James got nuthin' on this baby," as John Lennon wrangled a slippery solo from his lap steel guitar.

While his voice is best suited to buttery love ballads and chipper pop ditties, Paul McCartney's range is astounding, whether he's yelping like Little Richard or unleashing the feral growl, as one listen to "Helter Skelter" or "Why Don't We Do It in the Road?" from the "White Album" will surely attest. A composer of timeless melodies, Paul found the blues in its raw form too elemental, though he would occasionally borrow from the style in bits and pieces whenever needed, as with the punchy barrelhouse piano in "Lady Madonna," which bore unmistakable traces of Fats Domino's keyboard work. Throughout his solo career, McCartney continued to mine American roots music for inspiration. "Heart of the Country," from his second solo album, *Ram*, was reminiscent of a Mississippi John Hurt country blues number, to which he added a jazzy guitar riff that Paul doubles with his voice in the style of George Benson.

Under the gun to finish *Rubber Soul*, the Beatles returned again to Abbey Road on November 4, 1965, shortly before 11p.m. After knocking off Ringo's country rocker "What Goes On" in one take, the band began to jam on a Memphis-style blues number, with Lennon slashing away at the strings of his blue 1961 Fender Stratocaster in his best imitation of Steve Cropper. From Paul's count off, "12-Bar Original," the only unreleased track from the *Rubber Soul* sessions, bore an obvious resemblance to Booker T. and the MGs' 1962 hit "Green Onions." (The Beatles were far from alone when it came to falling under the spell of Booker T.'s irresistible groove. Blues singer/harmonica wailer supreme Sonny Boy Williamson would write a set of his own sultry lyrics to a very similar chord progression, which he released as a single titled "Help Me" the following year, in 1963.)

Keyboardist Booker T. Jones and his band had such great respect for the Beatles that they would release *MacLemore Avenue*, an instrumental tribute to *Abbey Road*, just months after the Beatles' final album was released in 1969. In homage to the Beatles' iconic album cover, the MGs were portrayed joyfully strutting their stuff across MacLemore Avenue, home to the Stax studios, where they cut their famous records.

Although just a twelve-bar blues jam, this tune allowed the Beatles to stretch out, with John and George trading riffs, years before the famous three-way guitar face-off in "The End," from *Abbey Road*. Toward the end of the number, George Martin suddenly lets his hair down, caressing the keys of the harmonium, whose thin, reedy folk timbre seems like an odd choice for an R&B number. (There is also some speculation that the keyboard part was played by the Fabs' faithful roadie Mal Evans, who is also credited with adding a dollop of Hammond organ to "You Won't See Me").

Allegedly mixed in just fifteen minutes on November 30, a mono version of the second take titled "12-Bar Original" was safely filed away, a relic to be cherished years later by hard-core fans. Lennon deemed the track "lousy" and most likely wouldn't have changed his mind even if he'd lived to see its release on the *Anthology 2* compilation in 1996. Beyond this rare outtake, the Beatles wouldn't touch the twelve-bar blues form again until 1967, with "Flying," a bit of groovy instrumental fluff from the *Magical Mystery Tour* soundtrack (and, like that for "Flying," the songwriting credit for "12-Bar Original" listed the whole band as equal partners: Lennon/McCartney/Harrison/Starr).

GET ON THE BUS

MCCARTNEY, INSPIRED BY SAN FRANCISCO BANDS like the Grateful Dead and Jefferson Airplane, was obviously feeling out of step with the flourishing psychedelic scene when he came up with the Magical Mystery Tour concept—as far away from their previous bus-inspired song "In My Life" as *Rubber Soul* was from *Meet the Beatles*. Ultimately it was Ken Kesey and his Merry Pranksters, whose acid-fueled adventures took them across America in their brightly painted bus (with legendary Beat figure Neal Cassady at the wheel), that would inadvertently spark the Beatles (under McCartney's direction) to produce their first unequivocal "failure," a half-baked homemade film that, although fun and quirky, ultimately led nowhere.

Perhaps even more embarrassing as a sign of the times was the Who's "Magic Bus." Although it was a catchy tune, written by Pete Townshend years before in 1965, inspired by Bo Diddley's trademark syncopated beat, the eponymous album, whose cover featured the band's name in a trippy scrawl, wasn't released until the fall of '68, over a year after the Summer of Love had withered and died on the vine. With violent protest to the Vietnam War on the rise, frequent shootouts between the Black Panthers and the police, the assassinations of Dr. Martin Luther King Jr. and Robert Kennedy, flower power and all its trappings suddenly seemed rather trite.

A year later, Lennon dove headfirst into the blues once more, recording the gut-wrenching "Yer Blues" for the "White Album." While some heard the song as a parody of popular "heavy" British blues bands of the day like John Mayall & the Bluesebreakers, Savoy Brown, and Cream, its deeply poetic lyrics (which reflected John's haggard psychological state of mind at the time as he howled, "Yes I'm lonely, wanna die . . .") were second only to Dylan's fleeting surrealist verse. "Yer Blues" (which includes a shout-out to "Dylan's Mr. Jones" from Bob's harrowing "Ballad of a Thin Man,") also revealed a bit of inspiration from classic blues songs like Gus Cannon's "Minglewood Blues" (later revived by the Grateful Dead as "The New Minglewood Blues"), in which the protagonist bragged of his mystical origins, claiming to be "born in the desert and raised in a lion's den." Jimi Hendrix, whose "Voodoo Child" went far beyond mere sorcery, took on the aura of a god as he claimed to be "standing next to a mountain," about to "chop it down with the edge of [his] hand." Such grandiose imagery evokes the likes of the luminous Vishnu or Hanuman, the Hindu monkey-god who not only changed size, but effortlessly leapt from the island of Sri Lanka to the mainland of India. Whatever Lennon's intentions, he (like Dylan before him) took the blues lyric to a whole new level as he sang, "I am of the universe and you know what it's worth."

"I've never bought the idea that ['Yer Blues'] was a spoof of British blues," said California singer/songwriter Peter Case. "It sounds dead serious." Case compared Lennon's lyric to Dylan's "Visions of Johanna," rating it as "psychedelic rock 'n' roll survival literature of the first order."

Strung out on junk, John screamed, "I feel so suicidal, even hang my rock 'n' roll," a harbinger of the emotional wallop that his first solo album, *Plastic Ono Band*, would pack. Lennon would perform "Yer Blues" live for *The Rolling Stones' Rock 'n' Roll Circus*, a made-for-TV special filmed on December 11, 1968 (which, for various reasons—the most obvious being the Who outshining the Stones' lackluster performance—remained shelved for decades, until its 1996 release), with an ad hoc supergroup dubbed the Dirty Mac, featuring Eric Clapton, Keith Richards (handling bass chores), and Jimi Hendrix's polyrhythmic drummer, Mitch Mitchell. John would perform the song again a year later on September 13, 1969, at the Toronto Peace Festival with Eric Clapton on guitar and Yoko standing close beside him, as an unearthly caterwaul erupted from her mouth.

21

"Think for Yourself"

"Think wrongly, if you please, but in all cases think for yourself."
—*Gotthold Ephraim Lessing*

In their early days, the Beatles had been a handful of rough-and-tumble teddy boys, done up in black leather. They smoked and cursed onstage, and got girls pregnant.

Just a few years before their debut on *The Ed Sullivan Show* on February 9, 1964, the cute and cuddly Paul had been charged with a paternity suit (which he successfully dodged, thanks to Brian Epstein's expert wrangling), back when the boys rocked the seedy red-light district of Hamburg's Reeperbahn. Unlike the Rolling Stones' Brian Jones, who sired a handful of illegitimate children by different young girls, John Lennon did the "decent" thing and married his art-school sweetheart, Cynthia, after she'd become pregnant with their son, Julian. The Beatles, as we were led to believe from Richard Lester's portrayal of the band in *A Hard Day's Night* and *Help!*, were a pack of jolly, good-natured lads, who only wanted "dance with you" and "hold your hand." It was a charming charade that lasted a few seasons until cracks began to appear in their cheerful veneer.

The first inkling was George Harrison's dour "Don't Bother Me" from the Fab Four's second LP, *With the Beatles* (better known in the States as their debut album, *Meet the Beatles*). The song came off rather abrupt, bordering on rude, in light of all that mop-top giddiness. You suddenly felt like an intruder with the door slammed in your face after having been invited to the world's greatest party. "I've got no time for you right now, don't bother me," George groused. As a young bloke seeking peace of mind in the maelstrom of Beatlemania, Harrison regularly turned a cold shoulder to both the press and fans, who he felt used the band as "an excuse to go crazy," as he complained.

From the start, Harrison was convinced the band was "doomed" if they couldn't somehow manage to get off the mad conveyor belt of fame and constant demand for new product.

"You need your own space, man. Everything needs to be left alone," said "the Dark Horse," as George later came to be known.

Harrison's "Think for Yourself" was somewhat startling upon first hearing. Over Paul McCartney's grungy fuzz bass, George tells off his ditzy lover, describing her mind as "opaque" while suggesting she start thinking for herself for a change, as he has no plans on being with her in the future. Everyone from Dylan to Jagger to the Sex Pistols, who "took the piss out of" Queen Elizabeth with their anarchist anthem "God Save the Queen," could appreciate that artful twist of that knife.

Although there are few clues within the lyrics to state his case, Harrison later claimed the song's inspiration came not from some flaky bird but from his distrust of and disdain for the British government. George's barbed accusation "You're telling all those lies about the good things that we can have if we close our eyes" might have been aimed at the prime minister as easily as at a lover. Somewhere in the blur of Beatlemania, Harrison's memory may have become fogged, and he may have confused "Think for Yourself" with his next major effort, "Taxman," the lead-off number from *Revolver*, written after he suddenly found himself in an obscenely high tax bracket after becoming "one of the beautiful people." In "Taxman" George handed political figures Sir Edward Heath and Harold Wilson their heads on a silver platter as he warned, "Declare the pennies on your eyes," to anyone planning on dying in the near future.

While Mick Jagger routinely spit mean-spirited misogynist lyrics in songs like "19th Nervous Breakdown," "Under My Thumb," and "Stupid Girl," Bob Dylan was not to be outdone in his follow-up to "Like a Rolling Stone." Recorded just four days after his controversial concert at the Newport Folk Festival on July 25, 1965, "Positively 4th Street" shocked his fans as Dylan's switchblade tongue turned from slicing up the faceless powerbrokers who inspired songs like "Only a Pawn in Their Game," and "Masters of War" to jealous old friends who he believed would "rather see [him] paralyzed" than become successful. Dave Marsh described the song as an "icy hipster bitch session"; there had never been anything like it in the history of pop radio. Startling as it was, "Positively 4th Street" didn't even bother with the etiquette of having a chorus. While no one would have guessed George Harrison capable of such vitriol, "the Quiet One" apparently wasn't as comatose as *The Rutles* (Neil Innes's hilarious parody of the Beatles) made him out to be.

Recorded on November 8, "Think for Yourself" (originally titled "Won't Be There with You") had an edge unlike most Beatle songs before it. The bitter resentment of Harrison's lyrics were driven not by a snarling guitar riff but by Paul McCartney's most sinister bass line to date. Known for his trademark violin-shaped Höfner, bought in 1961 at Steinway Musichaus in Hamburg and played since the Beatles' early days, slugging it out at the Cavern Club, Paul had recently switched to a Rickenbacker 4001S, which he first used on "Think for Yourself," saturated in fuzz tone.

While Abbey Road engineer Ken Townsend credits the distortion on Harrison's song to an in-house innovation devised by the sound technicians at EMI, it was actually an effects box known as the Tone Bender built by Gary Hurst, who'd given a prototype to Beatles earlier in '65.

Fuzz tone, as George recalled, was originally a mistake made during a Phil Spector session while recording Bob B. Soxx & the Blue Jeans in 1962, covering the Disney song "Zip-a-Dee-Doo-Dah."

"The engineer who set up the track overloaded the microphone on the guitar player and it became very distorted," Harrison said. "Phil Spector said, 'Leave it like that, it's great.' Some years later everyone started to try to copy that sound, and so they invented the fuzz box. We had one and tried the bass through it and it sounded really good."

According to Carol Kaye of L.A.'s legendary session band the Wrecking Crew, McCartney's grungy overdrive was hardly anything unusual. "Fuzz was used on the bass as early as 1956," explained the veteran session guitarist/bassist. "They'd take a tube out of an amp in the late 1950s to simulate fuzz tone. René Hall played the Dano [Danelectro] bass with that around 1956. People were using fuzz back then in the studio. It was common, though of course it was better with the actual fuzz-tone pedals built in the 1960s. But it was still before the Beatles' time."

Others have claimed that fuzz tone was accidentally born in a Nashville recording studio during the summer of 1960 when session guitarist Grady Martin plugged his Fender six-string bass into a malfunctioning mixing board while cutting "Don't Worry" for country star Marty Robbins (best known for his 1959 recording of the gunslinger ballad "The Streets of Laredo"). Robbins apparently liked the distorted sound, which Martin then used, not for the bass part but as the song's lead riff. Despite protests from his producer, "Don't Worry" sailed to number one on the *Billboard* country charts, opening the door for a long line of copycats.

The Tone Bender would make a triumphant return nearly three years later, in August 1968, adding its crunch and distortion to Lennon's smoldering anti-establishment anthem "Revolution."

Listening to the complete tapes of the session, one realizes that the constant banter that took place between Lennon and McCartney while recording the backup vocals for "Think for Yourself" must have driven George to the brink of madness. Ringo banged a tambourine while John hilariously sang, "Listen . . . do you want to hold a penis? Doo-wah-doo" (to the tune of "Do You Want to Know a Secret").

"Lukewarm baby gotta custard face," Lennon suddenly blurts out as Paul announces off-mic, "I just got in from Olympia. I lit the torch," before breaking into the Woody Woodpecker theme song. A moment later McCartney asks John, "Did ya see that Humphrey Bogart film?" "Wasn't Hump wund?" Lennon replies. George, frustrated by his partners' shenanigans, somehow manages to maintain his cool while trying to keep his mates focused on the task at hand. Meanwhile John continues to goof off as he stumbles over the song's complex harmony, having to sing "about the good things that we can have if we close our eyes" repeatedly. "I get something in me head and all the walls of Rome couldn't stop me," Lennon remarked.

"Somebody up there likes me! It's Jesus our lord and savior!" John begins another rant, this time in the voice of a wrathful preacher. "Okay . . . let's go!" George finally says, unable to stop himself from laughing at Lennon's shenanigans.

Surprisingly, it was their straitlaced producer George Martin egging them on in hopes the the Beatles might say something off-the-cuff that he could use as a greeting for their third annual Christmas record, a yearly premium the group sent out to faithful DJs and members of their fan club. Although there were quips aplenty, nothing really fit the holiday spirit, and the tape was shelved with a note, "This will eventually be issued," scrawled on the box. Three years later, six seconds of George and Paul singing "and you've got time to rectify" over and over again would be used in their new film, *Yellow Submarine*.

Of all the Fabs, George Harrison clearly had the least patience for all the hype and hysteria of Beatlemania. "I would never want that again," he wrote in his 1980 memoir *I Me Mine*. "It's like [Ken Kesey's novel *One Flew Over the*] *Cuckoo's Nest*, where you are sane, in the middle of something and they're all crackers."

Throughout the sixties both Dylan and Lennon repeatedly urged their fans not to follow their (or anyone else's) lead, but to forge their own unique path through life. "You make your own dream," Lennon told *Playboy*. "That's the Beatles' story, isn't it? That's Yoko's story. That's what I'm saying now. Produce your own dream. . . . People cannot provide it for you. I can't wake you up. You can wake you up. I can't cure you. You can cure you."

The 1960s acid guru Dr. Timothy Leary (whom Richard Nixon had dubbed "the most dangerous man in America"), best known for his slogan "Turn on, tune in and drop out," which instructed the burgeoning counterculture to leave the nine-to-five game of life behind and find inner peace and enlightenment through following a spiritual path comprised of yoga and meditation and frequent use of the "holy sacrament" of LSD, perhaps went a bit too far in trying to awaken the slumbering masses. "Think for yourself and question authority," another popular catchphrase of Leary's, soon appeared in his consciousness-raising lectures and writings. Whether or not the renegade doctor was inspired by the chorus to Harrison's song from *Rubber Soul*, no one can say for certain, but Leary adored the Fab

Four and considered them "mutants. Prototypes of evolutionary agents sent by God, endowed with a mysterious power to create a new human species, a young race of laughing freemen."

Along with Allen Ginsberg, Petula Clark, Dick Gregory, and the Smothers Brothers, Tim Leary would join John and Yoko for their Bed-In "happening" at the Queen Elizabeth Hotel in Montreal on June 1, 1969, to sing and record Lennon's anti–Vietnam War anthem, "Give Peace a Chance."

In April 1966, Lennon would buy a copy of Timothy Leary's book *The Psychedelic Experience: A Manual Based on the Tibetan Book of the Dead* (cowritten with Richard Alpert and Ralph Metzner), which sparked the opening lyrics, "Turn off your mind, relax and float downstream," to his first psychedelic opus, "Tomorrow Never Knows." Three years later, in 1969, when Leary ran for governor of California against Ronald Reagan, John Lennon asked if he could somehow lend his friend a hand. Tim suggested that John compose an anthem based on his campaign slogan "Come together—join the party." John returned the favor by composing "Come Together," which soon wound up as the lead-off song on *Abbey Road*, the last great song he would record with the Beatles.

Following George's own spiritual awakening, first sparked by an unexpected flash of LSD and then sustained and refined through daily meditation and the chanting of the Hare Krishna Maha Mantra, George's *Sgt. Pepper* offering "Within You, Without You" a few years later was a remarkable statement on the trap of the material world by a young rock star who had everything a young man could ever desire. George warns those of us "who gain the world and lose their soul" that the ultimate price of negative karma is not worth such fleeting wealth. Beyond the many Beatle fans who initially disliked Indian music and felt alienated by George's preachy lyrics, around the offices of Apple Records, Harrison was regularly referred to as "His Lecture-ship" for his strident beliefs and opinions. During his Dark Horse tour in 1974 it became painfully obvious that George's devotion to the blue flute-playing Hindu god far exceeded his passion for rock 'n' roll. As his devotion to Lord Krishna deepened, George groused, "I'm sick of all these young people just boogying [*sic*] around, wasting their lives, you know."

RUBBER COVERS: "THINK FOR YOURSELF"

Although the Yonder Mountain String Band's by-the-book arrangement of "Think for Yourself" brings nothing new to the song bass-wise or vocally, their take on Harrison's tune is unique enough, thanks to Dave Johnston's driving banjo and Jeff Austin's shimmering mandolin arpeggios. Bluegrass interpretations of Beatles tunes began in neither Kentucky nor Tennessee, but in Cambridge, Massachusetts, when the Charles River Valley Boys first gave the Fabs' music a bit of that high lonesome sound when they recorded *Beatle Country* for Elektra Records in 1966. Worried that their fans (mostly Harvard students) would accuse them of selling out, banjo picker Bob Siggins claimed their approach was to make the album "as hard-core bluegrass as we could." Not surprisingly, *Beatle Country* sold poorly and the band dissolved two years later.

"[Fiddler] Richard Greene and I first listened to *Rubber Soul* when we were down in Nashville when we were with Bill Monroe and the Bluegrass Boys," recalled Peter Rowan (lead singer of Old and in the Way, an acoustic spin-off band of the Grateful Dead that featured Jerry Garcia). Although they could appreciate the Beatles blending elements of folk and country in their new album, the music they'd been playing with Bill Monroe, Peter pointed out, was "much more authentic!"

Years later, in 2012, Pete Shelley transformed Harrison's song (for a Beatle tribute CD available from *Mojo* magazine) into an exhilarating punk anthem. Employing bludgeoning drums and crunchy guitar chords reminiscent of the Kinks' "All the Day and All of the Night," the ex-Buzzcocks' singer/guitarist took no prisoners.

22

"The Word"

*"It is love; love, the comfort of the human species,
the preserver of the universe, the soul of all sentient beings,
love, tender love."*
—*Voltaire*

Somewhere between "the good and the bad books" that John Lennon had read, he finally got the message loud and clear. "The Word," as he sang in a near evangelical fervor, was "more than just holding hands."

"The Word," as John told *Playboy* in 1980, "was written together, but it's mainly mine. It's about gettin' smart. It's the marijuana period. It's the love and peace thing. The word is love, right?"

While a wellspring of alternative consciousness—found in the Beat poetry of Allen Ginsberg and novels of Jack Kerouac and William S. Burroughs, and in the modern jazz of Miles Davis, Thelonious Monk, Ornette Coleman, and Charles Mingus—percolated just beneath its drab surface, Eisenhower's fifties had been a decidedly dull time in many ways, an age of black and white, not just from the flickering light emanating from television sets proliferating from coast to coast, but in the apartheid politics of segregated America as well. Rock 'n' roll had been a teenager's only hope, but with Elvis drafted into the army, Jerry Lee Lewis hounded from the stage in shame and degradation after marrying his thirteen-year-old cousin, Chuck Berry doing time for messing around with "jailbait," and Buddy Holly's plane tragically crashing in a frozen Iowa cornfield in February 1959, the music and flourishing culture that surrounded it was suddenly dead, gone with barely a trace. Listening to commercial AM radio programming in the early sixties made one wonder if the American cultural revolution had ever happened at all. A conveyor belt of prefab teen idols like Fabian and Frankie Avalon were now being groomed and peddled to the next generation of kids who'd been born too late to see and hear the real thing. Countering the teenybopper trend was a new folk music movement that spread amongst college students and young working adults who'd grown up tapping their toes to diner jukeboxes and now craved music with more integrity, something or someone who might possibly address a few of the world's mounting problems.

A clutch of apple-cheeked singers and guitar strummers from San Francisco known as the Kingston Trio would offer tidy interpretations of Celtic folk songs like "Tom Dooley" and clever novelty numbers including "M.T.A.," which unexpectedly shot to the top of the charts in 1959, triggering what soon became known as the "folk boom." With their clean-cut collegiate look and matching candy-striped shirts (which soon wound up on the backs of the Beach Boys), the Kingston Trio made folk music fun (and safe) again for the whole family, rather than the tool of Communist rabble-rousers like Paul Robeson and Pete Seeger, who many felt used the sing-along as a weapon of dissent.

Dylan, as usual, had gotten it before the rest of us. It's not like he had a running start, having grown up in a minuscule mining town in northern Minnesota. Bob's lifeline to the outside world had been late-night radio broadcasts of R&B stations coming out of Chicago, along with plenty of that high lonesome sound by way of Nashville's Grand Ole Opry. Hearing this passionate, exotic music made Dylan feel, as he said in Martin Scorcese's documentary *No Direction Home*, "like [he'd] been delivered to the wrong address, miles from where [he] was meant to be." Fleeing his hometown of Hibbing, Bob enrolled in and quickly dropped out of the University of Minnesota after reading Woody Guthrie's autobiography *Bound for Glory*. Inspired by the rapturous ramblings of the wire-haired Welsh poet Dylan Thomas, Robert Zimmerman (as he was known to his family) refused to go "gentle into that good night." With his cap and guitar and harmonica in a rack, "Dylan" soon lit out on his own personal Homeric odyssey, in search of postwar America while simultaneously reinventing himself.

It's hard to pinpoint exactly when the sixties began. Some say the Kennedy election represented the turning of the page, when hope suddenly arrived in the form of a charismatic Catholic senator from Massachusetts who barely beat out Eisenhower's unscrupulous vice president, Richard Nixon, in a neck-and-neck race that was said to have been bought for him in the end by his father, the bootlegging tycoon Joseph Kennedy Sr. The youngest president in American history, accompanied by his classy and fashionable wife, Jacqueline, "Jack" would replace the tired old warhorse Eisenhower, a bald general who had played a starring role in World War II and loaned his steady hand to steering the decade that forever bore his name, the "Eisenhower Era." Although Kennedy's "Camelot," as his presidency soon became known, offered a bright future where equality for African Americans as well as for women in the workplace was possible, many old prejudices and issues still lingered, particularly the threat of Communism, which nearly led the world to the "Eve of Destruction," (as Barry McGuire later sang). Jack Kennedy's winning smile, inspiring speeches, and smart style represented, for many, a new America, full of possibility.

Despite a myriad of exotic influences and new ideas, love was the main theme that resounded throughout *Rubber Soul*. But in a matter of months, the Beatles' lyrical landscape would take a decidedly surreal turn. Strange images unexpectedly leapt out at you, sparked by their drug-fueled imaginations. Everything and everyone from yellow submarines to pretty nurses "serving poppies on a tray" would change the way we looked at the world.

Nonetheless, whether under the influence of LSD or Lewis Carroll, John Lennon would soon fashion love as a symbol that was both simple and clear, a universal message that everyone everywhere could understand. Written over a two-week period in May '67 and performed on June 25 for *Our World*. the BBC's first satellite broadcast, where it was seen by an estimated 400 million viewers, Lennon's joyful romp "All You Need Is Love" took the ideas first expressed in "The Word" to the Age of Aquarius.

JOHN COLTRANE'S MESSAGE OF LOVE

"IN THE BEGINNING I MISUNDERSTOOD," Lennon sang like a man on a mission to rectify the chauvinist attitudes of his past as quickly as possible. "But now I got it, the word is good." Although 1967 would soon become known as the "Summer of Love," the seeds of this gentle philosophy had been planted over two years earlier when the Beatles, as well as the great jazz saxophonist John Coltrane, began infusing their compositions with the message that love was a universal power capable of saving mankind.

Romantic standards like "My One and Only Love" and "Nancy with the Laughing Face" would soon slip from Coltrane's set list as he began shifting his focus from the adoration of women to the love of God, singing the praises of the Creator with the deep, rich tone of his tenor saxophone.

"He [Coltrane] had gone through a spiritual change and he was praising God," the Byrds' Roger McGuinn told author Ashley Kahn. "And I was going through a similar kind of thing at the time, so I could relate to it."

"Thought waves, heat waves, all vibrations all paths lead to God," Coltrane reflected in his prayer/poem titled "A Love Supreme" (released in February 1965). "One thought can produce millions of vibrations and they all go back to God—everything does," he wrote. Considered one of the greatest jazz albums of all-time, *A Love Supreme* was recorded during one session on December 9, 1964.

"I think *A Love Supreme* attracted [the hippies] because it wasn't specific, it was not trying to shove a particular religion down your throat," McGuinn explained. "It gave people the opportunity to experience spirituality on a general level." Having overcome heroin addiction, Coltrane purified his spirit by pursuing "peace, love and perfection in everything."

Paul McCartney would later cite Coltrane's friend, the free jazz saxophonist/ sonic alchemist Albert Ayler's album *Spiritual Unity* as an influence. While not an obvious inspiration, perhaps, Ayler's radical style egged the band on to create some of their wilder moments like the swirling ending of "A Day in the Life," or the sonic mash-up of "I Am the Walrus," or the eight-minute, unedited version of George Harrison's overlooked psychedelic opus "It's All Too Much." Ayler's wailing horn and song titles like "Music Is the Healing Force of the Universe" spelled out his spiritual mission loud and clear for all to hear, including John Coltrane. For better or worse, Ayler, along with Pharaoh Sanders and Ornette Coleman, inspired Coltrane to abandon traditional structures of melody and rhythm and play free extended jams of strange, unrecognizable music that challenged and ultimately alienated a large portion of his audience, who suddenly dismissed his new spiritually based music as noisy, aggressive, and militant.

"We had one message for the world," said Paul. "Love. We need more love in the world." While millions ate it up with a paisley spoon, it came as no surprise that musical genius and grand cynic Frank Zappa wasn't buying it.

"There are more love songs than anything else. If songs could make you do something, we'd all love one another," he countered. Zappa's crew of enfants terribles, the Mothers of Invention, would release *We're Only in It for the Money* in 1968, with a cover shot that took aim not only at the Beatles' *Sgt. Pepper* (supposedly Zappa was aggravated by McCartney for "stealing his mustache") but at the flourishing hippie culture in general, with songs like "Flower Punk" and "Concentration Moon," in which Frank jokingly (he *was* joking, right?) offered "the final solution" for the growing hordes of long-haired "creeps" who were suddenly sprouting up from coast to coast.

A simple message demands a basic, uncomplicated melody and arrangement to help get it across. The best examples are often found in folk and gospel music. A song like "Oh Happy Day" by the Edwin Hawkins Singers (which inspired George Harrison to write "My Sweet Lord") conveys feeling with only a few words (repetitive as the song might be) while driving it into your consciousness with a tune you can't forget.

"To write a good song with just one note in it, like [Little Richard's] 'Long Tall Sally' is really very hard to do," McCartney pointed out. "It's the kind of thing we wanted to do for some time. We get near it in 'The Word.'" Whether he was joking or not when he called "Love Me Do" their "greatest philosophical song," McCartney's point behind the remark was earnest. "For [a song] to be simple and true means that it's incredibly simple."

The session began at 9 p.m. on November 10 and ran until four the next morning, beginning with the basic tracks to "The Word," with Paul on upright piano, John chopping tight, chunky chords on his Fender Stratocaster, and Ringo on drums.

McCARTNEY'S PIANO

"THE WORD" KICKS OFF with the loose, funky feel of McCartney's piano, his fingers tripping over one another, as if falling through a door in a slapstick routine. Although one of the finest and most inventive bass players in rock, Paul's keyboard work has not garnered nearly as much attention, being most often employed over the years to carry his classic ballads like "Long and Winding Road," "Let It Be," "Hey Jude," and later "Maybe I'm Amazed" (the original power ballad?). In tunes like "Penny Lane," McCartney's comping (a slightly clunky, yet immediately identifiable style) provides a simple, solid foundation that allows his voice to smoothly glide over the song's chords. On "The Word," Paul's rolling triplets reveal the influence of New Orleans piano master Huey Smith, whose rollicking "Rockin' Pneumonia" packed a punchy backbeat that may very well have influenced "The Word."

Paul would look to the Crescent City once more for inspiration in February 1968, when he hammered the eighty-eights (actually double-tracked) on "Lady Madonna" in an obvious imitation of Fats Domino (in fact, "the Fat Man" himself recorded Paul's hit song in 1968, though his version barely grazed the charts at number 100). The 2012 reissue of McCartney's *Ram* included an obscure outtake titled "Little Woman Love," built on a syncopated piano riff attributed to the legendary the King of the Mardi Gras, Professor Longhair. In March,1975, McCartney would hire "Fess" to play a party that he and Linda threw on the *Queen Mary*, in Long Beach, California. A fine live album of the performance was recorded and released that included many of Fess's standards, among them "Tipitina," "Stagger Lee," and "Mess Around."

With basic tracks completed on the third take, overdubs were immediately added, with Lennon double-tracking his lead vocal and McCartney and Harrison singing backup harmonies, while Starr briskly shook a pair of maracas and George Martin played long, dark, sustained chords on the harmonium.

Unhappy with the way his bass was getting lost in the mix, Paul began overdubbing his parts, giving the instrument more presence and bringing it to a new prominence in the music (as would Brian Wilson and John Entwistle of the Who). While George laid down his lead guitar part, Paul added an additional falsetto vocal track, stacking the Beatles' ethereal harmonies to the heavens.

Despite a pressing deadline to crank out new product for the

Christmas season, *Rubber Soul* represents a significant period of invention and playfulness for Lennon and McCartney, whose creative partnership (whether writing together or separately) was in full bloom at the time. After firing up a joint, John and Paul broke out a box of crayons and, like a pair of stoned schoolkids, began doodling a brightly colored lyric sheet of their latest song. Although they were now getting high on a regular basis (according to Ringo, the Beatles, by this point, were "smoking pot for breakfast"), the Beatles usually preferred to work straight, whether onstage, in the studio or while writing together, as pot, as Paul later told Barry Miles, only "got in the way of songwriting because it would just cloud your mind up."

The lyric sheet was later purloined by Yoko Ono, who, having recently arrived in London, came to Paul's house one day hoping to secure a musical score as part of a project she was curating for the avant-garde composer John Cage's fiftieth birthday. While Paul refused, John presented her with the cosmic crayon doodles that illustrate "The Word," and that were later reproduced in Cage's *Notations*. It is interesting to note that John Cage actually turned fifty in 1962, and "The Word" wasn't written until the fall of 1965. What exactly Ono was doing collecting a body of work in honor of Cage's birthday three years after the fact is unclear, but somehow fitting in light of her various dadaist art concepts.

Incidentally, the *Beatles* cartoon based on "The Word" (episode 31 from the second season) finds the lads "in the middle of the Egyptian desert."

THE BEATLES CARTOON SHOW

RUNNING FROM SEPTEMBER 1965 through September 1969, *The Beatles* was the first cartoon series based on the lives of actual people. It's easy to understand why John, Paul, George, and Ringo were less than thrilled about a cartoon portrayal of the band based on the stereotypes created for *A Hard Day's Night*. But once again Brian Epstein knew be$t, and every Saturday morning at ten-thirty the Fab Four could be seen in all their animated glory—John, the lazy wise-guy leader of the pack; Paul, charming, optimistic, and sincere; George, skeptical, witty, and cultured; and Ringo, somewhat dumb, frequently unlucky, but always lovable. The cartoon's action usually revolved around Ringo, who blamed his ongoing series of misadventures on the fact that his "mother dropped him as a baby." A cartoon Brian Epstein made just a few appearances.

The cartoon Beatles' endless tour took them from Egypt to Hollywood, from India to Transylvania, from Texas to Spain, where they met a plethora of monsters, tribal leaders, and desirous young women. The plots were idiotic, of course. It was a cartoon, after all. But any excuse to hear the Beatles was enough to make you switch on the TV for half an hour every Saturday morning (no matter how old or stoned you were) while you ate your cereal.

All told, there were thirty-nine episodes of *The Beatles* (nine of which were based on songs cut for during the *Rubber Soul* sessions). In 1972 (perhaps in a moment of nostalgia coming two years after the band's breakup), John confessed that "I still get a blast out of watching the Beatles' cartoons on TV."

Years later, in 1999, George admitted he "always kind of liked [the cartoons]. They were so bad or silly that they were good. And I think the passage of time might make them more fun now."

Whether life inspires cartoons or cartoons inspires life, it should be noted that both McCartney's second group, Wings, and the Archies (who "featured" two girl singers while Wings only had Linda) had more than sweet, chewy music in common. At one point both "bands" included session guitarist Hugh McCracken, who not only ghost-picked all of the Archies' fabulous lead guitar parts, but also added some tasty riffs on Paul and Linda's first jointly credited album, *Ram*.

After suddenly coming across a sinister sheik's "harem of beautiful girls" who've removed their veils in order to get a better look at the band, the Beatles are to be thrown to the crocodiles (in a desert? Hey, it's a cartoon!) for the crime of having gazed upon the women's lovely uncovered faces. Before the lads are devoured, the girls plead with their master to "let them play one song." The only thing that can save the Beatles from impending doom is to say "The Word" love, creating the premise for the cartoon. While a pair of the prettiest girls can't resist John and Paul, the most plump of the three chases George up a tentpole, while the camel falls head over hump for Ringo. The enchanted dromedary, it turns out, is actually a Trojan horse, filled with French Foreign Legion soldiers who have come to rescue the boys (did I mention it's a cartoon?!). Following a sixties-style action-packed sequence reminiscent of the TV show *Batman*, the Beatles break free and frantically flee across the desert. Despite containing every stale cliché about Bedouin people (the evil sheik actually speaks in a Russian accent rather than with an Arabic inflection), the cartoon, within its mindless antics, contains the simple moral that love, even in the animated realm, will always win the day.

RUBBER COVERS: "THE WORD"

Sixties lounge jazz duo Jackie and Roy's kitschy/cool cover of "The Word" is simply nothing short of "groovy." Jackie Cain sings with shimmering blonde locks and white lipstick while Roy Kral hammers out a Ray Charles–inspired electric-piano vamp that sounds like it might have inspired the Doors' "Riders on the Storm."

Austin, Texas's motley psychedelic garage rockers the 13th Floor Elevators performed and recorded a swirling, off-kilter version of Lennon's love anthem at San Francisco's Avalon Ballroom in September 1966. The band's front man, singer/guitarist Roky Erickson (who was diagnosed as a paranoid schizophrenic and was institutionalized between 1969 and 1972), an outspoken proponent of LSD, sounds as if he's hallucinating paisley pythons as he sings in nervous fits and starts (a style that later worked wonders for Talking Heads' David Byrne in the late seventies and early eighties).

Giving the song a cool, alienated feel (just this side of Devo) is the longtime New York performance ensemble the Blue Man Group. Blending elements of experimental theater (after all, their skin is blue and they have no ears!) and modern composition, the trio perform a funky version of "The Word," driven by drums, a clunky homemade PC-pipe marimba, a chiming hammer dulcimer, and a dollop of electric keyboards. The song's accompanying video, filmed at New Jersey's Turtle Back Zoo, is both fun and arty.

23

"You Won't See Me"

"I haven't broken it off, but it is broken off, finished."
—Jane Asher announcing the end of her engagement to Paul,
July 20, 1968

Jane Asher was just seventeen (as Paul sang in "I Saw Her Standing There") and still living at her family home on Wimpole Street when she met Paul McCartney. The sister of folksinger Peter Asher, of Peter and Gordon fame, Jane interviewed Paul for *Radio Times* on April 18, 1963, when, according to Pattie Harrison, "they fell in love at first sight." McCartney was not simply Jane's famous lover—he made many of the decisions in the relationship, including what clothes she wore and where they vacationed. But by the time Jane turned the corner on age twenty, her independence started becoming an issue for Paul.

Although McCartney claimed that he and Jane had "a perfectly open relationship," as he described it, it was only true from his side of the fence. While Asher's work as an actor took her out of town, McCartney maintained an ongoing relationship with Maggie McGivern, John Dunbar and Marianne Faithfull's nanny, and the pair were known to have met for trysts in Paris. The Fabs, like most of the baby-boomer generation, were a rather chauvinist lot, certainly throughout most of the sixties. Although they learned to talk the talk of liberation, they found walking the walk of true male/female equality much more challenging than previously imagined.

Artist Jann Haworth, wife of Peter Blake (the pair are best known for their album cover design for *Sergeant Pepper*), described Jane as a "very calm person," and "a wonderful balance for [Paul]" throughout the madness of Beatlemania. But while the Beatles were recording *Rubber Soul*, Jane decided to move to Bristol, to appear in the Old Vic's production of John Dighton's *The Happiest Days of Our Lives*, the play's title ironic, considering that her decision to take this role wound up causing the couple nothing but misery. Her absence put a terrible strain on their relationship, which finally came apart in July 1968.

In "You Won't See Me," a frustrated McCartney, after failing to get through to his lover, tells her to "act your age."

"You Won't See Me" features a tight Starr and McCartney rhythm section with an irresistibly punchy groove. Paul's bass part, as he later described it, was "very Motown flavored," inspired by the great session player James Jamerson. Jamerson was the "fabulous" (Paul's words) in-house bassist on many of Motown's great recordings, including the Temptations' "My Girl," the Four Tops' "Reach Out and I'll Be There," and Stevie Wonder's "For Once in My Life," to name a few. His feel and melodic approach to his instrument were not only unique but influenced both McCartney and the Beach Boys' Brian Wilson.

McCartney attributed the songwriting credit to "100 percent me as I recall, but I am always quite happy to give John a credit because there's always a chance that on the session he might have said, 'That'd be better.'"

Lennon, it turns out, did very little on the song other than shake a tambourine and add harmony vocals. One of the most curious credits on *Rubber Soul* goes to Mal "Organ" Evans, who allegedly held down one note on a Hammond organ as the song slowly fades. It's a subtle touch—barely audible, in fact. Beatles scholar Mark Lewisohn is adamant that Evans' cameo is undetectable. The credit is ultimately a tip of the hat to Mal (who briefly appears as a swimmer in *Help!* when he momentarily pops his head out of a hole in frozen lake to ask directions). The Beatles were always rather tight when it came to acknowledging outside musicians who contributed to their albums, as Eric Clapton discovered after playing a deeply emotive solo to George's "While My Guitar Gently Weeps."

"You Won't See Me" was also the longest record in the Beatles' canon up to this point. In contrast to Dylan, whose "Like a Rolling Stone" clocked in at over six minutes in order to accommodate his rambling poetic verse, the Fabs (along with the song's protagonist—Paul, in this case) just seem reluctant to let a good thing go. "Breaking Up Is Hard to Do," as Neil Sedaka once sang, but when that difficult time arrives, "You Won't See Me" should have you dancing out the door.

RUBBER COVERS: "YOU WON'T SEE ME"

While the Bee Gees' 1966 version of McCartney's funky breakup number is worth noting for being more nasal than the original, the honor for the most bizarre interpretation of a Fab Four song goes to the New York experimental psychedelic folk-rock band the Godz, whose 1967 recording of "You Won't See Me," was sung out of tune (whether intentionally or not) over a sparse harmonium and a pair of chattering maracas.

Once more Bryan Ferry leaned on the Beatles, recording "You Won't See Me" for his 1973 release *These Foolish Things*. As on the original recording, the upbeat music seems to contradict the troubled lyrics. As Ferry sings, "The days are few and filled with tears," over a punchy barrelhouse piano, Phil Manzanera steals the show with a soaring guitar solo.

Despite its slick production and soaring violins, there are a few funky moments on Anne Murray's poppy rendition of "You Won't See Me" including a growling fuzz bass, a rocking piano, and a soul choir laying down a coda of doo-doo-doo-doos. Murray's version peaked at number eight on the *Billboard* charts in the summer of 1974, and Lennon allegedly loved it, claiming it was one of his all-time favorite Beatle covers.

When Helmut Köllen sang, "I will lose my mind," on a surprisingly gentle, haunting rendition of the song, he sounded like he wasn't joking. The former bassist of the German prog-rock band Triumvirat, who died in May 1977, six months after recording it, at age twenty-seven, Köllen turned "You Won't See Me" into a ghostly suicide note. The string arrangement on the coda takes the melody to some dark, unexpected places as it fades to black.

McCartney came back to reclaim "You Won't See Me" thirty-nine years later, during his 2004 summer tour, casually confiding to a sea of faces at the Palace Square in St. Petersburg, Russia, "Sometimes you make a song and you finish recording it and mix it, maybe that's the last time you ever sing it." A moment later Sir Paul (on left-handed Les Paul) and his band broke into the third track from *Rubber Soul* as the crowd joyously bounced along to the song's funky chugging rhythm.

24

"Girl"

"A Bond girl must be a strong and independent woman,
but at the same time charming and sensual.
Those opposite qualities combined together make her interesting.
She must be strong but at the same time feminine."
—Olga Kurylenko

Before the world had ever heard of the Beatles, Stu Sutcliffe, not John Lennon, was the cool guy in the band. Although he'd taken only a few piano lessons and briefly dabbled with the bugle, Stu never actually learned to play an instrument. He was first and foremost a visual artist. His true passion was abstract expressionism but he dug rock 'n' roll enough to give the bass a go.

In the early days of rock, the guy with the least amount of talent and ability was routinely handed the bass and told to go stand in the back and keep the volume down while he fumbled around with the instrument long enough to figure out how to play it. McCartney, a perfectionist of the first order, known for pushing his mates to the brink of fisticuffs over musical details, soon became impatient and indignant over Sutcliffe's halfhearted amateurism. When Stu finally quit the band in July 1961 to concentrate on his painting, Paul dutifully took up the bass, as neither Lennon nor Harrison was up for the task.

"None of us wanted to be the bass player," Paul later confessed. "In our minds he was the fat guy who always played in the back." McCartney would certainly help change that image.

It is much easier to strum chords on a guitar and sing than to lay down a solid bottom while trying to put a song across. Beyond McCartney, there have only been a handful of great bassists who could handle such a chore and make it look easy—Brian Wilson, Jack Bruce, Rick Danko, Larry Graham, Phil Lynott, Lemmy Kilmister, and Sting—and the moment their respective bands fell apart, most of them moved to the piano or the six-string.

Stu and John had been pals since their days together at the Liverpool College of Art. While everyone in the band competed for Lennon's attention and approval, it was Stu who John admired most.

While John spent his time copping Chuck Berry riffs and filling notebooks with whimsical doodles and nonsensical verse, Stu regularly wrestled with weightier issues of composition and color. Beyond the brilliance of his canvases, Sutcliffe possessed something Lennon coveted more than anything else: Astrid Kirchherr. John didn't exactly desire Astrid, but admired what she represented—a cool, stylish girl with an all-consuming passion for life and art.

Lennon had already begun to grow bored with his bandmates, as well as with his young wife, Cynthia Powell, whom he had quietly married in August 1962 after she became pregnant with Julian. John dreamed of a girl he could collaborate with *and* make love to. Someone who he felt was "in [his] tree," as he would later sing in "Strawberry Fields Forever."

Given that Astrid was a German girl, and that World War II was less than twenty years previous, she seemed not only exotic, but somewhat taboo as well. Exchanging engagement rings in November 1960, Stu and Astrid couldn't have cared less when the boys snickered as they shared clothes or when she combed his chestnut-brown pompadour down into that silly pudding-bowl hairdo. All the while, Sutcliffe was unwittingly planting seeds in Lennon's mind as to what to look for in an ideal partner.

It would be a few more years before Yoko Ono arrived on the scene. On November 9, 1966, John was invited by Marianne Faithfull's then husband John Dunbar to the Indica Gallery to view the work of a strange, shy Japanese conceptual artist. Initially unimpressed, Lennon found himself atop a ladder, peering through a magnifying glass at the word *yes* printed on the ceiling above his head, and enthralled by Yoko's Zen-like nature. In the meantime, Cynthia was away on vacation, and John, bored to death in the suburbs, invited Yoko up to their Weybridge mansion one night to record a series of experimental tapes (which later became the *Two Virgins* album for which they posed together in the buff for its "pornographic" cover). As the sun rose that morning, they made love.

Overnight John dumped his wife of four years, along with his young son, from whom he would remain estranged for the rest of his life. Cynthia soon returned home to find Yoko traipsing about the house in her bathrobe.

The first Mrs. Lennon received very little sympathy from the public or the press as she was unceremoniously brushed aside. As far as Beatles fans were concerned, no one, other than perhaps Brigitte Bardot, would have been "good enough" for John. (Lennon had been infatuated with the pouty-mouthed French sex symbol, whom Cynthia tried her best to physically resemble. Lennon and Bardot actually met in May 1968, under terribly awkward circumstances. Not surprisingly, they had very little in common, as she spoke only French and John knew nothing but English. "It was a terrible night," Lennon later confessed, "worse than meeting Elvis.")

Falling head over heels for a petite, peculiar Japanese woman didn't win John any points with the public. Lennon's affair and subsequent marriage to Yoko seemed to simultaneously stir up resentment while heralding the end of the world's love affair with the Fab Four.

Lennon undoubtedly had crossed some sort of invisible line when he shacked up with "that Jap tart," as McCartney allegedly called Yoko while she and John were staying at Paul's Cavendish pad. Even before we had gotten an earful of Yoko's bizarre insect caterwauling, she'd already been branded "ugly" by the media. To begin with, she was seven years older than John, previously married, with a daughter and . . . Japanese. The brutal treatment that captured British soldiers received at the hands of the Japanese during World War II had not been forgotten by the older generation. That John Lennon, who already got a kick out of pushing the public's buttons, was now enthralled with a samurai's granddaughter did little to assuage his notoriety.

Ono's impact on Lennon seems to have been greater and more immediate than his influence over her. While her physical appearance seemed to barely change over the years, at least until Lennon's murder in December 1980, John, who was always something of a chameleon, began to part his hair down the middle in the style of his Japanese lover's, and began dressing in all-black or all-white outfits, as was Yoko's custom.

In their early days, John and Paul immortalized all sorts of girls in song, but none had been quite like this. "Girl" begins with Lennon lamenting over a minor chord. "Is there anybody going to listen to my story?" John pleads, his reedy voice brims with sorrow and regret. He sounds hopeless, like the type of fellow you'd do your best to avoid at a bar or stumbling down the street alone at night, forlorn, under a dark spell, begging, not for spare change, but for a kind word that might somehow ease his tortured mind. Despite his appeals and apologies, Lennon's ideal woman remains aloof. She is beyond cool. She is cold. But what kind of man would desire a woman who can't take a compliment, and in turn "puts you down when friends are there?"

The Mississippi-born jazz and blues/pianist/singer Mose Allison often tells a story about a college professor he knew who studied the Hopi Indians of the American Southwest. He found it strange that most Hopi music revolved around the theme of water. When he asked a Native American musician about it, the Indian explained, "We only sing about what we lack. Most of your music," he observed, "is about love."

With "Girl" the Beatles had come a long way since the bobble-headed exuberance of "Thank You Girl," written just two years earlier, and sung in appreciation of the constant flood of letters written by their female fans. This "Girl" was an altogether a different creature.

HITCHCOCK, BOND, AND THE BEATLES

BEAT GROUPS WERE ONLY PART of the British Invasion—the Beatles' road to success in America had already been paved thanks to the snuffling "Master of Suspense," Alfred Hitchcock, who had moved to Hollywood in 1939 and would produce his own weekly TV show. Yanks became enamored with his British accent and unusually dry sense of humor. Beyond his macabre skits, Hitchcock would appear unceremoniously before the camera to provide hilarious commentary on the foibles of his characters while taking pot shots at his sponsors. In addition to the Beatles and Hitchcock, James Bond films had done more to promote British culture (despite the fact that Sean Connery was a Scot) than anyone since William Shakespeare. The invention of the best-selling author Ian Fleming, 007, with his high-tech gadgetry and irresistible pickup lines, was the epitome of cool.

On the surface, *Help!* had seemed like just another light-hearted romp with the Beatles, only this time in color and filled with campy references to James Bond films (the other main component of the British Invasion).

But despite all the exotic locations, cartoonish ad guys, and the gorgeous "double agent" Eleanor Bron (who was rumored to have been amongst John's many extramarital affairs), the Beatles' new songs, John's in particular, revealed a creeping sense of insecurity. It wasn't just bejeweled Ringo who needed saving from some bizarre Kali-worshiping cult, but Lennon, growing fat and wallowing in the London suburbs, who was desperately seeking a way out before he wound up bored to death.

Inspiration soon arrived in the form of a new record that Paul played for his mates, called *The Freewheelin' Bob Dylan*. Lennon and Harrison were both stunned by Bob's rough sound and his uncanny ability to articulate his every emotion, whether through poignant protest songs like "Blowin' in the Wind," and "Masters of War," or the deliberately unsentimental breakup ballad "Don't Think Twice."

Although Bob was the first folksinger to sign to a major label, he was nearly dropped by Columbia Records, who couldn't see what visionary producer John Hammond (responsible for signing the likes of Billie Holiday, Count Basie, and Pete Seeger) already knew. Branded "Hammond's Folly," Dylan's debut (which contained few original compositions) initially sold poorly, failing to graze the *Billboard* charts. Yet it contained a raw rendition of "House of the Rising Sun," a smoldering dirge previously recorded by both Woody Guthrie and Lead Belly, which he pinched from legendary Greenwich Village folksinger Dave Van Ronk, that would soon hit number one after being overhauled by the Animals.

Bob Dylan's impact on John Lennon was incalculable. With the exception of Elvis and Smokey Robinson, no other American musician had inspired him so completely. Catching Bob live for the first time at the Royal Albert Hall in the fall of 1964 was an instant game changer for both Lennon and McCartney. They were both knocked out by his stark lyrics, his weary, scratchy voice, and his solid guitar chops, which inspired John to lay down his Rickenbacker Capri and delve more into the acoustic guitar, and more into the darker recesses of love relations and romance.

Lennon had already played the harmonica before discovering Dylan, laying down simple wailing blues riffs on the Beatles' 1962 single "Love Me Do." John had gleaned some pointers from Texas R&B singer Delbert McClinton, who'd earlier toured England in 1962 with Bruce Channel after blowing harp on his chart-topping hit "Hey Baby." George Martin claimed Lennon's wailing harmonica "had a definite appeal" and reminded him of Sonny Terry and Brownie McGhee records.

With "Girl," a creeping unease began to haunt the moptops' music. The relationship in the song is far more complex than anything they'd previously sung of, revealing traces of sadomasochism. It's clear who is in control here. Although the singer is in pain to the point of being distraught, he continues to justify his lover's every cruelty.

Before Yoko Ono burst into his life, John Lennon, by his own admission, had been very tough on his former girlfriends. His songs were filled with ultimatums. With "You Can't Do That," John laid down specific boundaries for his flirty bird who'd been seen chatting up some other guy. But behind his gnawing insecurity, it seems that the protagonist was more afraid of losing face than of losing his lover. With "Girl," the lovers, distant as they seem, are bound together by some unhealthy force. As George Harrison sang in the Beatles' earlier cover of Goffin and King's "Chains," "they're the kind that you just can't see."

Recorded during the last session for *Rubber Soul* on November 11, "Girl" was one of the album's most sophisticated songs both lyrically and musically. (While some have credited George's exotic guitar break as him playing sitar that is clearly not the case.) But in some ways "Girl" was not unique. Many sixties soul classics, like "Nowhere to Run" and "You Really Got a Hold on Me," portray a similar dynamic, where the singer struggles to escape the clutches of a lover who pervades his heart and mind to the point of obsession. Roy Orbison was one of the first men in rock (beyond Johnnie Ray, who was famous for pulling out his hair and feigning emotional breakdowns on stage) to openly wear his heart on his sleeve. For Roy, love rarely (at least until his later years) meant a happy, healthy balance. Most often it seemed he was deeply tormented by the object of his desire. Orbison's lyrics often revealed complex dark relationships that read more like a psychiatrist's casebook than like the average pop song. This "Girl" only torments the singer, playing with his emotions like toys. In the end he is imprisoned by his desire for her. Happy (perhaps) to remain tortured by some, aloof, unobtainable ideal.

As far as California singer/songwriter Jackson Browne was concerned, the Beatles had "hit the nail on the head" with "Girl," which "embodied the feelings [he] was living every day, completely burning with sexual desire, with almost a regret at being so overpowered."

In "Devil Woman," the great jazz bassist Charles Mingus (who claimed he heard the sound of "little marching men" in the Beatles' chart topper "Eight Days a Week") snarls and shouts, "I got a devil woman 'cause angel women don't mean me no good." While Lennon's dilemma in "Girl" was not so clearly defined, John claimed the song was actually inspired by his feelings about the Catholic Church and its concept that one must suffer before deserving any form of pleasure, a notion that Lennon flatly opposed.

John would later claim that the song's object of desire was Yoko Ono, only he hadn't met her yet. If that was indeed the case, his comment may shed more light on the true dynamic of their relationship than all of the performance art and cuddling they did in the name of peace.

As a young man, Lennon was something of a tough guy; a blue-jeaned, leather-clad teddy boy, more smart-ass than street fighter. As he was inspired to sing years later on his first solo release, *Plastic Ono Band*, his parents "didn't want me, so they made me a star." Not that they had raised him to be a child star of the stage or movies, but the Lennons fueled their son's enormous need for attention by first ignoring him, and then deserting him at a tender age. While John's father, Freddie, was a no-account seaman who had abandoned the family soon after

John was born, his mother, Julia, was too unstable to raise the child alone, and left the boy under the strict care of her sister Mimi. Julia was soon struck by a car and killed, leaving her son emotionally devastated. It seems that John Lennon had plenty of reasons to sing about love. Although he often dressed his songs with imagist poetry that rivaled that of Lewis Carroll, there was a deep sense of unfulfilled yearning in Lennon's lyrics that remained, right up through his last hit, "Starting Over."

Although "Girl" had originally been John's idea, McCartney claimed the song wasn't "fully finished" when he first heard it. According to Paul, it was Sam Cooke's 1960 hit "Chain Gang" that inspired such distinctly out-of-character phrases as "was she told when she was young that pain would lead to pleasure" and "a man must break his back to earn his day of leisure."

While the verse was moaned like an intimate confession, John's voice punctuates the chorus with a sharp, percussive in-breath (thanks to a compressor employed by engineer Norman Smith) that slices through the air like a radiator letting off steam. And then there's the matter of the background vocals. . . .

"It was always amusing to see if we could get a naughty word on the record," Paul told author Barry Miles, referring to the line from "Penny Lane" about "fish and finger pie," a euphemism for getting to "third base" with a girl. The original version of "Day Tripper" was said to contain the line "prick teaser," which was quickly (and understandably) replaced by "big teaser" as it was certain to have been banned off the radio if it happened to miraculously slip by George Martin or the watchdogs at EMI. Then there's the "tit tit tit tit" of "Girl."

"The Beach Boys," Paul told Miles, "had a song out where they'd done 'la la la la' and we loved the innocence of that and wanted to copy it, but not use the same phrase. So we were looking around for another phrase, so it was 'dit dit dit dit,' which we decided to change in our waggishness to 'tit tit tit tit,' which is virtually indistinguishable from 'dit dit dit dit' . . . If we could put in something that was a little bit subversive then we would," McCartney laughed. Even the well-respected critic Greil Marcus claimed that McCartney had snuck in a bit of profanity when he shouted "One-two-three-fuck!" in his passionate count-off to "I Saw Her Standing There."

Recorded during the last all-night session for *Rubber Soul*, which began at around 6 p.m. on November 11 and finally wound down at 7 a.m. the next morning, "Girl" was one of the album's most sophisticated tracks, both lyrically and musically. Although the old-world European melody at the end of the tune was written by Paul, (whether inspired during his vacation to Greece with Jane Asher, two years earlier, or by Mikis Theodorakis's enormously popular soundtrack to *Zorba the Greek*), there is some dispute as to whether George actually played it on a bouzouki or a twelve-string guitar. George Martin claimed Harrison picked the melody on the double-stringed, bowl-backed lute that he was given as a present on a recent trip to the Mediterranean, while McCartney recalled that he and George "just did it on acoustic guitars."

Paul would turn a similar old-world minor-key melody to gold in August 1968, when he produced Mary Hopkin singing "Dorogoi Dlinnoyu," a Russian folk song from the 1920s better known in the West as "Those Were the Days."

RUBBER COVERS: "GIRL"

In January 1966, the British pop group St. Louis Union recorded a lumbering soft-shoe version of "Girl," complete with melodramatic vocals and an uninspired saxophone solo. Sadly, this rather dull remake garnered considerable radio play, climbing to number eleven on the UK charts while at the same time an obscure mod duo from north London (Frank Aiello and Steve Jameson) with the unfortunate name of the Truth cut arguably the best cover of the song as a single for Pye Records. The Truth's interpretation (which features a righteous rendition of Bobby Darin's classic torch song "Jailer Bring Me Water" on the flip side) teems with teen angst and desperation, while a skillfully played harpsichord and tight string section add an air of baroque sophistication to the track.

It was inevitable that someone would deliver Lennon's biting lyric in the husky-voiced cabaret style reminiscent of Marlene Dietrich. In 1967 Mezzo-soprano Cathy Berberian would cut an entire album titled *Beatles Arias*, with a rendition of "Girl." Her version features a baroque harpsichord and swirling string quartet. Although nowhere as sultry as Dietrich or cerebral as

Lotte Lenya, Berberian brings out the Kurt Weill/Bertolt Brecht influence that lies at the heart of the song's eerie melody and disturbed verse.

With its old-world sound, "Girl" instantly appealed to singers across Europe and around the world, from Polish vocalist Halina Kunicka to Brazilian pop star Ronnie Von. Von recorded the vibrato soaked "Meu bem" in 1966, which could only be improved upon with a rhapsodic reading by the vivacious Italian songbird Dalida, whose "Amo," appeared on her 1967 album *Piccolo Ragazzo*. That same year, "the French Elvis" Johnny Hallyday sang "Je l'aime," complete with a noir-style accordion and a twelve-string guitar doing a fine imitation of a bouzouki on the song's bridge, transforming it into the 2/4 dance rhythm known in Greece as the hasapiko.

In an uncharacteristically deep voice, Tiny Tim, backed by the wacky Texas polka band Brave Combo, delivered a regretful reading of "Girl" in 1996. Ad-libbing over a mournful horn solo, the uniquely freaky singer begs dejectedly, "Why don't you understand? . . . Why am I wasting time?"

Echoes of Gershwin's "Summertime" reverberate through Joe Jackson's cover of "Girl." Jackson, who performs the song solo on piano with a powerful pounding left hand, breaks into a sultry tango that replaces the Greek sirtaki section. Joe's "Girl" appeared as a bonus track of his 2004 live album *Afterlife*.

25
After Geography

"If anything is left, we have left really good music.
And that's the important part, not the mop-tops or whatever."
—Ringo Starr

Famous for his quirky sense of humor, Ringo Starr suggested the ludicrous title *After Geography* for the title of the Beatles' next album (*Revolver*), to take the piss out of the Rolling Stones' latest album, *Aftermath*. The Stones were accused of routinely imitating the Fabs throughout the sixties, most often and vociferously by Lennon, who even sang about Mick and Keith's lack of originality in the nonsensical "I Dig a Pony."

While *Aftermath* actually bore little resemblance to *Rubber Soul*, beyond the occasional strains of baroque music in "Lady Jane" and Brian Jones's rocking sitar riff on "Paint It Black" (the lead-off number from the American release), their next two albums, *Between the Buttons* and *Their Satanic Majesties' Request* (their record sleeves in particular!) followed closely in the footsteps of the Beatles' latest ideas and innovations.

"They seemed to be paying too much attention to what we were doing," McCartney diplomatically told *Uncut* magazine in 2004, pointing out that *Satanic Majesties* was "their direct answer to *Pepper*. In that way, they took their lead from us."

With the release of *Revolver* in August 1966, it was clear the Beatles had taken control of their art, not just in terms of their songwriting, but in the way they'd begun to use the recording studio as well. The band had thrown the gauntlet down with *Rubber Soul*, opening a new world of possibility by adding a surprising array of instruments previously unheard of in rock 'n' roll (including sitar, harpsichord, and harmonium) and now, with *Revolver*, they took things a step further, not only in adding punchy brass to the mix (as in Paul's "Good Day Sunshine") but by stretching the capabilities of the recording studio by varying tape speeds and even playing their music backward, as on the coda to "Rain," in which John seemed to sing in a mystical gibberish. Most strikingly, their playful sound manipulations would lead George Harrison to meticulously fashion the exquisite "backward" guitar solo on Lennon's lazy/hazy "I'm Only Sleeping"

Whether they titled it *Beatles on Safari*, *The Magic Circle*, *Abracadabra*, or *After Geography*, *Revolver*—their seventh studio recording—showed the Beatles expanding on the concepts and themes of *Rubber Soul*. The funky soul vamp of "Drive My Car" echoed throughout *Revolver's* opening track, George Harrison's "Taxman," while Paul dug deeper into classical music with the elegant "Eleanor Rigby," which featured a double string quartet comprised of first violinist Tony Gilbert with three additional violinists—Sidney Sax, John Sharpe, and Jurgen Hess. The octet was rounded out by two violists, Stephan Shingles and John Underwood, and a pair of cellists, Norman Jones and Derek Simpson.

Harrison, who had previously thrown the door to the East open with his sitar on "Norwegian Wood," now sang "Love You To," backed by a band comprised solely of Indian musicians, without any help from his bandmates, either vocally or instrumentally.

Following "Rain" (the B-side to "Paperback Writer," McCartney's most recent hit single in June of '66), John seemed to have fallen down the rabbit hole into a netherworld of altered consciousness, writing "I'm Only Sleeping" and "And Your Bird Can Sing" (both of which were cut from the American release of *Revolver*, seriously compromising Lennon's contribution to the album). A psychedelic soup of a song built off the mesmerizing drone of Harrison's sitar, "Tomorrow Never Knows" featured a wash of sound effects, including snippets of McCartney's avant-garde home recordings, in which his laughter morphed into seagull squawks. Lennon had instructed George Martin to make his voice sound like the disembodied voice of the Dali Lama echoing across the Himalayas as he enticed everyone to "surrender to the void."

With "Here There and Everywhere," Paul continued to write and sing first-rate romantic ballads in the mold of "Yesterday" and "Michelle." Although a perfect vehicle for the band's pristine harmonies, the song seemed like a throwback amid an album brimming with innovation.

The songs of loss and sorrow that McCartney had composed about his troubled relationship with Jane Asher had now reached devastatingly new depths with "For No One." Originally titled "Why Did It Die," "For No One" was a stunning ballad about the existential emptiness one feels following the demise of a relationship. Following up where George Martin had left off with his "harpsichord" solo on "In My Life," Paul continued adding baroque touches to his songs, employing England's top French horn player, Alan Civil, to play a plaintive passage on the song's bridge.

At the same time, the album's single, "Yellow Submarine," revealed a new level of playfulness with its Spike Jones–inspired sound effects created by the Beatles and a gaggle of friends (including Brian Jones and Marianne Faithfull) who sound happily adrift "sea of green."

With *Rubber Soul* just six months behind them, there was no turning back. Never again would the Beatles crank out raw rock 'n' roll in a sweaty, grimy Liverpool cellar, nor would they struggle to sing their latest single over the din of delirious throngs in sports stadiums, nor bow to royals who, as instructed by John, shook their jewelry in lieu of applauding. The Beatles were not only the most successful pop group of their day but had suddenly, joyfully blossomed into "recording artists." With each consecutive album they grew in fantastic leaps and bounds. Although Lennon later denigrated *Sgt. Pepper* as "the biggest load of shit we've ever done," their June 1967 release immediately became the benchmark for every band of its day, challenging the accepted notion of the three-minute pop song formula as well as what instrumentation was now acceptable within the flour-ishing rock idiom. (While Brian Jones dabbled with dulcimers, marimbas, and the sitar, no one took this concept further than Brian Wilson with the Beach Boys' unreleased opus, *Smile*). Left and right, everybody except Dylan began isolating themselves in the studio, spending long hours and big bucks to create their masterpiece. For better or worse, the gilded age of psychedelic excess was suddenly upon us. With "I Am the Walrus," rock could no longer recognize its own reflection in the Summer of Love's fun-house mirror. Employing fragments of radio broadcasts, free-associative poetics, and nonsense syllables like "goo goo goo job," "Walrus" would frost the audio cake beyond most people's comprehension.

John, who touted himself the band's true roots rocker was temporarily seduced (with the help of plenty of LSD) by the endless possibilities the studio had to offer. But before he and his bandmates could "Get Back" to basics, Lennon would join forces with Yoko Ono, with whom he would twist and bend the parameters of rock beyond listenability and taste.

While 1968's "White Album" offered a wildly diverse sonic palette ranging from McCartney's raging rocker "Helter Skelter," to Lennon's avant-garde audio collage, "Revolution #9," to Harrison's wistful "While My Guitar Gently Weeps," the band, who were in the throes of disintegrating, managed to reconnect with the fading warmth and spirit of their best songs from *Rubber Soul* in spare acoustic ballads like "Julia," and "I Will."

In recent years, *Revolver* has routinely topped *Sgt. Pepper* in both critic and opinion polls. Although it may have been the band's perfect storm, there is little doubt the spirit of innovation the Beatles brought the world on *Rubber Soul* has triggered much of the great music of the late sixties, the seventies, and beyond.

Acknowledgments

Thanks to my "More Than Wife" Marilyn Cvitanic for her eternal love, support, and patience throughout the writing process; to Mitch Blank for his encyclopedic knowledge and fabulous collection of holy relics; to Glenn Wolff for his sensitive penmanship; to my brutal but truthful editor, Mike Edison; to my dearly departed pug, Louie; and all my friends and students who read the rushes and endured my gushes about this album for all these years. Special thanks to the family of Pandit Shiv Dayal Batish for permission to republish excerpts from his memoir. And to Radhanath Swami for his knowing smile.

All glories to Lord Krishna!

Bibliography

INTERVIEWS

Interviews conducted by the author for *This Bird Has Flown* include:

Felix Cavaliere (the Rascals)

Joel Dorn (producer at Atlantic and Warner Brothers Records)

Steve Earle

Barry Goldberg (Mitch Ryder & the Detroit Wheels, the Electric Flag, sideman to Bob Dylan)

Joshua M. Greene (author and Gita scholar)

John Hammond

Richie Havens

Carol Kaye (the Wrecking Crew)

Lenny Kaye (Patti Smith band, author)

Howard Kaylan (the Turtles, Flo & Eddie, Frank Zappa, T. Rex)

Steve Katz (the Blues Project, Blood Sweat & Tears)

Al Kooper (the Blues Project, Blood Sweat & Tears, sideman to Bob Dylan, Jimi Hendrix, the Rolling Stones, George Harrison, Roy Orbison, and others)

Bruce Morrow (radio personality)

Peter Rowan (Seatrain, Old and in the Way)

John Sebastian (the Lovin' Spoonful)

Betsy Siggins Schmidt (founder of the New England Folk Archive)

Terry Widlake

BOOKS

The Ballad of John and Yoko. Editors of *Rolling Stone*. New York: Doubleday/Dolphin, 1982.

Beatles, The. *Off the Record*. London: Omnibus Press, 2000.

Davies, Hunter. *The John Lennon Letters*. New York: Little Brown, 2012.

Guralnick, Peter. *Sweet Soul Music*. New York: Harper & Row, 1986.

Luckman, Michael C. *Alien Rock*. New York: Pocket Books, 2005.

Lewisohn, Mark. *The Complete Beatles Recording Sessions*. London: Hamlyn, 2005.

MacDonald, Ian. *Revolution in the Head*. Chicago: Chicago Review Press, 2007.

McMillian, John. *Beatles vs. Stones*. New York: Simon & Schuster, 2013.

Miles, Barry. *The Beatles: A Diary*. London: Omnibus Press, 1998.

Miles, Barry. *Many Years from Now, Paul McCartney*. London: Henry Holt, 1997.

Nash, Graham. *Wild Tales*. New York: Three Rivers Press, 2013.

Rodriguez, Robert. *Revolver: How the Beatles Reimagined Rock 'n' Roll*. Milwaukee: Backbeat Books, 2012.

Sawyers, June Skinner. *Read the Beatles*. New York: Penguin Books, 2006.

Schwartz, Francie. *Body Count*. New York: Straight Arrow Books, 1972.

Schwenson, Dave. *The Beatles at Shea Stadium: The Story Behind Their Greatest Concert*. New York: North Shore Publishing, 2013.

Swed, John F. *Space Is the Place*. New York: Da Capo Press, 1998.

Turner, Steve. *A Hard Day's Write: The Beatles*. New York: MJF Books, 2009.

PERIODICALS

Bachelor, Lisa. "Iconic Beatles Artwork Under the Hammer." *The Observer* (UK), June 16, 2007.

Cohen, John & Traum, Happy. "The Bob Dylan Interview." *Sing Out!* 18, no. 4 (October/November 1968).

Cleave, Maureen. "The John Lennon I Knew." *The Telegraph*, October 5, 2005.

Ghosh, Palash. "George Harrison and India: The Real 'Magical Mystery Tour.'" *The International Business Times*, November 17, 2011.

Glass, Philip. "George Harrison, World-Music Catalyst and Great-Souled Man: Open to the Influence of the Unfamiliar Cultures." *New York Times*, December 9, 2001.

Jones, Allan. "McCartney: My Life in the Shadow of the Beatles." *Uncut*, July 2004.

Shenk, Joshua Wolf. "The Power of Two." *The Atlantic*, July/August 2014.

"The Beatles 101 Greatest Songs." *Mojo*, July 2006.

WEBSITES AND BLOGS

Batish, Pandit Shive Dayal. "My Episode with the Beatles and George Harrison." Raganet.com. http://raganet.com/Issues/3/beatles.html.

The Beatles' Bible. http://www.beatlesbible.com.

Kingman. "When Shea Stadium Was Invaded by Cannibal and the Head-hunters." *Loge 13*, September 11. http://www.loge13.com/2012/09/when_shea_stadium_was_invaded.php.

Kezier, Brian. "Keith Richards Sings the Blues." *Cuepoint*. Accessed June 14, 2014. https://medium.com/cuepoint/keith-richards-sings-the-blues-8d7e73a0545c.

James, Gary. "Interview with Richard 'Scar' Lopez." Classicbands.com. Accessed May 3, 2014. http://www.classicbands.com/RichardLopezInterview.html.

McKie, Rod. "Things You Didn't Know You Didn't Know . . . About Charles Front." Personal blog, August 1, 2010. http://rodmckie.blogspot.com/2010/08/things-you-didnt-know-you-didnt.html.

Index